FIGHTING SPIRIT

the memoirs of

FIGHTING SPIRIT

major yoshitaka horie
and the battle of iwo jima

edited and annotated by
Robert D. Eldridge and **Charles W. Tatum**

NAVAL INSTITUTE PRESS
Annapolis, Maryland

This book has been brought to publication with the generous assistance of Marguerite and Gerry Lenfest.

Naval Institute Press
291 Wood Road
Annapolis, MD 21402

Library of Congress Cataloging-in-Publication Data
Horie, Yoshitaka.
 [Tokon Iojima. English]
 Fighting spirit : the memoirs of major Yoshitaka Horie and the Battle of Iwo Jima / edited and annotated by Robert D. Eldridge and Charles W. Tatum.
    p. cm.
 Includes bibliographical references and index.
 ISBN 978-1-59114-856-2 (hardcover : alk. paper) 1. Iwo Jima, Battle of, Japan, 1945—Personal narratives, Japanese. 2. World War, 1939–1945—Personal narratives, Japanese. 3. Horie, Yoshitaka. I. Eldridge, Robert D. II. Tatum, Charles W. (Charles William) III. Title.
 D767.99.I9H613 2011
 940.54'2528—dc22

                                                                        2010047536

Printed in the United States of America

19 18 17 16 15 14 13 12 11   9 8 7 6 5 4 3 2 1
First printing

this book is dedicated to
those who died in World War II

contents

editors' preface
to the english edition

ABOUT THIS BOOK

There are always two sides to any story, and sometimes more. The Battle of Iwo Jima has been well documented and recorded in numerous books and films by Americans, both veterans and historians.[1] The Japanese side of the story, however, is less well known.

One reason for this void in the literature is the simple fact that almost all of the important Japanese officers from Iwo Jima lost their lives. Only four Japanese officers of field grade (those with the rank of major or above) survived—Imperial Japanese Army majors Komoto Kumeji, Hara Mitsuaki, Inaoka Masaru, and Horie Yoshitaka, the author of this book.[2] Komoto, who served as a senior adjutant to Lieutenant General Kuribayashi Tadamichi, was back in Tokyo for liaison purposes at the time of the invasion, and unable to return, survived.[3] Hara was the commander of the 1st Battalion, 145th Infantry Regiment (Hohei Dai 145 Rentai), from Kagoshima, in the southwesternmost part of the island of Kyushu, and Inaoka was a surgeon in charge of the field hospital for the 2nd Mixed Brigade (Konsei Dai 2 Ryodan), hailing from the Kanto plain area around Tokyo and commanded by Major General Senda Sadasue. Horie, a native of Ibaraki Prefecture, was, as we will see in this book, initially assigned to Iwo Jima, but after arriving there was sent by Kuribayashi a few months before the actual battle in October 1944 to Chichi Jima,[4] 150 miles north of Iwo and about a quarter of the distance between Iwo Jima and Tokyo, in order to take charge of logistics and shipping, and thus was spared.[5]

While several enlisted men and others who survived the fighting have written memoirs of the battle,[6] and other monographs exist written by those with a connection to Iwo Jima, including family members of participants,[7] Horie is the only field grade officer from this command known to have left memoirs presenting the Japanese point of view.[8] (Extensive inquiries with leading Japanese authorities on the battle provided no additional leads or insights on this question.) Horie published the Japanese version of this book in March 1965 on the occasion of the twentieth anniversary of the end of the battle.[9] At the same time, as he makes clear in the foreword to the Japanese edition, he also worked on an English translation of the manuscript, apparently by himself, with the hope that it would in fact be read by a large number of people, especially U.S. veterans with whom he had become close (discussed below).[10] The English version was never published, however, and Horie subsequently passed away, in August 2003, without seeing it come out in book form.[11]

Horie, who would devote much of his postwar career to writing and teaching, was grateful to his English-language skills for the "ability to eat and live over the four decades after the war."[12] Interestingly, he was not a trained translator or interpreter.

Horie had studied English for ten years in middle school, the Imperial Japanese Army Academy, and the Army War College, but lamented later "about the extremely unfortunate situation in which I could only read English. My spoken English was completely useless."[13] He only seriously began studying English, as he makes clear in the pages that follow, when he was stationed on Chichi Jima, beginning in 1944, interrogating downed American flyers who had been taken prisoner and having them teach him English. Although some of the flyers were tortured, murdered, and in some cases eaten by some of the more sadistic captors, Horie befriended and tried to protect them.[14] For his actions, Horie came to be known by the Japanese soldiers and sailors on the island as *Chichi Jima no ryoshin,* or "Chichi Jima's conscience,"[15] which is in direct contrast to the "Tiger of Chichi," Major Matoba Sueo, who was primarily responsible for the prisoner abuse. Horie's descriptions of learning English, which appear in this book, are actually quite funny and suggest that humanity does occasionally show its face amid the tragedy of war.

It was Horie, importantly, who fingered Matoba and the others, including Lieutenant General Tachibana Yoshio, both eventually convicted of war crimes and hanged, after U.S. forces, which had landed on Chichi Jima in the fall of 1945, quietly began their investigation of the fate of the downed flyers, and confronted Horie with undeniable evidence and testimony and asked for his help.[16] As the star prosecution witness against those who had abused the prisoners, Horie was called an "American dog" by Tachibana. You can almost see the venom flying from Tachibana's mouth when he screamed at Horie during the trials, "You are not Japanese!"[17]

An American Marine officer, who was stationed on Chichi Jima in late 1945 and to whom Horie would give his sword, noted that indeed Horie was an "opportunist" but credits him with playing a crucial role: "had he not turned state's evidence most of those war criminals would be alive today."[18] Horie's sword and some of his correspondence remain well preserved today by the family of the American officer, who passed away in 2002 at the age of ninety (the officer and Horie would have been close in age).

Horie does not go into detail in this book about what happened to the flyers and his own role in initially covering up the tragedy and then in helping the prosecution. However, in a letter to Lieutenant Colonel James H. Tinsley Sr., the above American officer, Horie explains why he had not told the occupation forces earlier of the true fate of the flyers. "I am very sorry to say," Horie begins in the February 1, 1946, letter to the already stateside Tinsley,

> that there were case [*sic*] of cruelty to American aviators. I tried at first to keep the matter secret, but all came to light; we gave the truth and now Major [Robert D.] Shaffer's board [of investigation] is investigating the matter. I believe you can understand how I protected and loved [the] American aviators, but they suffered cruelties from one part of the Japanese [forces on Chichi Jima], how I was worried about this matter when Japan surrendered to America, finally we tried to conceal it to cover our senior officers when you came up here, but all was exposed and I told the truth to your fair and just board.[19]

Because of the grotesqueness and cruelty of the treatment the downed American flyers received, including being cannibalized in some cases, Horie seems to have avoided publicly discussing the issue in detail in his writings until he published an article in Japanese in 1984 entitled "The Chichi Jima Cannibalism Incident."[20]

When Horie was still on Chichi Jima, he also had the opportunity to brief a visiting general officer, Brigadier General Davis,[21] his staff of twenty-five officers, and the U.S. military leadership there in early December on Japanese defense strategy for Chichi Jima. "I was honoured," Horie explained in his letter to Lieutenant Colonel Tinsley a couple of months later, "to make a speech in English about the Defense Plan of Chichi Jima and they [the visitors] were very pleased."[22] Subsequently, Horie wrote two booklets, which the commanding officer on Chichi Jima, Colonel Presley M. Rixey, had printed up. One was entitled "Explanation of Japanese Defence Plan of Chichi Jima" and was dated December 23, 1945. It was based on Horie's briefing earlier that month. The other one was entitled "Explanation of Japanese Defence Plan and the Battle of Iwo Jima" and was dated January 25, 1946, one week before Horie had written to Tinsley. He left for Guam to participate in the war crimes trials shortly after this.

The editors decided to include these two reports, which have been referenced in the past in American writings on the Battle of Iwo Jima, in the appendix here, although they did not appear in the original Japanese edition of this book (published by Kobunsha Publishing) or the subsequent reissued editions (in 1973, also by Kobunsha Publishing, and in 2005, by Kojinsha Publishing).[23] The editors have been unable to locate Japanese versions of the reports and are led to believe that they do not exist because the original briefings were for U.S. officers and thus, as Horie alluded to above, probably written only in English. The English versions were fortunately published in the *Marine Corps Gazette* in February 1952 and July 1953, respectively.[24] Regarding the first of Horie's articles, the staff of the *Marine Corps Gazette* wrote, "In our opinion 'Japanese Defense of Iwo Jima' . . . is one of the most interesting articles we have read in years. Major Horie, general staff officer and last [*sic*] defender to leave Iwo alive, publishes for the first time the defense plan and progress of the battle from the eyes of the Japanese defenders. His comments on Marine use of naval gunfire, close air support, and tanks is [*sic*] both interesting and informative."[25]

According to letter from Horie to Tinsley at Christmas time in 1953, the colonel seems to have played a role in helping to get them published.[26] Horie thanked him profusely, and mentions how the honorariums received for each article, paid in dollars, helped him and his growing family in postwar Japan.[27] These articles were, it seems, Horie's first and second published pieces, at least in English. He was off to what would be a highly prolific career writing about World War II and translating military and political histories from English into Japanese. As is described later in this editors' preface, Horie had a full-time day job and used much of his spare time for writing and researching.

Referencing the letters of Lieutenant General Kuribayashi to his family between August 2, 1944, and February 3, 1945, which he translated and used with the permission of Kuribayashi's widow, Yoshii, Horie wrote about the last days of Kuribayashi on Iwo Jima. He published the article in the *Marine Corps Gazette* in February 1955, which included the translations of the seven letters.[28] In the fall of the following year, he published another article for the U.S. Naval Institute *Proceedings*, cited in chapter 2 of this book, about the difficulties encountered by the Japanese convoy escorts during World War II.[29] These four articles would provide much of the foundation for him to write this book about his experiences in World War II and problems with planning and executing the defense of Iwo Jima, Chichi Jima, and other islands in the Pacific.

In the early 1960s, Horie began working on a Japanese translation of *Strategy and Command: The First Two Years*, one of the volumes in the U.S. Army's War in the Pacific series, by Louis Morton, which he had been granted permission to do in early 1964.[30] It does not seem, however, that the massive book was ever published in Japanese. Nevertheless, in doing the translation, which he discusses in the foreword to the Japanese version, he certainly gained valuable insights into U.S. thinking and planning for the war. These efforts helped him tremendously when he wrote *Tokon* (Fighting Spirit), which, as mentioned above, was published in Japanese in March 1965. He, it seems, already had an English version ready as he writes in the foreword to the Japanese version.

With this said, Horie was far from fluent in English. As a result, the manuscript here had to be substantially edited and basically retranslated from scratch. Robert Eldridge, a resident of Japan since 1990 and fluent in Japanese, who was then working as a tenured associate professor of Japanese diplomatic and political history, checked the original Japanese text and reworked the English, trying to be faithful both to Horie's original intent and style while making the text more understandable and readable. Charles Tatum, an Iwo Jima veteran and prolific writer on World War II and Marine Corps issues, checked, and where necessary, edited passages concerning the battle, military terminology, and important facts and figures that only one who lived through that horrific battle would know.

Tatum had been given a copy of the manuscript by William Armond, the then-director of the Fifth Marine Division Association, shortly after attending the division's reunion in Baltimore, Maryland, in 1997. Tatum and Armond had been discussing the fact that few Japanese veterans had written about the war, and Tatum mentioned he had come into possession of Horie's "Explanation of Japanese Defense Plan and the Battle of Iwo Jima" (see appendix 2). Armond said he had a copy of it as well as of a typed, but unpublished, English manuscript called "Fighting Spirit." This news immediately caught Tatum's interest. Tatum asked Armond how he had come across it. According to Armond, as director of the division association, he had become friends with Horie, who had delivered speeches before the association about the battle. Horie had personally shared it with him in the hopes it would be published, distributed, and widely read. Armond later shared his copy with Tatum but told him, half-seriously, that if he did not return it he "would face a firing squad." Reading it, Tatum found Horie's descriptions of the defense plan and the politics and personalities behind Japan's efforts in Iwo Jima fascinating. Making a copy of it for himself, Tatum promptly returned to Armond his copy "so as not to face a firing squad."

After reviewing the translated copy, Tatum referenced it when writing his own memoirs, *Iwo Jima: Red Blood, Black Sand — Pacific Apocalypse*, but realized a lot of work was necessary on it if Horie's manuscript was going to get published.[31] He asked a close friend, a retired Marine and English professor named Howard Stark, to read it and make suggestions, after which it was retyped and further changes were made. However, even then, factually and otherwise, there was still much work to do, so the manuscript sat unpublished.

It was in the spring of 2008, when Eldridge was finishing his own book about the return of Iwo Jima to Japan (*Iwo Jima to Ogasawara o Meguru Nichibei Kankei*),[32] that he inquired with Richard Wheeler about Horie's manuscript, which he, too, referenced in writing his *Iwo*.[33] In the course of corresponding, Wheeler told Eldridge about the efforts of Tatum to revise the manuscript in the hopes of getting it published. Eldridge then flew to California in May that year and met with Tatum, and a pan-Pacific partnership was born to realize the publication of Horie's memoirs of the battle.[34]

Eldridge spent several months trying to locate Horie's family in order to seek out their permission and to interview them. Eldridge had difficulty, however, and finally traveled to Horie's hometown in Ibaraki Prefecture, but was still unsuccessful and had just about given up hope when an enthusiastic local official did some homework on his own and got the contact information for two of Horie's surviving children (discussed below). Their support for and assistance with this project was instrumental in bringing about this book.

It should be mentioned at this point that there are at least two limitations to Horie's version of events. One is the normal, subjective nature of memoirs, in which the information transmitted is almost certainly biased personally or organizationally, intentionally or otherwise. The other is the fact that Horie was not actually on Iwo Jima at the time of the battle, and thus some information may not technically be correct in every case. The editors were aware of these concerns and have made efforts to provide corrections (in the form of annotations) where appropriate. Nevertheless, we believe that the manuscript is important enough to warrant its publication in English. Not only is it significant, but the memoirs are an invaluable contribution to our understanding of Japan's defense of the islands and its decision making in military matters during the final years of the war.

In recent years, the story of Kuribayashi has become well known in both the U.S. and Japan through the release of the movie *Letters from Iwo Jima*, produced by Clint Eastwood, and *So Sad to Fall in Battle*,[35] one of several books that have appeared in English about Kuribayashi based on letters to his family shortly before the battle. Now, through the writings of Horie, who served on Kuribayashi's staff, we can learn the dynamics behind some of the local and national decisions made and the people involved beyond just the figure and image of Kuribayashi. The editors, representing two generations (World War II generation and the post-Vietnam generation) and two walks of life (a veteran and a civilian academic), hope that this book will help fill the gap in the literature on Iwo.

The editors would like to thank Susan Todd Brook, the senior acquisitions editor at the Naval Institute Press, for supporting this project from its early stages; Howard Stark, for his earlier work on the manuscript; the late Richard Wheeler and his cousin, Judge Jacqueline Russell, for their assistance on several matters relating to the manuscript; Robert Aquilina, assistant head, reference branch, Marine Corps History Division, for numerous reference materials; several Japanese military historians for insights and advice along the way with regard to the battle, especially Tobe Ryoichi of the National Defense Academy (NDA; Boei Daigakko) and Major Takeichi Ginjiro, Japanese Ground Self-Defense Force (Ret.) and formerly with the NDA; Suzuki Takashi of the Sakai town office in Sashima County, Ibaraki Prefecture (Horie's hometown); Colonel and Mrs. James H. Tinsley, Jr., USMC (Ret.), for information and materials about their father's relationship with Major Horie; Lieutenant Colonel Robert D. Shaffer, USMC (Ret.), for information on the Chichi Jima investigations, which he led, and his postwar relationship with Mr. Horie; the Suntory Foundation for its support toward the research and publishing of this manuscript; and our families for their constant support and understanding. Most important, the editors would like to thank the surviving children of Major Horie for their permission to translate, edit, and publish this work, and for all the assistance they provided with photos, background materials, and insights into the life of their father.

On a final note, we would like to make the following dedications. Eldridge would like to dedicate this book to Colonel Danny L. Melton, USMC, for his superb leadership, correct judgment, and warm friendship at Marine Corps Bases Japan.

Tatum would like to dedicate this book to Gunnery Sergeant John Basilone, who was killed in action on Iwo Jima on February 19, 1945, and Captain Wachi Tsuneo, Imperial Japanese Navy, who served as the first commander on Iwo Jima through the fall of 1944.

ABOUT MAJOR HORIE YOSHITAKA

Before concluding this editors' preface, it is necessary to provide some biographic background on the author to provide the context of who he was and where this book fits in his postwar writing career.

Horie was born on August 15, 1914, in the village of Yagihashi, in Sowa Town, Sashima County (Sashima-gun), Ibaraki Prefecture, in the heart of the Kanto region. The prefecture is located northeast of Tokyo on the other side of Tokyo's immediate neighbor, Chiba Prefecture, and is surrounded by Chiba to the south, Saitama Prefecture to the southwest, Tochigi Prefecture to the west, Fukushima to the north, and the Pacific Ocean to the east. Ibaraki Prefecture, which was formed in 1871 when the feudal domains were dissolved and reorganized into modern administration units called prefectures (a policy called *haihan chiken* in Japanese), was formerly known as Hitachi Province. Its major industries today are electrical equipment, machines, chemical products, and agriculture, and iron and steel export items.

Sashima-gun is one of the westernmost counties comprising modern Ibaraki, and Sakai-machi, where Horie attended school, is the largest town in the county, with a population of about 27,000. Town and city mergers over the years have greatly changed the administrative landscape of Japan, a trend that has increased dramatically recently due to the declining population in rural communities and drop in revenue of local governments. Most recently, Horie's hometown of Sowa, which until a few years ago belonged to Sashima-gun, merged with Sanwa Town and Koga City to form an enlarged City of Koga on September 12, 2005, and split from Sashima-gun.

The population of Koga City today is 144,198, of which there are slightly more men than women. Koga, which was once called Kyo-ga, is more than 1,300 years old, but really began to develop in the Tokugawa Period (1603–1867) as a castle town. The remnants of the castle are no longer visible today, although a marker shows its once proud presence. The area itself became known as the Koga Province (Kogahan). Unlike other parts of the county, which is predominantly agricultural in nature, growing rice and vegetables, National Highways 4, 354, and 125 all pass through the town, as does the national rail line, and thus the town is more industrial. Although administratively a part of Ibaraki Prefecture, it has greater economic and cultural relations with its closer neighbors Saitama and Tochigi prefectures.

Prior to the establishment of the modern Ibaraki Prefecture, Sashima County once belonged to the province of Sekiyadohan, which was centered in Noda City in present-day Chiba Prefecture, and had developed and prospered by waterways trade on the Tonegawa, a 332-kilometer river originating in the mountains of Niigata and Gunma Prefectures and running to the Pacific. Mount Fuji is visible from the embankment of the river next to the town, but it does not seem that the town truly benefited from its proximity to Tokyo.

The river caused widespread damage postwar as a result of the September 1947 Hurricane Kathleen (Typhoon No. 9, in Japan), so named because Japan was under Allied occupation and followed the American practice at the time of naming the storms after females. The Category 2 storm killed approximately two thousand people and injured an equal number. Sashima County was heavily damaged. Storm-related flooding had also caused extensive destruction in August 1910, during the Meiji Era, as well.

Horie's birth in 1914 came shortly after the end of the Meiji Era, the period from 1868 to 1912, when Japan sought to modernize after centuries of feudalism and self-imposed isolation, as a result of seclusion policies. The year 1914 corresponded with the third year of the Taisho Era (1912–26), a period of enlightenment and the expansion of "democracy" and political rights (including government by party politics rather than influential but autocratic elder statesmen). That same year, Japan had entered World War I on the side of the Allies, as it had been in a formal alliance with England since 1902 and was able to gain a great deal without the risk of losing too much since German forces were too preoccupied with the fighting in Europe to protect its possessions in China and the Pacific. Japan easily scooped them up, having been increasingly confident in its victories over China in its 1894–95 war and over Russia in 1904–1905. It was this military, confident but increasingly xenophobic and unwilling to tolerate domestic dissent (eventually snuffing out Japan's short-lived democracy by the early 1930s), that Horie would later join.

Horie's parents gave him the name Yoshitaka (芳孝), which means "good" and "filial piety." He was the second of three children, and his name combines the Chinese characters used in his siblings' names. His brother, Yoshioki (芳興), was two and a half years older than he was, and his sister, Koko (孝子), was seven years younger. Sadly, his older brother, who was a school teacher and whom Horie talks about in chapter 7, died in a tragic accident in the spring of 1958 when he was hit by a car as he was returning from the school he taught at on his bicycle one night after work.

Horie graduated from the prefecture-administered Sakai Middle School (Ibaraki Kenritsu Sakai Chugakko), which is now Sakai High School (Ibaraki Kenritsu Sakai Koto Gakko), also run by the prefecture.

Horie's father was a landowner, and the family was fairly well off, until an investment his father had made failed and they lost just about everything. A loan collector came to the Horie home one day when Yoshitaka was in the fifth grade. Yoshitaka cried to the man that there was nothing more to give. His father would die shortly thereafter, probably sad and broken over the fate that had befallen the family.

Although Horie was academically gifted enough to go on to university, his family's financial situation prevented this. Instead, Horie chose to attend the Imperial Japanese Army Academy (Rikugun Shikan Gakko), or IJAA, where he would receive a modest stipend. As the second son in the family, tradition did not bind him to the family home as was usually the case with the eldest son. He left for Tokyo in the spring of 1932 and entered the academy in April 1932.

The IJAA had its origins as the Heigakko (later the Heigakusho), which opened in 1867 in Kyoto, and then in Osaka as the Heigakuryo, to train infantry officers. In 1871 it was moved to Tokyo, which had replaced Kyoto as the center of both ritual and real power domestically. In 1874 the IJAA officially came into being. It initially followed the French military education system, but in 1887, it switched to the Prussian style after the French defeat in the Franco-Prussian War in the decade before. The school continued until it was disbanded after World War II as part of the demilitarization of Japan during the Allied occupation (1945–52).

Horie was still in the IJAA when Tokyo experienced a failed coup d'état by the Kodo-ha (Imperial Way Faction) of the Imperial Japanese Army on February 26, 1936. The coup leaders, young ultranationalist officers, seized key government buildings, including the Diet (parliament) building, Army Ministry headquarters, and Tokyo Metropolitan Police Headquarters. They also attempted to occupy the Imperial Palace but were turned back when the Imperial Guard (Konoe Shidan) resisted and surrounded the palace, sealing it off. They assassinated Finance Minister Takahashi Korekiyo, Lord Keeper of the Privy Seal Saito Makoto, and Inspector-General of Military Education Watanabe Jotaro before their three-day rampage ended when Emperor Hirohito declared martial law and called on the army and navy to crush the rebellion.

The so-called 2-26 Incident is one of the most significant events in prewar Japan, and although the coup failed and its leaders were punished through execution, it ended up strengthening the hand of the military in political affairs. It also led to the collapse of the cabinet of Okada Keisuke, who only escaped assassination when his brother-in-law was mistakenly killed instead, the following month. Japan eventually joined an anti-Comintern pact with Nazi Germany on November 25, 1936, under Okada's successor as prime minister, Hirota Koki.[36] It is uncertain how Horie, then twenty-one, observed these events, but it is safe to say that while he was a patriot he was not a nationalist.

Upon graduation in June 1936, Horie was commissioned as a second lieutenant, on October 1, 1936, and attached to the 7th Company, 2nd Infantry Regiment (Hohei Daini Rentai Dainana Chutai), based in Mito City, eighty-five miles northeast of Tokyo. Shortly after this, he became the regimental flag bearer as well as an instructor of the army's Officer Candidate School (Rikugun Kanbu Koho Gakko). He was sent to Northern China in August 1937 as a communications officer after the outbreak of fighting there that year and was promoted to first lieutenant in December. Two years and twenty-seven battles later, in December 1939, First Lieutenant Horie, in the city of Kaifeng, in eastern Henan province, was shot several times during his twenty-eighth battle. Wounded in the head, he suffered nerve damage to his legs. He was also hit in the chest and the bullets would probably have killed him had it not been for some coins he had in his wallet. Presented with the Order of the Golden Kite (Kinshi Kunsho), a military award recognizing bravery, leadership, and command in battle, and a second one for having been severely wounded, he returned to Japan in January 1940. He walked with a limp for the rest of his life, which may explain one of the reasons Kuribayashi directed him to go to Chichi Jima rather than Iwo Jima, where the terrain was rougher and U.S. forces were expected to land. But as we'll see below, Horie also possessed unique skills, experiences, and insights, especially his connections with the navy and knowledge of shipping, transportation, and logistics, and it is probably these values that Horie could bring to the fight which Kuribayashi most recognized.

Horie recovered, and six months after being promoted to the rank of army captain, was married, on February 25, 1941, to a young lady Sumiko, five years his junior. As was the tradition at the time, it was an *omiai*, or arranged marriage. According to Horie's son Yoshibumi (born in 1948), his bride apparently had someone else in mind to marry, but her father, being a military man himself, made her marry Horie. The fact that Horie was from the same region (Sumiko was from neighboring Chiba Prefecture, across the Tonegawa River) no doubt added to his credentials in her father's mind.

In December the year before his marriage, when his superiors thought he had recuperated enough to resume his military career, Horie entered the Army War College (Rikugun Daigaku), which had been established in 1882. He would graduate from the two-year course in November 1942. He was a classmate of Prince Mikasa (Mikasa-no-miya Takahito Shinnō), Emperor Hirohito's youngest brother.

That same month, Horie was temporarily assigned to the General Staff Headquarters (Sanbo Honbu) and then in January 1943 to the Army Shipping Headquarters (Senpaku Shireibu) and subsequently to the 1st Marine Escort Service (Dai Ichi Kaijo Engotai). Horie, who became a major in August 1943, became the army's liaison officer to the Kaijo Goei Soshireibu (Marine Escort Headquarters) in December 1943, a month after its creation. He continued in this capacity, gaining, as he writes, invaluable experience, insights, and information simultaneously from both the navy as well as the army, until June 1944. In that month, he was assigned to the staff of the 31st Army although aerial attacks on Saipan prevented his going there. In July, he was thus assigned to the staff of the 109th Division. He helped plan, along with

Lieutenant General Kuribayashi Tadamichi, the defense of Iwo Jima, as a major in the Imperial Japanese Army. During the preparations for the Battle of Iwo Jima and the actual battle itself, as mentioned earlier, Horie served as the detached commander on Chichi Jima, and thus survived. Following Kuribayashi's death, he was appointed the chief of staff to Lieutenant General Tachibana, who had assumed the command of the 109th in March 1945.

After testifying at the Guam war crimes trial in 1946, Horie returned to Japan and saw his wife and daughter, Yoshiko (芳子—who was given the same *Yoshi* Chinese character as her father and was born in 1942), for the first time in almost two years. (Horie writes about her in chapter 7 of this book.) He and Sumiko gradually expanded their family, with a second daughter, Reiko, being born in 1944, and a son, Yoshibumi (芳文— also with the same *Yoshi* Chinese character) mentioned above. Horie appears to have been a dedicated father, and was able to provide for his family after the war in part through the networks he had built during the occupation of Chichi Jima and through his intensive English study and ability to use it when Japan was under the Allied occupation.

After the war, Horie worked from October 1946 to March 1950 as the "Japanese Manager and Advisor" for the Far East Air Material Command at Tachikawa City, having been recommended by Major Robert D. Shaffer, who had led the investigation of the war crimes on Chichi Jima.[37] Subsequently, he became a representative of Tachihi Industrial Co., Ltd., the successor to Tachikawa Aircraft Co., Ltd., and later served as general manager, but eventually returned in a full-time capacity to work at Tachikawa Air Base in the Suggestion Awards Branch as a translator and in the procurement division (Shizai Chotatsubu), where he specialized in the purchase and acquisition of parts and materials from abroad. "Despite his noticeable limp," the Kanto Base Command's *Plainsman* newspaper wrote about him in an Iwo Jima supplement on the occasion of the reversion of the Ogasawara (Bonin) Islands to Japan, "he projects a proud yet congenial air."[38]

Through his work at Tachikawa, Horie was able to more fully develop his English ability and began to specialize in commercial English, which he later taught to adults. In addition to writing on World War II, discussed below, he also began teaching English during this time. His son, Yoshibumi, who was an elementary school student at the time, remembers about ten of the neighborhood children in elementary school and middle school studying English under his father's tutelage at their home from about 1954 to 1960.[39] Subsequently, from 1960 until 1966, he taught Asian history and Japanese in the University of Maryland extension program on base.

Horie retired from Tachikawa Air Base in early 1969, after almost twenty-five years there, and joined the faculty of Takushoku University, in Tokyo, as a lecturer *(koshi)* of English. His appointment was signed by Nakasone Yasuhiro, a Diet member who also served as president of the university (from 1967 to 1971).[40] A popular and outspoken politician, Nakasone had also become director-general of the Defense Agency in 1970 and would later become Japan's seventy-first (and seventy-second and seventy-third) prime minister, serving from November 27, 1982, until November 6, 1987.[41] Horie continued teaching at Takushoku, a school originally founded as the Taiwan Association School (Taiwan Kyokai Gakko) in 1900 to produce graduates to help in the development of Taiwan (acquired as a result of the Shimonoseki Treaty ending the 1894–95 Sino-Japanese War), until March 1986, although he had been working as a part-time lecturer *(hijokin koshi)* since 1977.

He was seventy-one at this point but continued writing and other projects. As mentioned above, he had a productive career as a translator and author. Most of his writings came out in the 1950s, 1960s, and 1970s, but he did have a few articles and chapters in books in the 1980s. Horie published most of these works through Kobunsha Publishing, which as explained above, was the publisher of the original version of Horie's memoirs. "Kobunsha," incidentally, takes its name from the Chinese reading of the founding president's first name, the man Horie speaks of in the preface.

Some of the translations, not including those of reissued or revised books, that he worked on after the release of *Fighting Spirit* in 1965 include: *Memoirs*, volume 1, *Year of Decisions*, and *Memoirs*, volume 2, *Years of Trial and Hope* (by Harry S. Truman) in February 1966; *The Decision to Drop the Bomb* (by Len Giovannitti and Fred Freed) in January 1967; *The Broken Seal* (by Ladislas Farago) in January 1967; *General Wainwright's Story: The Account of Four Years of Humiliating Defeat, Surrender, and Captivity* (by Jonathan M. Wainwright) in May 1967; *Subhas Chandra Bosu and Japan* (by Joyce Lebra-Chapman) in November 1968, *Bastogne: Ballantine's Illustrated History of World War II*, volume 29 (by Peter Elstob) in May 1972; and *Iwo* (by Richard Wheeler) in March 1981.

Horie did not simply translate books, however. He was also a prolific writer of books and articles. In addition to the articles mentioned above and *Fighting Spirit*, Horie wrote the following books: *Tokon, Peri-ryuto: Periryu-Angauru Ryoto Gyokusaiki* (Fighting Spirit, Peliliu: An Account of the Fight to the Death on the Islands of Peleliu and Angaur), published by Kobunsha in February 1967; *Ogasawara Heidan no Saigo* (The Last Days of the Ogasawara Force), published by Hara Shobo in 1969;[42] *Shito! Iwoto-Okinawa* (Fight Until the End! Iwo To and Okinawa), published by Gakushu Kenkyusha in 1972;[43] *Iwoto: Gekito no Kiroku* (Iwo Jima: A Record of Heavy Fighting), published by Kobunsha in January 1973;[44] and a biography entitled *Tsuji Masanobu: Sono Ningenzo to Yukue* (Tsuji Masanobu: Who He Was and What Happened to Him), published by Kobunsha in 1980.

After this biography of Tsuji, a pre–World War II and wartime tactician of the Imperial Japanese Army who murdered Allied prisoners and local civilians in China and Southeast Asia but escaped a war crimes trial, Horie also wrote several articles and book chapters, including two mentioned earlier, "Chichi Jima Jinniku Jiken: Shidancho mo Kutta" (The Chichi Jima Cannibalism Incident: The Commanding General Also Ate [the Flyers]), for a history journal, *Rekishi to Jinbutsu* (History and People), in 1984, and "Iwoto Kessen Kaiko" (Recollections of the Decisive Battle of Iwo Jima) in a special edition of the military affairs magazine, *Maru*, in July 1989. He did regular interviews, some of which were published. For example, while he was still working at the Kanto Base Command at Tachikawa Air Base, his story appeared opposite an American veteran's, Master Sergeant John Ostronic, who had served in the U.S. Air Force (as commander of Detachment 1, 2132nd Communications Squadron, at Iwo Jima Air Base) in the *Kanto Plainsman* base newspaper.[45] Around the same time, he was interviewed by a prewar expert on the Japanese military, Alvin D. Coox, for an article about the postwar military (the Self-Defense Forces, or Jieitai) in the *Marine Corps Gazette* in 1965.[46] He also wrote an unpublished essay, "Onshuo o Koete: Beikaihei Dai 5 Shidan Zaikyo Gunjinkai to Watashi" (Beyond Love and Hate: The U.S. Marine 5th Division Association and Me), which provides rare insights into his unique relationship with U.S. veterans of Iwo Jima.[47]

During the postwar, Horie also provided assistance to veterans and researchers in their own writings, including military historian John Toland, who bases much of his chapter on the Battle of Iwo Jima in his huge 1970 book, *The Rising Sun*, on information and contacts provided by Horie.[48] Toland's *Rising Sun*, published by Random House, went on to win the 1971 Pulitzer Prize. The two men spoke of Horie possibly translating it into Japanese, but eventually it was done by a team hired by one of national newspapers, the *Mainichi Shimbun*. Some of the assistance Horie provided including introducing other veterans and researchers to the family of Lieutenant General Kuribayashi, and taking them around Japan and to Iwo Jima as well.

For example, on February 19, 1970, the twenty-fifth anniversary of the start of the Battle of Iwo Jima, Horie participated in and interpreted for a ceremony on top of Mount Suribachi with fifty-four American and twenty Japanese veterans of the battle.[49] Also in attendance was Major General William K. Jones, who had fought in the Pacific during World War II and flew in from Vietnam for the ceremony.

Before and after this, Horie gave many speeches in the United States, and in Japan as well, to veterans groups and Japanese chapters of the Lions Clubs. His talks, especially one given at the annual meeting of the 5th Marine Division Association, whose members he had become close with, received wide coverage on American television networks.[50]

Horie caused a bit of a sensation in one of his talks about the Battle of Iwo Jima when he stated that Kuribayashi had been murdered by one of his subordinates after the commanding general decided to surrender, in essence refuting the more well known account (including the one given in this book) that Kuribayashi died a more glorious death, after leading his remaining forces into battle and being wounded, either dying by *seppuku* (literally, slicing one's stomach) and decapitation or by handgun. This speech Horie gave was before the Japanese Ground Self-Defense Force's Fuji School (Fuji Gakko), a school that opened in 1954 to train ground forces in artillery and combined arms.[51] It was part of a lecture series by combat veterans to students at the school.[52]

In fact, Horie had publicly discussed this account in his February 1955 article about Kuribayashi that appeared in English in the *Marine Corps Gazette*.[53] He also discussed it in a chapter in a book about the battle in November 1989.[54] Moreover, while not widely known, Horie spoke about this version of events in an oral history for the War History Office (Senshishitsu) of the National Institute for Defense Studies (Boei Kenkyusho).[55] This oral history was labeled secret for four decades but was opened for viewing in June 2003, a couple of months before Horie's passing. The varying accounts, their defenders and detractors, and the controversy surrounding them perhaps go to show that significant figures, like Kuribayashi, including their lives, leadership, and circumstances of death, will be the subject of never-ending debate.

Horie had become so close over the years to the Fifth Marine Division Association that it made him an honorary member (a fact he proudly writes of in the foreword).[56] One of those who had become quite friendly with Horie was Iwo Jima veteran Charles Early, president of the association in the early 1970s, who came to Japan in 1969 and then again heading a delegation of veterans to Japan and Iwo Jima in early 1970.[57] Another one was John Downer, who succeeded Early, and whose home in Los Angeles Horie stayed at on his way to an association's twenty-fifth reunion gathering in Washington, D.C., in July 1970. Yet another American veteran Horie became close with was the author Richard Wheeler, who had written a bestseller about the battle, titled simply *Iwo*.[58] Wheeler had read Horie's self-translated manuscript *Fighting Spirit* and, very impressed with it, had asked Horie to translate his book into Japanese, which Horie did, and which appeared the following year (1981).[59] Horie also helped John Keith Wells, an Iwo Jima veteran, who visited Japan in June 1983 and spoke before a large group of Ground Self-Defense Force officers and personnel about the battle. There are several photos of Horie, who served as interpreter and host, in Wells' book, *Give Me Fifty Marines Not Afraid to Die: Iwo Jima*.[60]

As mentioned earlier, Horie had also stayed in touch with his former USMC counterparts from his days on Chichi Jima. In the early postwar years, he kept up a correspondence with Lieutenant Colonel Tinsley, and well into the 1970s, he was in touch with Major (later Lieutenant Colonel) Robert D. Shaffer, who had led the investigations into the fate of the downed flyers. Horie visited Shaffer at the latter's home in Salt Lake City, Utah, where the two men reminisced. When Eldridge met with Shaffer, then ninety-two, in the summer of 2009, his memory was outstanding, no doubt helped by the perfect records he kept and detailed photo albums, including many photos from Chichi Jima and of a visit by Horie to Utah a few decades ago.

After retiring, as Horie got older, he found it harder to get around his home with his bad leg. He became increasingly frustrated with his condition and irritable and in 1990 his family had him enter a senior citizens' home. After this, it appears he no longer wrote anything. In the late 1990s, he developed Alzheimer's disease, but was otherwise in good health and lived until a week shy of his eighty-ninth birthday. He died on August 6, 2003, which happened to be the sixty-third anniversary of the dropping of the atomic bomb on Hiroshima.

Horie was survived by his sister, Koko, his wife and two of their children—their second daughter, Reiko, who lives in Chiba Prefecture, and Yoshibumi, who lives in Kanagawa Prefecture. Their oldest daughter, Yoshiko, about whom Horie wrote in this book, had died seven months earlier, in January 2003, at the age of sixty.

Horie's final years were quiet, especially when compared to his pre-retirement years, but the significance of his contributions throughout his entire life to promoting U.S.-Japanese relations in general and better relations between World War II veterans of both sides, especially those from Iwo Jima, in particular, deserve much greater attention and recognition, as does his service to his country during the war and his efforts to educate his fellow citizens after the war about the history of that period.

We hope this editors' preface has been able to shed some light on Horie's work and the significance of this book.

Robert D. Eldridge and Charles W. Tatum

foreword

I was a staff officer of the Iwo Jima defense command. In the twenty years following the end of World War II, I have regularly heard voices critical of the war. Sometimes I have shared that feeling, and other times I have been upset by the criticism about the war. However, when people speak of the battle of Iwo Jima, they show only admiration and respect for the greatness of the fighters, both Japanese and American, and find no reason for criticism. The U.S. Marine Corps and Navy, likewise, continue to describe Iwo Jima as the worst battle in world history, and I have gotten many letters from Americans asking about the battle.

After some time on Iwo Jima, I was assigned to the island of Chichi Jima to handle transportation and supplies. This occurred in the summer of 1944, after the U.S. military began its air raids, and thus I was spared when U.S. forces attacked Iwo Jima. Having returned home alive, I wanted to write for the sake of the bereaved families about the battle and of those who had died. The president of the Japanese publishing house Kobunsha, Ikeda Tsuneo, and his staff members Kusano Goichi and Shimizu Toshio approached me about publishing this book on the occasion of the twentieth anniversary of the battle, and I found the courage to do so.

To discuss the Iwo Jima campaign, we must know why the bloody battle occurred there—an island isolated and essentially impossible to support or reinforce. We must also look at the reality of what was happening in the Pacific at the time, which the Japanese public was not being told, and at the relationship between the Imperial Japanese Navy

(IJN) and Imperial Japanese Army (IJA). Before I left for Iwo Jima, I was a liaison officer for the army with the navy in Tokyo and am able to write of the events of those days based upon this unique experience and the insights gained then.

I believe the facts must be allowed to speak for themselves and thus will hold nothing back. For some, the manner in which these facts are presented may seem to be rude or discourteous, but I hope that those offended will understand that I wish to simply present the truth as I saw it and do not want to alter the details. Because two decades have passed, there may be some mistakes with dates, numbers, and places, etc. I would be grateful for any suggestions for corrections that readers might have. Also, the reader might notice some discrepancies regarding dates and figures in statements by individuals who appear in these pages. Respecting their original remarks, I have chosen not to make any changes.[1]

In writing this book, I gratefully acknowledge the help of the families of Lieutenant General Kuribayashi Tadamichi and Rear Admiral Ichimaru Rinosuke; the wife of Baron Nishi Takeichi; the staff of the Repatriation Division of the Ministry of Health and Welfare (Koseisho Hikiage Engokyoku); Omoto Takeo, formerly major and adjutant to Lieutenant General Kuribayashi; survivors; and Sakurai Naosaku, the president of Iwo Jima Industry Co.

I also owe a great debt to the U.S. Army's Office of the Chief of Military History, who gave me permission to translate into Japanese Dr. Louis Morton's *The United States Army in World War II: Strategy and Command,* from which I have quoted and from which I learned much about both U.S. and Japanese decision making.[2] I have also drawn heavily on the figures appearing in that great work. I am also indebted to Dr. Morton himself, who is currently a professor at Dartmouth College but served a long time in the Pacific during the war and spent almost fifteen years writing the book as the deputy head of the Army's Office of the Chief of Military History (from 1946 to 1959), and to members of that office, including Colonel Walter B. McKenzie, chief, Editorial and Graphics Division.[3]

Lieutenant Colonel James H. Tinsley, 1st Battalion commander, 3rd Marine Division, U.S. Marine occupation forces, Chichi Jima, who went to the island right after the end of the war, became one of my horseback-riding friends, along with Colonel Presley M. Rixey, commander of the occupation forces, and Major Robert D. Shaffer, the deputy commander. Using one of the fourteen horses on the island, I used to ride, talk, and drink with these officers. Later, Tinsley was assigned, in 1954, to the Sixth Fleet in the Mediterranean as the fleet marine officer and promoted to full colonel. It was just before this that he wrote to me recommending that I write something about the Iwo Jima operations based on the lectures I had given to my riding buddies on Chichi Jima.[4] Subsequently, the *Marine Corps Gazette* published some of my articles about the Iwo Jima campaign, under the heading of "military commentator."[5]

Since then, over the past fifteen years, we have been like brothers, in a mutually beneficial relationship. With the planned publication of this book in Japanese, I wrote the *Gazette* authorities, and Lieutenant Colonel W. L. Trayno promptly sent many pictures of the battle to me by airmail, and thus most of the pictures in this book are from the collections at the *Marine Corps Gazette*.[6] The editors also wrote to say that they looked forward to its publication in English. I have written this in both Japanese and English and hope that with their help this manuscript can one day be published in English and be read widely in the United States. I am grateful to my former riding friend, Colonel Tinsley, and to Lieutenant Colonel Trayno for their assistance with this book.

Finally, I wish to thank everyone at Kobunsha Publishing for their assistance in the publication of the Japanese version of the book.

August 15, 1965
Horie Yoshitaka

chapter one

THE TOUGHEST BATTLE
IN WORLD HISTORY

THE LAST DAY ON THE ISLAND OF DEATH

I can only imagine what that last day was like from my interaction with the radio operator on Iwo Jima.

Several hand grenades exploded near the entrance of his cave. Men near him were groaning in their cave, "Water! Kill me now, please!" His fellow troops were in a pitiful state. Through the smoke and shelling, the enemy could be heard on his loudspeakers yelling: "Give yourselves up and you will be protected." The radio operator still had three more messages given to him by Colonel Nakane Kaneji to send to Tokyo through our Chichi Jima radio station. They had already burned all the codebooks, and, I learned later, apparently unable to decode the messages I was sending them in their final days. They were getting ready to destroy the radio. Could his men hold out defending the cave's entrance until he finished sending the messages? His hands must have been shaking. The oppression of the heat and death in that cave was probably unbearable. As soon as he finished sending the messages, if in fact he could, he would then have to go out and make a banzai charge. He somehow got all the messages off. The sweat was no doubt pouring down his face. At the end, he included a message from the commanding general, Kuribayashi Tadamichi, who had been promoted to full general on March 18 but was unaware of it. It read, "Goodbye to my dear friends of Chichi Jima." Using a pick, the radio operator destroyed the radio and tore out of the cave on a banzai charge.

It was March 23, 1945, when the above radio operator died. Three days later, on March 26, organized resistance by the Japanese defenders ended.

1

The *Asahi Shimbun* had reported the following on March 20:

Led by the commanding general at the front, all officers and men gloriously attacked [the enemy]. Our troops on Iwo Jima have fought tenaciously for the past month after the landing by the enemy. Particularly after March 13, 1945, there has been heavy fighting around all pill boxes and caves in the North Village and Higashiyama area. Reaching the final stages, the Imperial Japanese headquarters received the following message: "Praying for victory for the mother country, we, with the commanding general leading the charge, will make a glorious attack on the enemy at midnight on March 17, 1945." There has been no more communication between Iwo Jima and Tokyo. Iwo Jima has finally fallen into the hands of the enemy. After invading Iwo Jima, the enemy has continuously surrounded the island with twenty or thirty vessels and fired four thousand [to] eight thousand rounds of naval fire per day, and has covered the sky with two hundred to eight hundred carrier planes. Moreover, according to enemy announcements, they have fired in the first two days alone more than eight thousand tons of ammunition onto the island.

Twenty years ago, the Pacific war, perhaps the fiercest and most tragic war in world history, thus ended, covering Iwo Jima with an overpowering smell of death. The battle caused more than 23,000 Marine casualties and 19,000 Japanese deaths.[1]

WHAT IWO JIMA SHOWED THE WORLD
There are many reasons why the Iwo Jima campaign is so famous. Below are some of the main ones.

The first reason has to do with Japanese tradition. The twenty thousand warriors of the Imperial Japanese Navy and Army put up a determined fight on Iwo Jima, despite being completely isolated with no support. Their situation was beyond desperate; it was hopeless. The brave defenders resisted death until the last moment like sheep being surrounded by a hundred tigers. Major General Jonathan M. Wainwright, who had raised a white flag on Corregidor Island, became a hero among the Allies. So did General Douglas A. MacArthur, who had fled from the Philippines. Major General Edward P. King Jr. of Bataan and Lieutenant General Arthur E. Percival of Singapore were also counted as heroes. But for the Japanese officers on Iwo Jima, they never really had the option to give up. There was only victory or death. Fighting until their last breath was the Japanese way. This came from Japanese tradition.

The second reason was the commanders. With no hope for air or naval support, and realizing he and his forces had to fight on alone by themselves, Lieutenant General Kuribayashi, an expert on modern tactics with the benefit of a six-year stay in the United States and Canada as an exchange officer and military attaché, fought a primitive battle out of necessity, with firm determination and without fear of the American forces. In addition to this, Rear Admiral Ichimaru Rinosuke, a calm and brave man, cooperated fully with the general.[2] Iwo Jima was fortunate to have these two men in command.

Third, the lessons of those who had gone before us and died were important. The lessons from the battles of Guadalcanal, Attu, Makin, Tarawa, Saipan, Tinian, Guam, Peleliu, etc., taught the Iwo Jima warriors, caught like sheep, how to prepare against the attacking wolves.

Fourth, the unrealistic schedule of the U.S. military, its huge losses, and numerous news releases of the U.S. side also led to the battle being so famous. Underlying this were the efforts of the U.S. Pacific Fleet, led by Admiral Chester W. Nimitz and urged on by Chief of Naval Operations Admiral Ernest J. King, to advance to Japan through Iwo Jima and Okinawa by adopting the same tactics as before on an extremely tight timeline that had Iwo Jima falling in just a few short days, well before the start of the Okinawa battle. The U.S. decision and planning was simply unrealistic. U.S. planners tried to employ traditional tactics in an untraditional setting. The cat ended up being bitten by the trapped mouse. In light of the unexpectedly heavy losses, the press paid special attention to the battle.

The fifth reason was terrain. The main landing beach was limited to the southern beach. This gave the garrison a special advantage and a chance to put up strong resistance.

The sixth reason was the arms and ammunitions of the garrison. The Imperial Japanese Headquarters (IJH), or Daihonei, gave medium and small arms, such as machine guns, antitank guns, 25-mm machine guns, howitzers, propelled guns, etc., which could be used in caves and helped Kuribayashi in his tactics to hold out as long as possible and fight until the end. In other words, the arms and ammunitions fit the terrain.

The seventh reason was the policy of nonintervention by Imperial Japanese Headquarters in local strategy and tactics. The IJH had

belatedly come to realize the actual strength and ability of U.S. forces
through several crushing defeats over the past couple of years and
stopped giving instructions at every turn, such as "Annihilate the enemy at the beach," "Make counter attacks," "Move under darkness at
night and attack the flanks of the enemy," etc. The IJH, instead, at this
point left everything up to Kuribayashi's own discretion, in a sort of
reverent manner, knowing that it was he and his men who were going
to die there resisting the enemy. Kuribayashi was thus able to choose
the type of tactics for the battle that matched local realities, without
outside meddling.

IWO JIMA'S POET, COMMANDING GENERAL KURIBAYASHI

Another important reason that Iwo Jima is so famous was the power
of the pen and Kuribayashi's intellect. There were battlefields besides
Iwo Jima that saw heavy fighting. Tarawa was one such battle and was
unmatched in fierceness. There were other terrible battles as well—
Guadalcanal, Biak, Imphal, Myitkyina in Burma, Salamaua-Lae in New
Guinea, Hengyang in China, etc. No one can talk about or listen to these
stories without shedding a tear, for either side.

In Okinawa, the Himeyuri monument, named in honor of the
several hundred high school girls who had met a tragic fate, is well
known.[3] In Peleliu, the 2nd Infantry Regiment and other troops under
the command of Colonel Nakagawa Kunio used tactics similar to those
employed later at Iwo Jima, inflicting heavy losses among the famous
1st Division of the United States Marine Corps.

But the majority of the war historians throughout the world have
named Iwo Jima as the "Number-one battle" in the Pacific. I have read
many war histories and memoirs written by Americans, British, Rus-
sians, and Germans. It is a common conclusion that the turning point
in the war in Europe was Stalingrad and for the Pacific, Midway. They
list El Alamein in North Africa, Iwo Jima, and Stalingrad as the three
"toughest battles." Why?

One reason is that the battles at Tarawa, Guadalcanal, Imphal,
and Peleliu are not as well known, having had to be kept secret by the
Allied forces and Japan in those days; only a few announcements were
made. A second reason had to do with the fact that Japan still had some
strength left in the Combined Fleet, and the Japanese army had some
ability to move troops in the Pacific area. A third reason was that Iwo
Jima belonged to the Tokyo metropolitan area and thus the defenders would fight that much harder, to protect the entrance to mainland

Japan. A fourth reason was the broadcast of the "Iwo Jima Song" at midnight on March 17, 1945, by NHK (Nippon Hoso Kyokai) when the defenders of the islanders were making their last staged attack. This broadcast helped to make the Iwo Jima campaign famous throughout Japan.[4]

Yet another reason exists for Iwo Jima being so famous. There was a poet and writer on the island, the force of whose prose cannot be overlooked. This poet and writer was the commanding general of the island, Lieutenant General Kuribayashi himself. His reports, sent word for word to Tokyo by wire through the radio station at Chichi Jima, were composed in a cave under candlelight with his small penciled letters until his leading the final banzai charge. I believe these reports can be compared to any first-rate literary work. In his reports, I am reminded of the melodies found in "Prayer" (Akatsuki ni Inoru) and "Horse Song" (Aiba Koshinkyoku), which he participated in selecting following contests he helped organize when he was still a colonel working in the War Ministry in Tokyo as the section chief of administration for horses.

chapter two

ISOLATED ISLAND
Where No Planes or Vessels Could Go

Now let us examine why Iwo Jima was isolated. What was the real reason? Why was something this unthinkable—this unbelievable—allowed to happen at the gateway to the Japanese homeland, the first territory historically Japanese to be invaded during the war? In those days, the people of Japan often said that "Saipan is the key point of war" or that "Leyte is the deciding point." To tell the truth, these opinions were nothing more than bluster and gossip. We must carefully analyze what actually happened in the Pacific, which was not announced at the time due to the necessity of secrecy and from the desire of the Imperial Japanese Headquarters to prevent the issue of war weariness in the people from rising. We were deceived.

AT MIDWAY, JAPAN LOSES THE PLANES
THAT HAD ATTACKED HAWAII

On June 4 and 5, 1942, just six months after Pearl Harbor, the Japanese Combined Fleet (Rengo Kantai) lost most of its 1st Air Fleet (Daiichi Koku Kantai), which had led the surprise attack on Pearl Harbor under the command of Vice Admiral Nagumo Chuichi. Four aircraft carriers, the *Kaga, Soryu, Akagi,* and *Hiryu,* and about four hundred aircraft and their pilots were lost at Midway.[1] Admiral Yamamoto Isoroku's statement of defiance on the eve of Pearl Harbor that "I can promise to give them hell for a year or a year and a half" was no longer heard.[2]

Louis Morton wrote in the chapter entitled "Transition" in his World War II history *Strategy and Command* that "The cost of these scattered holdings in planes, trained pilots, and carriers had been enormous.

Until these losses were replaced and the superiority lost at Midway regained, as it never could in a race against American production, the Japanese would have to go on the strategic defensive. The tide of victory had finally turned."[3]

As a result of the Lend-Lease Act pursued by Secretary of State Cordell Hull, in accordance with the big shipbuilding plan after 1939, the United States began producing vessels for the war at a rapid pace. The tables were turned, and the American advantage grew increasingly large over the Japanese as time went on.

During the war of attrition at Guadalcanal from August 1942 to February 1943, Japan lost not only many naval vessels, aircraft, and pilots, but also many high-speed merchant ships—approximately 400,000 tons in total. According to *Strategy and Command*, air power had been a "critical" factor in Guadalcanal, but Japan "had clearly lost the lead to the Allies. During the struggle for Guadalcanal alone they had sacrificed about 900 naval planes, one-third of them carrier-based."[4]

During the period from March 1943 until the end of the year, Japanese forces lost not only the main portion of their naval air power but also more than two hundred army planes of the 4th Air Army (Dai 4 Kokugun) under the command of General Imamura Hitoshi in operations around the Rabaul–Solomon Island area and in New Guinea. Morton writes that

> by late 1943 the high command of the Imperial Navy felt that conditions were ripe for a decisive fleet engagement. Twice in the autumn of that year Admiral Koga Mineichi, Commander in Chief, Combined Fleet, sallied forth from Truk in an effort to engage the U.S. Central Pacific Fleet. Both times he failed to discovery his adversary. In the end he retired to Truk and allowed most of his carrier air strength to be diverted to the Rabaul area, where two thirds of it was lost. In the spring of 1944, as American forces threatened to press farther into western Pacific waters, the Japanese prepared another plan, *Operation A-Go*, in the hope of forcing a major fleet engagement.[5]

Moreover, regarding the comparative battle strength of Japan and the U.S., as shown in *Strategy and Command*, the U.S. Navy had, as of December 31, 1943, the following listed strength. Interestingly, the strength of the Japanese navy was less than half of that for the U.S. Navy, except in heavy cruisers.

U.S. NAVY STRENGTH IN THE PACIFIC (AS OF 31 DECEMBER 1943)

Battleship (new)	6
Battleship (old)	7
Aircraft Carrier (large type)	7
Aircraft Carrier (ten-thousand-ton type)	7
Escort Aircraft Carrier	14
Heavy Cruiser	12
Light Cruiser	13
Destroyer (new)	175
Destroyers (old)	13
Submarines (new)	105
Submarines (old)	18

Carrier-based planes:

Bombers (medium, small, dive, and torpedo)	386
Patrol Bombers (heavy, medium, and small)	660
Fighters	384
Photo-Reconnaissance Planes	36
Reconnaissance Planes	36
Troop Carrier Planes	72

Land-based navy Planes:

Torpedo Bombers	519
Fighters	884
Reconnaissance Bombers	432
Others	106

Army planes cooperating with the navy:

Bombers	745
Reconnaissance Planes	118
Fighters	973
Troop Carrier Planes	312

Thus, around the end of 1943, Imperial Japanese Headquarters had the unpleasant task of sending Imperial Army troops to each of the isolated islands to make those places into unsinkable aircraft carriers while rebuilding the Combined Fleet. In the meantime, it immediately sent off the 52nd Division (Daigojuni Shidan) to Truk in December 1943.

Admiral Yamamoto, who had opposed the war with the United States but nevertheless successfully launched the surprise attack against Pearl Harbor, became a popular and highly respected figure in Japan.[6] However, Yamamoto had to overcome the opposition of the Imperial Japanese Headquarters when conducting the Midway and Guadalcanal campaigns. Although he was eventually given approval for those campaigns, he had to conduct them against great internal opposition. It is unfortunate that as a result of the failure of both campaigns, many war historians in the United States assess Yamamoto lightly. I also think it is a shame that, as I learned after the war, the Japanese codes had already been broken by a retired U.S. Army lieutenant colonel prior to the outbreak of war, leading to Yamamoto's untimely death during an ambush by American P-38 fighters while his plane was en route to Buin on April 18, 1943.

SHIP DAMAGE DUE TO U.S. SUBMARINE ATTACKS

Graduating from the Army War College in November 1942, I worked in the Army Shipping Headquarters (Rikugun Senpaku) as a staff officer and then spent one year, from June 1943, as a liaison officer between the army and the navy at the 1st Convoy Escort Fleet (Daiichi Kaijo Goeitai) and later at the Convoy Escort General Fleet (Kaijo Goei Shirebu). I was able to witness much in these positions, which I will share below.

In the spring of 1943 Japan had the following types and tonnage of merchant vessels:

A group (merchant ships chartered by Imperial Japanese Army)	2,200,000 tons
B group (merchant ships chartered by Imperial Japanese Navy)	1,100,000 tons
C group (remainder of merchant ships in Japan)	2,400,000 tons
Total	5,700,000 tons

Shortly after the start of the war, Japan had about 6,200,000 tons of merchant shipping, including some captured ships. Based on the estimates of the Imperial Japanese Navy General Staff (Gunreibu) about the likelihood of damage and new production of ships, the Cabinet Planning Board (Kikakuin) and the General Staff (Sanbo Honbu) were thinking that 5,800,000 tons might be enough to fight a war of long duration. Thus, the above figure of 5,700,000 tons was not seen as so bad.

In those days, the 1st Convoy Escort Fleet was located at Takao, Taiwan (present-day Kaohsiung City). The fleet was commanded by Vice Admiral Nakajima Torahiko, and Rear Admiral Horie Giichiro was his chief of staff.[7] With such good leaders, I was happy to be there. However, it was the first time for me to serve with the navy, and the poor condition of the convoy escort system greatly surprised me. About ten old destroyers, such as those of the *Kuretake* class, some submarine chasers, and a few newly built coastal defense ships represented the entire strength of the 1st Convoy Escort Fleet.[8] This strength was not only responsible for convoy escort operations in the Southwest Pacific area, but was also the main strength of the Japanese convoy escort ships. Sad dispatches came one after the other into the headquarters—"this ship was sunk" or "that ship was badly damaged." Other messages regularly inquired about how ships moored in different harbors and, thus exposed, should be handled. The fleet was basically vulnerable, without defenses against the enemy submarines.

I had read the World War I memoirs of Winston Churchill. I highlighted the part about the menace of the submarines and printed three hundred copies of it, distributing them to high-ranking army and navy officers all over Japan.[9] They seemed to have been very much surprised when they read it. Both Vice Admiral Nakajima and Rear Admiral Horie admitted that the Japanese navy had done nothing in the area of convoy escort following World War I. They joked, "Don't blame only the navy. The Japanese people as a whole do not like to talk about defense issues in general, and we good men have been forced to do the work on their behalf." The status of the Japanese convoy escort system was thus quite low.

From the autumn of 1943 until the end of the year, Japan sent Anami Korechika, the commanding general of the 2nd Area Army (Daini Homengun), to the northern coast of New Guinea in an operation code-named *Kame Sakusen* (Operation Tortoise). I was sent to Manila to be the liaison officer for sea transportation and convoy escort operations. We had a staff meeting in General Anami's presence at the Manila Hotel every morning. I was responsible for reporting about troop shipping conditions to New Guinea from Japan proper, China, and Korea, mostly through Manila. I had to inform him that I was unable to tell him the expected arrival date and the number of troops and supplies for each destination, as the rate of damage due to sunken ships increased every day.

In November 1943, the Japanese navy was reorganized as follows. The whole navy was divided into two groups, the Combined Fleet and the Convoy Escort General Fleet (Kaijo Goei Sotai). The Combined Fleet was to be in charge of the Pacific Ocean area outside the Truk–Palau–

Singapore line. The Combined Escort General Fleet—composed of the 1st Convoy Escort Fleet, 2nd Convoy Escort Fleet (Daini Kaijo Goeitai), which was in charge of convoy escort between Tokyo and Rabaul), and all naval stations and ports—would be in charge of the Pacific Ocean area inside the Truk–Palau–Singapore line. At that time, I was in Soerabaja, Java, on an official trip, and I received an emergency telegraph from the vice chief of the General Staff which ordered me back to Tokyo immediately. I returned at the end of the year and started work at the Convoy Escort General Fleet Headquarters (Kaijo Goei Soshireibu), located in Tokyo, on January 2, 1944.

The headquarters had very good officers. The commander in chief was Admiral Oikawa Koshiro, the chief of staff was Rear Admiral Shimamoto Hisagoro (who later became the vice chief of staff of the General Staff, and Vice Admiral Kishi Fukuji came aboard as chief of staff), and the senior staff included Captain Goto Jitsuni and Commander Oi Atsushi, in charge of operations. The other members of the staff were also first-rate. Neither this headquarters nor the 1st Convoy Escort Fleet ever discriminated against my being from the army. I still have respect for them today. This fair treatment by them was one of the strong points of the old Imperial Japanese Navy. In the morning, I read the telegrams and reported the damage to shipping from the previous evening to the General Staff. Afterwards, I would continue to read more telegrams and attend meetings. I went to the General Staff in the afternoon, explained the naval situation to the army officers concerned, and then read the army telegrams. At night I returned to the Convoy Escort General Fleet Headquarters and slept in a room at the Navy Ministry with Rear Admiral Shimamoto and Commander Oi.

I was surprised here again. In the navy, the Combined Fleet was the key actor, and the Naval Staff was simply there to take care of administrative details. Furthermore, the Operations Section (Sakusenka) of the Naval Staff was under the orders of the 1st Section, Naval Administration Division (Gunmu Daiikka). The 12th Section of the Naval Staff (Gunreibu Daijunika), which was in charge of convoy escort operations, was behind the scenes. The Combined Fleet, under the command of Admiral Koga, was located at Truk but was too busy to pay attention to convoy escort matters. The officers of the Combined Fleet, having been influenced by the U.S. Navy strategist and instructor of the 19th century Admiral Alfred T. Mahan, through Lieutenant Commander Akiyama Saneyuki about eighty years ago, insisted on there being a decisive battle to fatally knock out the enemy's naval power and did not like the prolonged and conservative convoy escort duty.[10] Their ideas had been also influenced by the specific character of the Japanese people—a dislike of defensive operations in favor of offensive first strikes.

The Convoy Escort General Fleet, therefore, only had less than fifty vessels composed of old destroyers, coastal defense ships, and submarine chasers. Because the Naval Staff was not powerful enough to control the whole navy, the Combined Fleet cooperated with the Convoy Escort General Fleet operations only with great reluctance. Vice Admiral Kishi said to me, both jokingly and sarcastically, "Because there are fifty-seven admirals under the control of Yokosuka Naval Station, we at least would like to have fifty-seven vessels." Later, the 101st Air Squadron (Daihyakuichi Kokutai), which was land-based, four small escort aircraft carriers (*Kaiyo* class), and some army aircraft came under the command of the General Fleet.[11] However, when we compare this with the fact that Navy Minister Churchill decided to fire the British Convoy Escort Fleet commander, believing him to be no more than a technocrat without creativity, and replace him with Commander Archibald R. Henderson, who helped lead the establishment of the British Convoy Escort Fleet in World War I and the cooperative relationship between the convoy fleets of the British and Americans in World War II, our situation would be very weak.

ANTISUBMARINE POLICY OF THE IMPERIAL JAPANESE HEADQUARTERS IN THE SPRING OF 1944

In those days, the truly outstanding officers in the navy were Admiral Shimada Shigetaro, chief of the Naval Staff, Vice Admiral Oka Takazumi, vice minister of the Navy Ministry, Captain Yamamoto Yuji, chief of the 1st Section, Naval Administration Division (Gunmu Daikka), Rear Admiral Tomioka Sadatoshi, director of the 1st Division (Daiichibu), which handled operations, Commander Suzuki Hide, in charge of general operations, and Commander Genda Minoru, in charge of air operations. Moreover, Commander Sogawa Kiysohi, a member of the 12th Section of the Naval Staff (Gunreibu Daijunika), was quite modest and kind, but he was pushed around by the other officers.

The navy was quite different from the Army General Staff, which was able to hold most of the power. Within the army, the leading officers were General Tojo Hideki, chief of the General Staff, Lieutenant General Hata Hikosaburo, vice chief of the General Staff, Major General Sanada Joichiro, director of the 1st Division (Daiichibu), for operations, Colonel Hattori Takushiro, chief of the 2nd Section (Operations) of the same division (Daiichibu Daijunika), Major Sejima Ryuzo, senior operations staff, Colonel Arao Okitsugu, chief of the Shipping Section (Senpakuka), and Colonel Nishiura Susumu, chief of the Army Affairs Section (Gunjika) of the War Department.

Nevertheless, Japan continued to lose ships. In the first half of 1944 alone, the number and tonnage of ships sunk by submarine or lost due to other reasons were as follows:[12]

MONTH	NO. OF SHIPS LOST	TONNAGE LOST
January	87	340,000 tons
February	115	520,000 tons
March	60	230,000 tons
April	37	130,000 tons
May	70	280,000 tons

The total losses of Japanese ships in 1944 were as follows:

No. of ships lost by submarine attacks	565	2,480,000 tons
No. of ships lost by aircraft attacks	234	1,230,000 tons

I remember someone said during this time that "we are losing the equivalent of the island of Shikoku every night."[13]

The estimates, introduced above, that 5,800,000 tons would be enough for Japan to sustain the war over a long period of time were now "ancient history." From a humanitarian perspective, it had become a very desperate situation, because the Convoy Escort General Fleet had to think about the escort of petroleum convoys, bauxite convoys, and iron ore convoys more than that of troop convoys as a national policy, just to keep the industries going back home. The army was angry with the navy and resorted to the unusual step of bringing the issue before Emperor Hirohito at a meeting (gozen kaigi). As the escort of convoys was a critical part of the war effort, the army decided to commit more and more aircraft for convoy escort duties and sent a convoy inspection mission headed by Lieutenant General Suzuki Sosaku (Lieutenant Colonel Miyoshi Sadamu and Lieutenant Colonel Ureshino Tsuki joined this mission from the Shipping Section, Lieutenant Commander Kami Naomichi, responsible for air operations, from the 2nd Section, Commander Eguchi Eiji and the author from the Convoy Escort General Fleet) to the Okinawa–Formosa–Philippines–Borneo area and ordered the Kanegafuchi Textile Co., Ltd., to conduct the test manufacture of a petroleum-carrying submarine. I went to participate in the test of this army petroleum-carrying submarine from Yodogawa Plant in Osaka to Wakanoura Bay in Wakayama Prefecture, immediately south of Osaka. At nine in the morning, as soon as Colonel Arao received my report concerning the loss of ships of the previous night, the chief of the Shipping Section reported it to General Tojo immediately. Tojo called Admiral Shimada right away and they started discussing the issue of convoy escorts.

Tojo used to say that the convoy escorts were the key to the conduct of the overall war and worked hard on this problem. Admiral Shimada cooperated with him, and as a result was criticized as "Tojo's briefcase-carrying aide" by many of his fellow navy officers. The concern within the senior leadership of the army and navy about the convoy escorts, however, was real. From my perspective, the situation at the time could be described in the following analogy. The father (General Tojo) of a poor family who was worried about his relatives (troops), who were sick, decided to send his lovely daughter (ships) to nurse and help them. But his wife (Admiral Shimada) did not have any train fare to give to the daughter, and so the daughter had to go alone at night along a dark road, where many hungry wolves might appear. The parents asked their oldest son to go with her, but this son (the Combined Fleet) was too busy with other business. The second son (Convoy Escort General Fleet), who obeyed his parents despite suffering from a serious illness, got out of his sick bed and went out to escort his sister. Immediately after their departure, the poor brother and sister immediately became prey to the wolves.

U.S. VIEWS OF THE DAMAGE TO THE JAPANESE FLEET

In the chapter entitled "Carriers and Submarines" in Maurice Matloff's history of the Second World War, *Strategic Planning for Coalition Warfare*, the following is written about the role of U.S. submarine warfare:

> U.S. submarines received little publicity, since the very nature of their work demanded tight security measures if they were to stand a chance of returning safely to their home bases. As the U.S. submarine fleet in the Pacific increased, its impact upon Japanese naval and merchant shipping mounted. Operating individually during the first half of the war, U.S. submarines in the Pacific theater had sunk seventeen naval vessels and 142 merchant ships plus four probables, totaling 666,561 tons by the end of 1942. The

pace quickened during the first six months of 1943 when nine naval vessels and 125 merchant ships were sent to the bottom—Japan lost 575,416 tons. During mid-1943, the U.S. undersea raiders operated in small wolf packs as well as singly, and the addition of new and improved submarines made the last half of the year a most fruitful period. From July through December, twelve Japanese naval vessels and 166 merchantmen were destroyed for a total bag of 793,673 tons. Japan was not in a similar position; its limited shipyard facilities made full replacement impossible. With the Army Air Forces using low-altitude and radar bombing techniques against Japanese shipping and [Major General Claire L.] Chennault employing fighter bombers to destroy inland merchant shipping in China, further inroads were made upon the enemy's dwindling merchant marine. The rising rate of Japanese losses imposed restrictions upon her offensive capabilities and even made maintenance and repair difficult.[14]

REINFORCEMENT OF CENTRAL PACIFIC DEFENSE—
TSURU SAKUSEN (OPERATION CRANE)

In February 1944, Truk was attacked by an American task force. The Japanese Combined Fleet fled to Palau, but in March, Palau itself was attacked and the situation of the Combined Fleet became quite desperate. At the end of March, Admiral Koga went missing, and the remaining force of the Combined Fleet fled to the anchorage of Tawi Tawi Island, located south of Halmahera Island. The Imperial Japanese Headquarters established a Central Pacific Fleet (Chubu Taiheiyo Homen Kantai) under the command of Vice Admiral Nagumo, who had been in charge of the execution of the Pearl Harbor and Midway attacks. The 11th Air Fleet (Daijuichi Koku Kantai), a land-based air force established and headed by Vice Admiral Kakuta Kakuji and the 31st Army (Daisanjuichi Gun), headed by Lieutenant General Obata Hideyoshi, was organized under Nagumo. The chief of staff of the 31st Army was Major General Iketa Keiji. Colonel Shimamura Noriyasu had already been assigned to the Combined Fleet, and now Major General Tamura Yoshitomi was assigned to the Central Pacific Fleet, and both men served as advisors for the commanders in chief of the Combined Fleet and the Central Pacific Fleet, respectively, regarding the use of army forces for the defense of the islands in the Pacific.

From March to May 1944, the so-called *Tsuru Sakusen*, or "Crane Operation," was carried out to reinforce the defense of the islands in the Central Pacific. Some fifty thousand troops were sent—the 14th Division (Daijuyon Shidan) to Palau, 43rd Division (Daiyonjusan Shidan) to Saipan, 29th Division (Dainijukyu Shidan) to Guam, along with some independent brigades and independent regiments. The damage to shipping was not so bad during this operation, with the exception of the loss of the *Sakito-maru*, which was carrying the 29th Infantry Regiment (Hohei Dainijukyu Rentai), and resulted in the sinking of its personnel. It was later learned, after the end of the war, that the period of Operation Crane occurred at the same time as the rotation of U.S. submarines, thus the relatively high success rate in avoiding attacks by the American navy.

One Saturday afternoon I went home in the car of Vice Admiral Kishi. On our way home, Kishi said, "Major Horie, I have heard that General Tojo told the chief of the Naval Operations Division that he could reinforce Saipan, making it impregnable, with the help of the convoy escort by the navy. What do you think?" I found it difficult to answer, so I replied, "He might have said so, under the assumption that the Combined Fleet might still be strong enough to stand up to the U.S. Navy." Later, after U.S. forces did take Saipan, and in light of the atmosphere at the time within the General Staff, it does appear that Tojo had actually made such a declaration.

At the time, I used to say that those who are in charge of the conduct of the war should at least experience the hell of life aboard a merchant ship or convoy escort ship (I, myself, had done so aboard a submarine chaser from Formosa to Manila). Without this experience, the leadership cannot understand the total picture, a view I still believe was correct.

In those days, the navy regularly conducted study meetings. About twenty to thirty officers, including Admiral Nagano Osami, Admiral Shimada, Captain (and Prince) Takamatsu Nomiya, and Admiral Oikawa, attended. I was the only one in a khaki army uniform among them. Symbolic of how serious they were, one participant (I think it was Admiral Nagano) said, "The people of Japan believe that the army started the war but that the navy is losing it. We must restore our reputation."[15] Very often, I was so moved by these statements that my eyes filled with tears. Out at sea, enemy submarines were using radar with deadly effect, and our submarine crews were fighting only with their eyes. The outcome was clear. Captain Oka Takasumi, sitting beside me, said, "With our ships twenty years behind, how can we fight this war?" He concluded that the difference in the levels in technology would decide the victor.

MY LECTURES TO THE ARMY CONCERNING
ANTISUBMARINE TACTICS

Working day and night in this desperate environment, I was very glad to have been asked by the Army Education Administration (Kyoiku Sokanbu) of the army to lecture before army officers at the headquarters of the Eastern Army (Tobugun), Central Army (Chubugun), and Western Army (Seibugun), as well the Army Academy, the Military Preparatory Academy (Rikugun Yoka Shikan Gakko), and the Toyohashi Army Noncommissioned Officers School (Toyohashi Rikugun Kyodo Gakko), etc., in accordance with the schedule prepared by the Army Education Administration. Because the lectures on antisubmarine tactics were seen as necessary (with many of the troops to deploy abroad in light of the worsening war situation) and the fact that many of those in attendance wanted to escape at least for a little while the depressing atmosphere of their work, the talks were well attended (100 percent attendance), and the participants listened carefully, anxious to know the situation of the Pacific. I still remember the frozen faces of Lieutenant General Makino Shira, the superintendent of the Military Preparatory Academy, who was later killed in action at Leyte as the commander of the 16th Division (Daijuroku Shidan), and Lieutenant General Ushijima Mitsuru, then the commandant of the Military Academy, later killed in action at Okinawa as the commander of the 32nd Army (Daisanjuni Rikugun).

I still remember one time as I was about to finish my lecture in the large auditorium of the Military Academy, Major Kuroiwa Toichi, who was with the Army Education Administration and had accompanied me, ran up and said, "Your lecture was so pessimistic that the listeners may lose their fighting spirit. Please tell them that our Imperial Army still has fighting spirit at the end of your speech." I did it, albeit with somewhat mixed feelings.

chapter three

SAIPAN WAS SAID TO BE IMPREGNABLE

I AM TO BE TRANSFERRED TO THE 31ST ARMY AT SAIPAN

On June 10, 1944, I set out for Ujina in southern Hiroshima in order to attend a ceremony commemorating the fiftieth anniversary of the establishment of the Army Shipping Headquarters (Rikugun Unyubu).[1] I arrived there on the evening of the 9th and immediately went to report to Lieutenant General Suzuki Eisaku, who was like a father to me, about recent convoy escort operations.

He regularly asked me to provide him with information on the Combined Fleet, because, in his opinion, it was the main strength of the Japanese armed forces in the Pacific. We often talked about General Ugaki Kazushige, Lieutenant General Nagata Tetsuzan, and General Imamura Hitoshi in connection with the Army Education Administration, and he would say that if General Nagata had been alive, Japan would have not found itself in this situation. Suzuki used to say that the greatest evil of the army was the fact that many officers had come to erroneously worship General Yamashita Yasufumi, Lieutenant General Ishiwara Kanji, and Colonel Tsuji Masanobu, and he spoke about the difficult times he had as chief of staff of the 25th Army (Dainijugo Gun) in Malay when General Yamashita and Colonel Tsuji would not speak to each other for two, sometimes three, days at a time.

The skies were clear on June 10. I attended the solemn ceremony in the morning and moved to the dining hall just before noon. Although the times were gloomy, thanks to the efforts of Lieutenant Sasaki Akira, an actor in civilian life, the atmosphere was livened up by bringing in some top movie stars, including Miura Tamaki, Hara Setsuko, and Todoroki Yukiko, and planning many activities for the day.

After lunch, while I was busy in conversation with the actress Hara (she and I were talking about my visit last year to her Toho Production studios, when I helped write the script for the film *Unsosen*, or "Sea Transport"), Colonel Matsuo Eiichi, adjutant to Lieutenant General Suzuki, came to me with a frozen look on his face and said there was a telegram waiting for me. He took me to see General Suzuki and read the telegram to the general and me: "Major Horie is to be transferred to the 31st Army as of June 5, 1944." It was already about 1330, June 10, then. I asked one of the staff to go purchase a ticket on a sleeper carriage for me to return to Tokyo that night.

In the evening, General Suzuki, Major General Isoya Goro, the chief of staff, and some ten staff officers held a farewell party for me. I thought that it would be the last time for me to see them and thus thanked them for their kindness. Then I left Hiroshima for Tokyo.

I arrived at the General Staff in the afternoon of June 11. They told me that the focus of the war was shifting to the Central Pacific and that I would need to work with the navy to help supply the 31st Army. The next morning, June 12, I went to the Convoy Escort General Fleet Headquarters and explained about my transfer to the 31st Army to Rear Admiral Shimamoto and Oi, who had since been promoted to navy captain in March 1944. Then I went to the 12th Section of the Naval Staff to ask Commander Sogawa to provide air transportation from Kisarazu Airfield, in Chiba Prefecture, to Saipan. Sogawa made some inquiries and found out that air transportation was available only every four days, that the plane had already departed that day, and the next one was leaving on the 16th. Realizing that was the earliest I could go, I filled out the necessary paperwork and thanked him. I then went back to the Convoy Escort General Fleet Headquarters to look at the messages that had come over the past several days. I found one that read, "A large American convoy that left Ulithi is moving northwest."

Members of the General Staff and the Naval Staff had different opinions as to what this meant. The enemy might come to Palau, some said. No, they might come to Saipan, others argued. No, they will come to Guam, another person said. Ten people, ten opinions. Dispirited, I went to the Army Medical Department (Rikgunsho Imukyoku) to see Lieutenant Colonel (Doctor) Takatsuki Tamotsu to get a packet of potassium cyanide. No matter what happens, I would not let myself get caught by the enemy, I thought. After explaining my reason, he very kindly gave it to me immediately. When I returned to the General Staff, someone said to me, "Horie! The enemy just started bombing Saipan."

Hasten there! I am afraid you might not be in time." I went to the Shipping Section quickly and began reading the messages. One of them read: "The enemy task force is bombing Saipan. Behind them there are many ships. From the chief of staff, 31st Army."

On June 13, I went to my hometown, in Ibaraki Prefecture, to see my mother and to pay my respects before the graves of my ancestors. I told my mother that my wife would send thirty yen to her every month and asked that if I were killed that she help my wife and daughter. However, I explained, she should let my wife go back to her own family, should she chose to do so, if I died. My mother said to me, "You escaped by a hair's breath in northern China." (In 1938, I was machine-gunned during our attack against the Chinese army defending Kaifeng. I was a first lieutenant at the time and was hit by five bullets, one of which penetrated my skull on one side and went out the other. It took away some portion of the motion-nerve of my legs, making me crippled. Two bullets, which lodged in my wallet in my breast pocket, broke bones in my shoulder. Two others went through the inner sides of my thigh.) "I am sure you will return alive this time, too." She added, "I built a small shrine and I pray for you every day and night. Don't worry about death."

When I returned from the cemetery with my mother and older brother, one of my cousins was there waiting at the house. She had returned to Japan in March from Saipan with her two daughters, leaving her husband there.[2] I finally told her that I was going to Saipan. While I was talking with my mother in front of the Buddhist altar, she boiled about ten eggs and wrote a letter to her husband telling him that she and the children were fine. She asked me to take the letter and eggs to her husband on Saipan. Bringing these items with me, I returned to my home in Tokyo by night train and got my things in order at home.

On June 14, I went to the General Staff in the morning and the Convoy Escort General Fleet Headquarters in the afternoon and read the messages that had come in. Everywhere, everybody was busy. One message read, "Several hundred vessels of the enemy are now surrounding Saipan," and others said, "Another enemy convoy is seen," "The enemy started naval gun firing," etc. There were many messages about sunken ships, but no one paid any attention to these anymore.

On my way to the Naval Staff to see Commander Sogawa, I ran into Rear Admiral Horie. We both said to one another at the same time, "Long time no see." He told me that he had just arrived at the Naval Staff because he had been assigned to work there as the director of sea transportation. I told him that I had been transferred to the 31st Army. He said, "Then, I will introduce you to the main members of the Naval Staff and the Navy Ministry. These contacts will help you in the future in your work." He took me to two or three rooms and introduced me to the navy officers inside. Everybody looked annoyed and had no time for my greetings. Rear Admiral Horie did not know what to do.

Back in the hallway, I met Commander Sogawa. "Major Horie," he said, "You can't go to Saipan on June 16. Air transportation has been canceled." By the time I could thank him for letting me know, he was gone. I told Rear Admiral Horie that I would go back to the Convoy Escort General Fleet Headquarters and check on things. As I returned to the headquarters I saw Admiral Oikawa at the building's entrance. He smiled at me and said, "I heard you are leaving this headquarters tomorrow." I told him that that was true, and he said, "Well, come by to my office about ten minutes prior to the farewell ceremony, as I would like to give you a gift." When I entered the staff room, I overheard some heated arguments about whether or not Japan should send the Combined Fleet into this operation.

The Naval Staff had already instructed the commander in chief of the Combined Fleet to prepare Operation *A-Go*, the code name for the decisive naval battle to take place [in the Philippines] in early 1944 against the U.S. Pacific Fleet. Admiral Toyoda Soemu, commander in chief of the Combined Fleet, had ordered Vice Admiral Ugaki Matome, commander of Operation *Kon*, the code name for the operation to reinforce the inland defenses of Biak Island, to stop his operation and move north to join the main task force off the east coast of the Philippines.[3] Toyoda had also directed Vice Admiral Ozawa Jisaburo, the highly respected commander in chief of the 1st Task Force—the main strength of the Combined Fleet—to move north and command Ugaki's fleet and be ready for Operation *A-Go*. In those days, operation orders for the Combined Fleet were issued as "GF [the navy used to call the Combined Fleet this] Operation Order (number)" and those for the 1st Task Force as "1KDF Operation Order (number)."

I left the headquarters around 4:00 PM that day, mentioning that I would be leaving for good at 1:00 PM the next day. I had no desire to stop off at the General Staff, because there was nothing I could do without knowing the intention of the enemy.

U.S. FORCES BEGIN THEIR INVASION OF SAIPAN ON JUNE 15, 1944

On the morning of June 15, I did in fact end up going to the General Staff. The enemy had started the invasion of Saipan that day. This was the first time I saw the office this busy. The men there were displeased with the situation in Saipan. "What an ignoble army the 31st is! What a failure of a man Major General Iketa is! Why were they so weak to allow the enemy to land?"

The reason Major General Iketa was spoken ill of like this was that he was in charge of the island in the absence of General Obata Hideyoshi, commanding general of the 31st Army, who was off Saipan inspecting Palau with his chief of staff, Major General Tamura Yoshi-tomi, when the enemy launched its attack on Saipan.

Someone said, "Iketa should be relieved. He is careless and weak. We had better bring Major General Cho Isamu from Manchuria to replace him."

Lieutenant Colonel Miyoshi of the Shipping Section told me, "Major Tsukamoto Kiyohiko made some recommendations to General Tojo and ended up getting him angry. He was to be exiled to Saipan. You had better talk with him about getting there." I spoke with Major Tsukamoto, and we agreed to go to Saipan by air, not by sea, because we could not expect to be able to arrive there safely by ship. But, how could we get there? I sent a message to Major General Iketa to ask for some guidance.

I doubted it was true that the 31st Army was weak. However, the reputation of the 31st Army was very bad within the General Staff, and I, a low-ranking officer, could not say anything to change their mind. I did not know what to do and felt paralyzed. The bold declaration of Tojo's that "Saipan was impregnable," which Vice Admiral Kishi had told me about, began to haunt me.

Incidentally, Major General Iketa, assisting Lieutenant General Saito Yoshitsugu, commanding general of the 43rd Division (Daiyon-jusan Shidan), did a very good job in commanding the forces on the island. In particular, the 31st Army suffered big losses on the beaches at the beginning of the battle, and Iketa expertly led a fighting retreat. The U.S. official history of the battle has discussed this retreat operation and noted that U.S. forces had a difficult time. Based on the lessons from the fighting on Saipan, American forces extended by one month the period of prelanding bombardment of Guam. Iketa knew that Tokyo would be vulnerable to air attacks if Aslito Airfield on Saipan fell to the enemy even before he received the orders from the Imperial Japanese Headquarters to "defend to the death" the airfield. When Iketa finally launched the banzai charge in the northern end of the island on July 7, he was as skinny as a ghost, like Saito. This fact tells us how hard Iketa fought. The instructions sent by him became the basis of the tactics for the Peleliu and Iwo Jima campaigns.

I ran to the Convoy Escort General Fleet Headquarters in time to attend my last lunch there, and then I prepared to attend the ceremony honoring me. In those days the Japanese navy had a custom of seeing off departing officers, with all the officers and men in attendance. The atmosphere of this headquarters was completely different from that of the General Staff. There was a pall in every room. Everyone looked at me as if I were a sheep going to be butchered. They offered me words of comfort or sympathy. Several female clerks, students who had been drafted into wartime service, said to me, "So long!" with handkerchiefs on their cheeks. What a difference between the Japanese armed forces there is!

At 1:00 PM, I entered Admiral Oikawa's office as I had been instructed. He was the leading expert within the navy on Chinese literature and was reading a big book when I came in. He stopped reading, stood, and said to me, "You know the war situation. The GF has left already." He could not fight back the tears and just cried. With his trembling hands, he presented me one of his portraits with his signature done with a writing brush in the upper right corner. For the past six months, he had told us ribald stories at lunch about young women that made us laugh. Now his crying moved me. Suddenly tears came to my eyes, too.

All the staff of the Convoy Escort General Fleet Headquarters lined up in front of the headquarters and saw me off. I heard some people sobbing. Just outside the headquarters I asked my driver to wait for about ten minutes, and I went to the 12th Section of the Naval Staff to see Commander Sogawa. All the navy officers I met on the way in said, "Is there any chance for Admiral Ozawa Jisaburo to win? Victory or defeat will come in a few days." Nobody spoke about Saipan. In other words, the key point was the success or failure of Operation *A-Go*. I agreed with these people completely, and I prayed for victory of our Combined Fleet.

THE PLAN TO RETAKE SAIPAN

I went to the General Staff and visited with Colonel Hattori Takushiro. He told me, "Tomorrow, Major General Cho, who is to become the chief of staff of the 31st Army, will arrive here. With him, you are to make a plan to retake Saipan." I was given some maps of Saipan. He went on to explain the situation: "The strength to be used for the retaking operation will be the 109th Division (Daihyakukyu Shidan) and the 9th Division

(Daikyu Shidan). The 5th Fleet will cooperate with our counterlanding. The 145th Infantry Regiment (Hohei Daihyakuyonjugo Rentai) is moving to Yokohama from Kagoshima. The 9th Division is coming to Pusan, Korea, from Manchuria. The 5th Fleet is rushing to Yokohama from the northern Pacific."

I went to the General Staff early the next morning (June 16) and tried to meet with Colonel Hattori or Major Sejima. Both of them were too busy to see me. I left the Operations Section on the second floor and went downstairs to the Shipping Section on the first floor and read a message that said, "Enemy planes are all around above Saipan and several hundred vessels are bombarding the island from offshore. The enemy is landing on Saipan!" Lieutenant Colonel Miyoshi showed me a message that had arrived from Saipan which read: "To Major Horie, Come to Saipan! Major General Iketa." Major Tsukamoto was busy cleaning out his desk.

As I wanted to know the situation of the Combined Fleet, I went to the Convoy Escort General Fleet Headquarters, from which I just "retired" the day before, to see the navy's messages. There were many dispatches laid out on the tables. Everyone was interested in the messages related to Operation *A-Go*. Nobody paid any attention to the reports of convoy operations. One message read, "The fate of our Empire depends upon this single battle," and another said, "Z flag was raised." These messages were issued by the Combined Fleet Headquarters, then located at Kisarazu, and by the 1st Task Force Headquarters (Daiichi Kido Kantai), under the command of Vice Admiral Ozawa. We could follow the situation of each plane and each vessel. On the other hand, some dispatches had arrived from the 11th Air Fleet, under the command of Vice Admiral Kakuta Kakuji, stating that it had been bitterly fighting against the enemy air raids. They said that Guam, Tinian, Rota, and Palau had been raided. One staff member who had visited the Convoy Escort General Fleet Headquarters from the Combined Fleet explained, "The enemy has many more carrier planes. However, we have a chance to win. After taking off and attacking the enemy, our planes can land on Guam and refuel, then they could go and attack the enemy again and again."

We learned soon thereafter that this story was completely wrong. The airfields on Guam had been badly damaged by enemy air raids and our planes landing there were all destroyed.

I returned to the General Staff at about 11:30. I was surprised when I saw Major General Cho, because he was very tall. We were given a room on the second floor. He asked me what the situation at Saipan was like. I told him what I knew, based on the dispatches sent from Saipan and the navy messages. He said to me, "Until we know the results of Operation *A-Go*, there is nothing we can do. Take it easy for the time being."

Throughout the building, however, the situation was the same as the day before. The General Staff continued to speak ill of the 31st Army. Someone from the Army Department brought in two No. 5 radios for us, saying that they were for the counterlanding operations at Saipan. Major General Cho and I just looked at him and said something to the effect of, "Oh, okay," without any emotion.

In the afternoon, I went to the Convoy Escort General Fleet Headquarters again to read dispatches. I could more clearly "see" the movements of the fleets of both Ozawa and Ugaki. On the other hand, many planes of the 11th Air Fleet (Daijuichi Koku Kantai) disappeared after the communication, "I am attacking an enemy vessel." The attrition of the planes of the 11th Air Fleet was serious. We anticipated the decisive battle between the Combined Fleet and the American Fifth Fleet on June 19.

On the morning of June 17, Colonel Ikeda, commander of the 145th Infantry Regiment, visited me in my room on the second floor of the General Staff to ask me for guidance. Soon after, Major Nakazawa Mitsuo, a staff officer of the 9th Division, came to ask me for guidance as well. I told Nakazawa to wait until the afternoon of June 19. At this time, I also received a dispatch from Major General Iketa telling me to go to Palau to join General Obata.

That afternoon, I borrowed a sidecar and a driver from the 145th Infantry Regiment, put the radios in it, and went to Yokohama Harbor. I gave a lecture on antisubmarine and antiaircraft warfare to the officers and men gathered in the harbor on *Noto Maru*, one of the best remaining ships, which could travel at fourteen knots.

I then went back to the Convoy Escort General Fleet Headquarters to find out about the status of Operation *A-Go* and called a staff officer at the Yokosuka Naval Base (Yokosuka Chinjufu) to ask him to inform the staff there that I would visit the cruiser *Yubari*, the flagship of the 5th Fleet, to discuss the operations to retake Saipan.

The dispatches said that enemy troops were advancing into the interior of Saipan and that Japanese forces were fighting desperately. The members of the 6th Fleet (Dairoku Kantai) in Saipan, a submarine fleet whose chief of staff was Rear Admiral Shimamoto, missed the opportunity to go out to sea and decided to stay and fight with the ground forces. What a sad message.

I went by sidecar to Yokosuka on June 18 to meet with the staff of the cruiser *Yubari*. The commander from *Yubari* met me. I was ushered to the officer's cabin, and we began our meeting to discuss retaking Saipan.

The navy officers were energetic, which surprised me. I heard one interesting story when I was with them. A lieutenant said, "We are very happy. The enemy is the Fifth Fleet, and coincidentally we belong to the 5th Fleet (Daigo Kantai). We are honored to fight against the same-numbered fleet."

When I asked the commander how many vessels and aircraft he had left in his fleet, he replied that they had two cruisers, eight destroyers, and two aircraft carriers. I stayed quiet for a moment. I was moved by the maintenance of secrecy of the navy and the purity of the officers of the fleet and did not have the heart to tell them that I had heard that the U.S. Fifth Fleet had more than 150 vessels and one thousand aircraft. I told them I would let them know the results of Operation *A-Go* and left *Yubari* around 4:50 PM.

I was struck by the valor of the General Staff and the boldness of the 5th Fleet, and I thought the Chinese poem "I shall not be afraid of ten million people if I am right" reflected the mood that night. Emboldened, I began not to worry about anything, thinking it all right if I too gave up my life for the cause. I checked my pocket to see if the cyanide tablets were still there.

I went to Yokohama Harbor to *Noto Maru*. Colonel Ikeda met me. I asked him to allow me to stay overnight on the ship, and he kindly made his cabin available for me. I told him not to do so, but he insisted. Colonel Ikeda, his adjutant, and I had dinner in the cabin. We had a bottle of beer, which tasted good.

On the ship, I heard another funny story. One lieutenant colonel of the Ship Engineering Regiment (Senpaku Kohei) came to see me. He gave me a piece of paper and asked me to write my name, then my wife's name, in order to tell my fortune. When I finished writing them, the color in his face changed. "The number of Chinese character strokes to your name and that of your wife's causes me to expect your death. You should change your name and also your wife's name tomorrow. If you change them, you will be able to return alive, I am sure." I remembered that when I was a second lieutenant in the 2nd Infantry Regiment (Hohei Daini Rentai), Colonel Ishiguro Senkyunosuke asked me to buy and distribute some books from one of the new religions, and I thought that the same thing was happening here. I told him, "Don't worry about me. I have given up hope, and I have no time to change my name officially." I tried to get away from him by going up on the deck, but he followed me. I guess he felt he had to try one more time to keep me from dying. Finally, his attention moved to Colonel Ikeda. Relieved to be rid of him, I gathered the battalion commanders on the deck and explained the war situation to them.

OPERATION *A-GO* LOST

The day Japan's fate was sealed finally came. It was June 19, 1944. Japan was like a patient with a fever who expected to recover despite the illness actually becoming worse. Delirious with the success of the surprise attack against Pearl Harbor and the fall of Singapore, the patient Japan had experienced the dislocation of its pelvis and legs at Midway and then suffered from arteriosclerosis in the convoy escort operation in the Pacific. However, having received some emergency treatment, the patient somehow expected his recovery. The full seriousness of the patient's condition became apparent on this day, June 19. The heavens could not help the patient, and he became paralyzed. This dire situation was Japan in the second half of June 1944.

The Japanese fleet was destroyed in Operation *A-Go*. The 1st Task Force (Daiichi Kido Kantai), which was still in the process of rebuilding, had all of the pride and hope of the Japanese nation behind it, but in the end was completely defeated. Aircraft carriers and their aircraft could be built again, but as at Midway, the experienced pilots were lost forever. June 19 was the death of Japan indeed. Praying for the happiness for the brave pilots now sleeping at the bottom of the Pacific, let us read from Philip A. Crowl's *The War in the Pacific: Campaign in the Marianas:*

> On 11 June the Japanese admiral received word of Mitscher's carrier strike against Saipan and immediately suspended the *Kon* operation, ordering the task force bound for Biak to join forces with the main body of Ozawa's 1st Mobile Fleet.[4] Ozawa himself sortied from Tawi Tawi two days later, and on the morning of the 15th Operation *A-Go* was activated. Contrary to earlier Japanese expectations, the Americans had chosen to attack the Marianas rather than the Western Carolinas. Hence the scene of the impending "decisive fleet engagement" could only lie somewhere in the

Philippine Sea—that vast stretch of ocean between the Philippines and Marianas. On the evening of 15 June Ozawa's Fleet had completed its progress from Tawi Tawi up the Visayan Sea and through San Bernardino Strait into the Philippine Sea. On the next afternoon it was joined by the *Kon* force that had been diverted from Biak. Both fleets were sighted by American submarines, and it was apparent that the Japanese were heading in a northeasterly direction toward the Marianas. All together, Ozawa had mustered 5 carriers, 4 light carriers, 5 battleships, 11 heavy cruisers, 2 light cruisers, 28 destroyers, and 430 carrier-based combat aircraft. He was outnumbered by the Americans in every respect except in heavy cruisers. Spruance had at his disposal 7 carriers, 8 light carriers, 7 battleships, 8 heavy cruisers, 13 light cruisers, 69 destroyers, and 891 carrier-based planes. The mammoth American fleet was divided into four carrier task groups under Adm. Mitscher, Commander, Task Force 58. Mitscher was in tactical command, but his major tactical decisions had to be approved by Spruance as Commander, Fifth Fleet. By the morning of 18 June all four American carrier groups had rendezvoused and were steaming in a southwesterly direction toward the approaching enemy. Spruance had ordered: "Action against the enemy must be pushed vigorously by all hands to ensure complete destruction of his fleet," but had added the precautionary note, "Task Force 58 must cover Saipan and our forces engaged in that operation." That night Adm. Mitscher learned the full meaning of this qualification when his superior ordered him to change course to the east and maintain it until daylight. Mitscher protested but was overruled. Adm. Spruance was fearful that Ozawa might attempt an end run under cover of darkness and put the Japanese fleet between him and Saipan. . . . On the morning of the 19th, after the American carriers had turned west again, Ozawa's planes, which were lighter and less well armed and therefore capable of greater range than their American rivals, delivered the first blow. In four separate raids, delivered for almost five hours Japanese planes roared over the horizon in a futile effort to knock out Mitscher's mighty fleet. Out of all the American surface vessels present, only one was hit—the battleship *South Dakota*, which lost 27 men killed and 23 wounded, but was not seriously damaged. . . . By evening the "Great Marianas Turkey Shoot" was over with disastrous results to the Japanese. Out of 430 carrier planes, Ozawa lost 330. Some went down under the fire of American ships and planes; others were destroyed on Guam and Rota; and still others were counted as operational casualties. Against this, only twenty-four American planes were shot down and six lost operationally. The same day, two Japanese carriers, *Shokaku* and *Taiho* (Ozawa's flagship), were sunk by American submarines operating well to the south of Mitscher's fleet. That night Ozawa changed course to the northwest hoping to put distance between him and the American fleet and to allow him opportunity to refuel. . . . Mitscher immediately launched a twilight air attack that succeeded in destroying about 65 of Ozawa's remaining 100 aircraft, sinking the carrier *Hiyo*, hitting another carrier and a battleship, and damaging the fleet oilers to the extent that they had to be scuttled. American plane losses came to 100, mostly incurred through crashes when the returning planes tried to land on their carriers after dark. Personnel casualties were not so heavy, coming to only 49. . . . In the opinion of Samuel Eliot Morison, "Thus, the Japanese land forces on Saipan, Tinian, and Guam were doomed, no matter how bravely and doggedly they fought."[5]

SAIPAN HAS TO BE ABANDONED

After June 19, we awaited each and every report from our aircraft and ships, but only bad news came. That same day Colonel Omura and some of his officers came to Tokyo from the Army Shipping Headquarters at Ujina to participate in the preparations for the counterlanding at Saipan. At noon on June 20, Colonel Arao Okikatsu held a farewell luncheon party for me, Colonel Omura, and some other officers. I was grateful to Colonel Arao for his thoughtfulness, but I was so anxious to know the results of Operation *A-Go* that I left the party early and went by taxi to the Convoy Escort General Fleet Headquarters to read the dispatches coming from the headquarters of Ozawa's fleet. The men looked like they were attending a wake. No good news came, either on the 20th or 21st.

At 1400 on June 22, the two service chiefs, General Tojo and Admiral Shimada, went to see the emperor. They went to report to the emperor that they could find no alternative to abandoning Saipan. With this, the war situation entered a new stage.

Shortly before then, at noon, I had received a memo at the Shipping Section from Major Tsukamoto. It read: "Horie-kun, I made every effort to find you. Because of the time, I am leaving ahead of you. I am sorry. Major Tsukamoto." Apparently, earlier that day, Major Tsu-kamoto had gotten word that a bomber was going to leave Tachikawa Airfield (Tachikawa Hikojo) at about ten o'clock. The plane was headed for Formosa. He tried to find me, in accordance with our promise that we would go together by air. Failing to find me, he left a memo for me and went to Tachikawa without me. I was angry and said to Lieuten-ant Colonel Miyoshi, "Major Tsukamoto had promised to go with me. He broke his promise. He is good for nothing." I turned my attention to thinking how I could find other air transportation to get to General Obata's side.

Major Tsukamoto went to Palau via Taipei and Manila. He joined General Obata and Major General Tamura there. They went to Guam by a navy plane but were killed in action when American forces invaded Guam. While it was only for a few days that we were together, I remem-ber Major General Cho, Major Tsukamoto, and I being in the same office on the second floor of the General Staff saying, "Let's ensure we die together." Now, twenty years have passed since Tsukamoto was killed on Guam, and Cho on Okinawa. I have since forgiven Tsukamoto for leaving without me.

chapter four

IWO JIMA IS NEXT!

ESTABLISHMENT OF THE OGASAWARA ISLANDS FORCE AND 32ND ARMY

After losing Operation *A-Go*, the Imperial Japanese Headquarters decided to strengthen the defenses of the Ogasawara Islands and Okinawa. The Hattori–Sejima line was in force because the army still had dozens of divisions intact.

However, it was unlikely that these divisions could be used in the Pacific, even if it was appropriate to try to do so. In essence, this was the problem, but Japan in those days was like a ship that had already been launched—there was no alternative now at this point. On July 1, 1944, the Ogasawara Islands Force (Ogasawara Heidan) and 32nd Army (Daisanjuni Gun) were established, and the troops that had been garrisoned in the Ogasawara Islands were separated from command of the 31st Army and came under the direct command of the Imperial Japanese Headquarters. The 32nd Army, on the other hand, came under the command of Lieutenant General Ando Rikichi, the commanding general of the 10th Area Army (Daiju Homengun), based in Taiwan.[1]

AREA COMING FROM	HARBOR DEPARTING FROM	TROOPS
Kagoshima	Yokohama	145th Infantry Regiment (Hohei Daihyakuyonjugo Rentai)
All over Japan	Pusan	26th Tank Regiment (Sensha Dainijuroku Rentai)
Kanto	Shibaura (Tokyo Bay)	109th Divisional Headquarters (Daihyakukyu Shidan Shireibu)

AREA COMING FROM	HARBOR DEPARTING FROM	TROOPS
All over Japan	Shibaura	109th Division Communication Unit (Daihyakukyu Shidan Tsuhintai)
All over Japan	Yokohama	109th Division Radar Unit (Daihyakukyu Shidan Keikaitai)
All over Japan	Yokohama	109th Jet Propelling Gun Battery (Daihyakukyu Shidan Funshinho Chutai)
Hiroshima	Hiroshima	3rd Battalion, 17th Independent Mixed Regiment (Dokuritsu Konsei Daijunana Rentai Daisan Daitai)
Northeastern area of Honshu	Shibaura	Iwo Jima Provisional Ammunition Service Unit (Iwo Jima Rinji Heikisho)
Northeastern area of Honshu and Kanto	Shibaura	Iwo Jima Provisional Material Service Unit (Iwo Jima Rinji Kamotsusho)
Kanto	Shibaura	2nd Mixed Brigade Field Hospital (Konsei Daini Ryodan Yasen Byoin)
Kyushu and Chugoku	Yokohama	20th Special 25-mm Machine-Gun Unit (Tokusetu Dainiju Kikanhotai)
Kyushu and Chugoku	Yokohama	21st Special 25-mm Machine-Gun Unit (Tokusetu Dainijuichi Kikanhotai)
Kyushu	Yokohama	5th Fortress Construction Company (Yosai Kensetsu Kenchiku Daigo Chutai)
Kanto	Yokohama	8th Independent Antitank-Gun Battalion (Dokuritsu Sokushaho Daihachi Taitai)
Kanto	Yokohama	9th Independent Antitank-Gun Battalion (Dokuritsu Sokushaho Daikyu Taitai)
Kinki (Osaka-Nara area)	Osaka (By cruiser)	10th Independent Antitank-Gun Battalion (Dokuritsu Sokushaho Daiju Taitai)

AREA COMING FROM	HARBOR DEPARTING FROM	TROOPS
Shimane and Hiroshima	Yokohama	11th Independent Antitank Gun Battalion (Dokuritsu Sokushaho Daijuichi Taitai)
Kanto	Yokohama	1st Independent Machine-Gun Battalion (Dokuritsu Kikanju Daiichi Taitai)
Northeastern area of Honshu	Yokohama	2nd Independent Machine-Gun Battalion (Dokuritsu Kikanju Daini Taitai)
Kyushu	Yokohama	2nd Medium Howitzer Battalion (Chuhakugekiho Daini Taitai)
Kanto	Yokohama	3rd Medium Howitzer Battalion (Chuhakugekiho Daisan Taitai)
All over Japan	Yokohama	109th Charge Company (Daihyakukyu Shidan Totsugeki Chutai)
All over Japan	Pusan	20th Independent Howitzer Battalion (Dokuritsu Kyuho Dainiju Taitai)

TOTAL STRENGTH: ABOUT THIRTEEN THOUSAND TROOPS.

The 109th Division was ordered to be the main strength of the Ogasawara Islands Force, and the 9th Division was ordered to go to Okinawa.

On June 23, Colonel Hattori told me that Major General Cho would be sent to Okinawa to become chief of staff of the 32nd Army and that I would be going to the Ogasawara Islands. "Thank you, Major Horie," the tall general said to me. "So long," he added, and left our room.

Lieutenant Colonel Miyoshi and Major Tomida Minoru of the Shipping Section said to me, "There is no harbor at Iwo Jima, so you will probably end up at Chichi Jima. Continue to give us information after you leave here. The Ogasawara Islands Force will come under the direct command of the Imperial Japanese Headquarters." They were always kind to me.

COMMITMENT OF 13,000 TROOPS TO IWO JIMA
Major Sejima, who was in charge of general operations, Major Haruki Takeshi, who was in charge of operations in the Central Pacific, and

Lieutenant Colonel Itagaki Toru, in charge of logistics, worked with the members of the Organization Section (Henseika) of the General Staff and the Ammunition Section (Heibika) of the Army Department to help dispatch the above-listed troops to Iwo Jima. Some of the troops—namely, the detached 109th Divisional Headquarters (Daihyakukyu Shidan Buntai) and 109th Division Communication Unit (Daihyakukyu Shidan Tsushintai)—stayed on at Chichi Jima. Furthermore, about 1,700 men of the 17th Independent Mixed Regiment (Dokuritsu Konsei Daijunana Rentai), minus the 3rd Battalion (Daisan Daitai), also went to Chichi Jima from Hiroshima.

SHIPMENT AND CONVOY ESCORT

Major Tomida of the Shipping Section made plans for shipment, and Captain Oi Atsushi prepared for the naval escort of these troops.[2] The two of them were quite busy.

With the exception of a very few troops that went straight to Iwo Jima, most of the above troops were sent to Chichi Jima Harbor by some transports with escort vessels; there I would unload them, disperse the supplies and equipment at night, divide them into small groups, put them on fishing boats and sailboats the next evening, and send them on to Iwo Jima via Haha Jima, which is thirty-two miles south of Chichi Jima and 125 miles north of Iwo.

ANTISUBMARINE AND ANTIAIRCRAFT TACTICS

American submarines were waiting right outside the harbors of the Japanese mainland. Moreover, no one knew when enemy task forces would show up and attack our convoys.

I went to the ship *Noto Maru* at Yokohama Harbor and asked Colonel Ikeda to buy some bamboo stalks for the 145th Infantry Regiment. If the ship was sunk, they could float on the sea with the help of these stalks and might have a chance to be rescued by escort vessels or other passing ships.

I am now fifty years old. During the past several decades, I have had many opportunities to stand at a lectern, and today I teach almost every night to both Japanese and American students. However, I think that those instructing the troops on board the ships about antisubmarine and antiaircraft warfare had the best job, because the students listened to them in earnest. They were listening because their survival was at stake, not simply for a degree or a job. They were not just being nice, sincere, or even serious. It was more instinctive: they absolutely needed the information to survive.

In March 1944, as a member of a special mission sent by the Imperial Japanese Headquarters, I taught antisubmarine and antiaircraft tactics to the officers of the 14th Division (Daijuyon Shidan) at Dairen and the 35th Division (Daisanjugo Shidan) at Tsingtao, both in China. Because of the poor level of technology and the lack of defensive capabilities, these innocent army men had to go to sea and face many threats there. As their instructor, I felt very sad that I had to tell them life-or-death stories of individual sacrifice.

I remember Lieutenant General Inoue Sadae, the commander of the 14th Division, Colonel Tada Tokechi, chief of staff of the division, Colonel Nakagawa Kunio, commander of the 2nd Infantry Regiment (Hohei Daini Rentai), Lieutenant General Ikeda Shunkichi, commander, 35th Division, Colonel Imada Shintaro, chief of staff of the division, and Colonel Ikeda, commander of the 145th Infantry Regiment, all begging me to help them at least to reach their destinations. "Help us," they said. What pitiful words these were!

I also read the following dispatches issued by the commanders of the convoy escort vessels: "We have stopped trying to rescue floating personnel at sea." I understood the position of the escort vessel commanders. They did not have time to continue rescue operations, due to the necessity to complete their original duties. They also had to worry about their own vessels being hit or sunk. However, I am still sad when I think how the men who were not rescued ended up drowning after having held out hope for as long as they could. During the war, a huge number of soldiers and sailors came to lie at the bottom of the Pacific. Of course, the situation of the crews of the escort vessels and merchant ships was also quite miserable.

Below is a list of the approximate loss of the crews of Japanese merchant ships during the war.

Total Merchant Ship Crew	137,044 men
Total killed	103,000 men
By enemy submarines	67,000 men
By enemy aircraft	21,000 men
By mines	14,300 men

According to an official U.S. war history, the following American submarines were in the Pacific as of December 31, 1943: 105 new submarines and 18 old submarines, for a total of 123.

About 40 to 50 percent were always combat ready, which means that about fifty to seventy submarines were out and about at any given time. After the war, I had dinner with a U.S. Navy commander who was a submariner. He told me the following story. "The biggest difference between U.S. submarines and their Japanese counterparts," he began, "was the ability to be detected. American submarines operated quietly, while Japanese submarines were noisy. As soon as they were found, they were sunk. However, Japanese torpedoes, at least in the beginning of the war, were more advanced, and the U.S. Navy was afraid of them."

After mid-1943, the American navy operated in small wolf packs of three or four submarines together, but the Japanese submarines could not operate that way, as they were concerned about friendly fire and sinking one another by mistake.

Despite these problems, the work of the Shipping Section in Tokyo was really spectacular. The men there labored without sleep, or even breaks, in the spirit of sacrifice for a common cause. Their combined effect on the sea shipments was large.

But in those days the Tokyo Shipping Branch Office, located at Shibaura, worked very hard for us. I sincerely thank the officers and men of that office for working behind the scenes like they did.

chapter five

IWO JIMA
An Island of Pineapples and Jungle

HISTORY OF IWO JIMA

Iwo Jima, which is almost always hot, as in summer, is located at latitude 25° 10' N and longitude 141° 20' E. It is less than six kilometers from north to south and no more than three kilometers from east to west in size. There used to be many bananas, papayas, and pineapples growing there. Prior to the battle, there were jungles and valleys on Iwo Jima. The battle literally changed the landscape.

In 1890, Iwo Jima was clearly shown as a part of Japan, through Imperial Ordinance No. 190, as a part of the Ogasawara Islands. Before then, the territorial relationship of the island was not clear; in some maps, it apparently was shown as Spanish territory. This was a result of the tragedy of the seclusion policy of the Shogunate Tokugawa government (1603–1868), which had essentially shut Japan off from much of the world. In 1903, a small group of people moved to Iwo Jima from Haha Jima and began to engage in farming and fishing.

There are three islands lying in a row north to south—North Iwo Jima, Middle Iwo Jima, and South Iwo Jima. This book focuses on the campaign that took place on Middle Iwo Jima, otherwise known simply as Iwo Jima.[1] In 1913, a village office was established for all three islands, and on April 1, 1940, Iwo Jima was placed under the ordinary town-village administration system of which other rural areas of Japan were part.

ARRIVAL OF JAPANESE FORCES AND EVACUATION OF INHABITANTS

Sakurai Naosaku, director of the Iwo Jima Industry Co., Ltd. (Iwo Jima

Sangyo Kabushiki Gaisha), who now lives in Tokumochi-machi, Ota Ward, Tokyo, told me the following.

I was born in Gunma Prefecture, but I lived on Iwo Jima for twenty-four years. First, I was sent to Iwo Jima as a manager of the company. In those days our company was called the Iwo Jima Sugar Manufacturing Co., Ltd. (Iwo Jima Seito Kabushiki Gaisha). However, our business was not going well, and we later changed the company's name to the Iwo Jima Industry Co., Ltd., and primarily dealt in medical herbs. We bought up about 90 percent of the land on Iwo Jima. The other land was held by about ten or so landowners, with the Forestry Agency (Eirinsho) of Japan having a small portion too. There were four officials in the village office, which belonged to Ogasawara Office (Ogasawara Shicho) at Chichi Jima. There was one eight-year school and a vocational school, and seven teachers took care of both schools. The schools were in session until just prior to the evacuation of the inhabitants to the mainland. Some of the senior students went to work for the military, I recall. There was one inn named Taihei-Kan, for which the governmental officials used to be the main customers. There was one bar in which three of the island women used to work. There was no movie theater. Ships visited about six times a year. In 1940, the Yokosuka-based Mabuchi Construction Company (Mabuchigumi) came and started the construction of the First Airfield under the direction of the Imperial Japanese Navy. In the spring of 1941, Lieutenant Takarada Akira brought ninety-three navy men and started construction of gun positions in the middle of Iwo Jima. Around this time, about two thousand laborers came to the island to help construct the airfield. I established the Ogasawara Food Co., Ltd. (Ogasawara Shokuhin Kabushiki Gaisha), and became the managing director. I sold dumplings *(dango)*, udon noodles, pineapples, coffee, tea, sweet bean cakes *(manju)*, etc., to the workers. Imperial Japanese Navy personnel also came to buy food. In late 1942, Commander Wachi Tsunezo came with more than a thousand garrison troops. I sold watermelons, eggplants, and cucumbers to his troops. Water, which was scarce, was collected in gutters installed under roofs and in tanks placed under rocks. In the beginning, the rainwater was colored, and when we made rice, it looked brown. There were papayas, mangoes, bananas, etc., on Iwo Jima. There were white-eyes, bulbuls, doves, booby gannets, and Japanese buntings, but no other birds. Around April 1944 Colonel Atsuchi Kanehiko brought about a thousand Imperial Japanese Army troops with him. Mainly, however, I had contact with Commander Wachi, and I met Colonel Atsuchi only four or five times. Lieutenant General Kuribayashi showed up on Iwo Jima, suddenly, on June 13, 1944. He asked me if he could borrow my house until the headquarters was built. Very soon communication troops completed a telephone net, making my reception room the command center. I was surprised at the speed and efficiency of the army. The American task force launched its first air raid against the island on June 15, 1944, which took me by surprise. There were some 1,150 islanders at the time. Through the village office, we were ordered to draft some young men and prepare the evacuation for the rest. The evacuation of the inhabitants was as follows:

GROUP	DEPARTURE	NUMBER DEPARTING
1st group	July 3, 1944	about 320 islanders
2nd group	July 7, 1944	about 500 islanders
3rd group	July 12, 1944	about 300 islanders

I sent my wife and children back by ship, and I myself evacuated Iwo Jima by a naval plane Commander Wachi specially arranged. The plane left Iwo Jima for Kisarazu [Chiba Prefecture] on July 25, right after a heavy rain. The manager of Taihei-Kan stayed a little bit longer and was evacuated at the beginning of August. There were about twenty-five men, younger than forty years old, who were drafted by the army. Another five men, who had married island girls, were also drafted, and so about thirty islanders were drafted in total. Out of these men, about five returned alive after the war. I used to dine quite often with General Kuribayashi on my porch and was impressed with his attitude about saving water. Colonel Hori Shizuichi, the chief of staff, who had quite a moustache, and Lieutenant Fujita Masayoshi, adjutant to the general, would join us. At the beginning of July, when we heard the broadcast telling us of the fall of Saipan, I said to Lieutenant General Kuribayashi, "General, the enemy will be lured to Iwo Jima and be crushed now, right?" The usually cheerful general, however, replied, "We are powerless. I am very sorry that we are causing a great deal of disruption to you here. We are unable to do anything more." I was shocked by his answer.

JAPAN'S ARMED FORCES ON AN EXPOSED ISLAND

Lieutenant Musashino Kikuzo, the former commander of the Engineer Company of the 2nd Mixed Brigade (Konsei Daini Ryodan Koheitai), who returned alive after the battle, wrote about the situation of Iwo Jima in those days as follows:

I went to Iwo Jima on March 23, 1944, taking one engineer company. At the time, Iwo Jima was exposed and completely defenseless. One infantry battalion, commanded by Lieutenant Colonel Watanabe Junya, had been stationed at the southern beach. Everyone walked around saying and believing that those who want to return home alive must help construct fortifications. By the end of March, there were about seven thousand troops, Imperial Army and Navy combined. They worked on the expansion of the Second and Third Airfields and on fortifications for the island. On June 19, U.S. carrier-based planes appeared for the first time. One hundred one of our land-based navy planes scrambled immediately, and an air battle took place about five of six thousand meters above us for about fifteen minutes. None of our planes returned. Those who had been watching the battle were sad when they realized none of the planes would return. Subsequently, about ten or twenty planes came to Iwo Jima from Japan proper, but they were all destroyed in enemy air raids, and by the time the enemy landed there were no more planes or ships left. After his arrival on June 13, 1944, Lieutenant General Kuribayashi stayed with me for about one month. Except during official duties, he was just like a colleague. We talked and laughed like friends. He was a scholarly general indeed. One time he told me, "I was in the United States for about five years. If war comes, the great peacetime industries of America can be converted into a wartime industry at a moment's notice, with just one command. Japan's war planners did not realize this. They did not understand this no matter how many times I tried to explain it to them. There is absolutely no chance for Japan to win this war. But we must continue to fight until the end."

THE TERRAIN OF IWO JIMA AND THE ENEMY'S LANDING POINT

The northeastern coast of Iwo Jima is composed of a series of cliffs, and it was apparent that a landing there was impossible. Mount Suribachi is found at the southwestern corner of the island. Between Mount Suribachi and [the then-village of] Motoyama is a wide sandy area which housed a navy airfield known as both "First Airfield" and sometimes "Chidori Airfield." It was possible to land either on the southern beach or the western beach, but the western beach was narrow in width and quite shallow for some distance from the shore.

There was no harbor at Iwo Jima, and the waves were rough. There was no breakwater. Both boarding and discharging passengers and cargo at the southern shore were dangerous.

Near the middle of the island was a shrine called Iwo Jima Jinja, but I am not sure which deities were celebrated there.

Sulphur gas gushed out just about everywhere on Iwo. Wherever one dug, the ground immediately became hot.

Mount Suribachi was about 169 meters in height, and the village of Motoyama was about 110 meters at its highest point.

Looking at Iwo Jima, therefore, it was quite clear—even to an amateur on military affairs—that the enemy would land at the southern beach. Kuribayashi knew it, too.

chapter six

THE OGASAWARA ISLANDS FORCE AND THE U.S. PACIFIC FLEET

OGASAWARA ISLANDS FORCE AND THE 27TH NAVY AIR DIVISION

Even with the outbreak of World War II, the Ogasawara Islands continued to be a peaceful area. There were some military installations—the Imperial Army had the Chichi Jima Fortress (Chichi Jima Yosai Shireibu) and the Imperial Navy had a special naval base headquarters (Tokubetsu Konkyo Chitai) at Chichi Jima. There was also a health and rehabilitation resort for sick personnel. Moreover, Iwo Jima was a staging island for navy planes, and Chichi Jima had Futami Harbor serving as a port of call for navy vessels going to Rabaul from Japan proper. But, for the most part, no one in the army or navy looked at Ogasawara seriously as a center of military operations.

Major General Osuga Kotau served as the commander of the Chichi Jima Fortress, but after 1943 he commanded all army troops in the Ogasawara Islands. In March 1944, Osuga and his troops came under the 31st Army when the latter's headquarters was established at Saipan.

At the time, naval air forces at Yokosuka used Iwo Jima as a staging base between Japan proper and the Marianas. In June 1944, the 27th Navy Air Division (Dainijunana Koku Sentai) was established under the command of the 3rd Air Fleet (Daisan Koku Kantai) Headquarters at Kisarazu.

Around the same time, when the 109th Division was being established, the Imperial General Headquarters ordered Major General Osuga to organize and lead the 2nd Mixed Brigade (Konsei Daini Ryodan), assembling five infantry battalions, one artillery battery, one company of pioneers, one communications unit, etc. Subsequently, he was instructed to move his brigade from Chichi Jima to Iwo Jima.

Major General Tachibana was then ordered to go from Tokyo to Chichi Jima to become the commander of the 1st Mixed Brigade (Konsei Daiichi Ryodan), which consisted of troops from Chichi Jima and some others sent from Japan proper. Colonel Kaido Chosaku, commander of the Chichi Jima Fortress's artillery, took some of his weapons to Iwo Jima. He was in charge of the artillery and some antiaircraft guns at Iwo Jima. About three thousand army troops, led by Colonel Masaki Hitoshi, were sent to garrison Haha Jima, along with some navy forces.

The Ogasawara Islands Force was provisionally organized, and it could be said that the only regular troops were essentially the 145th Infantry Regiment and the 26th Tank Regiment (Sensha Dainijuroku Rentai). The 145th Infantry Regiment had been left at Kagoshima because of the lack of ships after the 46th Division (Daiyonjuroku Shidan), headed by Lieutenant General Wakamatsu Tadaichi, was sent early to the Sunda Islands. The regiment had about three thousand men. The 26th Tank Regiment came from Manchuria, and it had about 760 men. Almost all the battalion commanders of 1st Mixed Brigade and 2nd Mixed Brigade were reserve officers. They were lieutenant colonels and about sixty years old.

It was only in February 1944, after Truk was attacked by the enemy task forces and the Combined Fleet forced to flee, that the Imperial Japanese Headquarters started to seriously begin preparing for the defense of the Marianas. In those days we called the line of Kurile Islands–Hokkaido–Ogasawara Islands–Marianas–Palau–Northwest New Guinea the Absolute National Defense Line, or Zettai Kokudo Boeiken. It was only after the enemy came to Saipan in June 1944 that Japan started its defensive buildup of Iwo Jima and Chichi Jima. Thus, in June, the Ogasawara Islands still remained basically defenseless.

MOVEMENT OF AMERICAN FORCES IN THE PACIFIC
The following is an outline of the situation of American forces in the Pacific, based on a U.S. official history.

Throughout the Second World War, the Combined Chiefs of Staff conducted an Anglo-American strategy. It was led on the U.S. side by: Admiral William D. Leahy, chief of staff to the president; General George C. Marshall, chief of staff, Army; Admiral Ernest J. King, chief of Naval Operations; and General Henry H. Arnold, chief of the Army Air Forces. On the British side it was led by Admiral of the Fleet Sir Dudley Pound (succeeded in 1944 by Sir Andrew B. Cunningham); Field Marshal Sir Alan Brooke, chief of the Imperial General Staff; Air Chief Marshal Sir Charles F. A. Portal, chief of the Air Staff; and Field Marshal Sir John Dill, chief of the British Military Mission to Washington.

They adopted the plan to defeat Germany first, with the Pacific theater being the secondary area. However, the main strength of the U.S. Navy was in the Pacific, and Admiral King, chief of Naval Operations and commander in chief, U.S. Fleet, was proud of being able to say that the U.S. Navy was the main force waging war against Japan and insisted that the commander in chief of the Southwest Pacific area, General Douglas A. MacArthur, should come under the unified command of Admiral Chester Nimitz. However, the U.S. Army did not concede this point. Admiral Nimitz and General MacArthur would continue to conduct the war against Japan in parallel. (Actually, MacArthur was under the Joint Chiefs of Staff [JCS], but Nimitz, who had large carrier task forces and was under the commander in chief of the U.S. Fleet, had greater forces and freedom of action than General MacArthur.)

It was after November 1943, when the British-American conference was being held in Cairo, that the U.S. government began to hasten the war against Japan. From this time, the U.S. Joint Chiefs of Staff shifted the main offensive of U.S. efforts to Nimitz's front. Nimitz's forces led a surprise attack against Truk in February 1944, and afterward U.S. efforts became focused on the Central Pacific.

Around February 1944, not only the U.S. Navy but also the Army Air Forces started looking at the Marianas. The Joint Strategic Survey Committee began insisting to the Joint Chiefs of Staff that the Central Pacific front was closer to Japan proper than any other front. It suggested that the main offensive be directed from the Central Pacific area and that the war effort in the Southwest Pacific and China-India-Burma areas be reduced. Even General Marshall concurred with this proposal.

Actually, the Joint Chiefs of Staff directed Admiral Nimitz to plan the following invasions (Secret Order No. 5137):

TARGET	D-DAY
Saipan	June 15, 1944
Palau	September 15, 1944

However, when the U.S. forces invaded Saipan, President Franklin D. Roosevelt, the Joint Chiefs of Staff, and other leading military members were in London in connection with the cross-channel operation. (The invasion of the Normandy Peninsula began on June 6, 1944.) On

June 12, 1944, Marshall and King were visiting the front in Normandy with General Dwight D. Eisenhower, supreme commander of the Allied forces in Europe. That is to say, the U.S. Joint Chiefs of Staff were paying too much attention to the European theater and failed to exploit the victory of the Fifth Fleet.

In connection with the occupation of the Marianas (Saipan, Tinian, and Guam), the Army Air Forces planned B-29 attacks against Japan proper by the end of October 1944 and expected to place 784 B-29 aircraft on the seized islands by February 1945. In light of this, the Matterhorn Plan, by which a wing of B-29s from the 20th Air Force, under the direct command of General Henry H. Arnold, had been introduced into China and operated from Chengdu against Japan, was shut down in March 1945.

After the invasion of the Marianas (Saipan, June 15–July 7; Tinian, July 24–July 30; and Guam, July 21–August 10), Nimitz was ordered to prepare for the invasion of Formosa, but due to unexpected delays in defeating Germany (the Combined Chiefs of Staff had expected Germany to surrender in October 1944), the Joint Chiefs of Staff believed that a diversion of the resources from Europe for the invasion of Taiwan would be impossible. Instead, the JCS decided to support the invasion of Ogasawara and Okinawa. The official order to take the Ogasawara Islands and Okinawa was issued on October 3, 1944, and it set in motion the final preparations for those terrible battles.

chapter seven

LET'S SINK IWO JIMA INTO THE OCEAN

THE 31ST ARMY'S PLAN TO ANNIHILATE THE ENEMY AT THE BEACH LINE

After my arrival at Iwo Jima, I heard the following story from Major General Osuga, Colonel Atsuchi, and Lieutenant Colonel Nishikawa. One day in May 1944, General Obata and Major General Tamura made their first visit to Iwo Jima and Chichi Jima. They gathered all the officers and Tamura gave a big speech, asking them at the outset of his talk what "beach line" meant.

After no one was able to give him the right answer, he said that the beach line meant the border between water and land, which changes due to the tide. The beach line had to be defended at all costs, he stressed, emphasizing his determination to annihilate the enemy at the beach. It was an eloquent speech. This approach was called the Tamura Doctrine, they told me.

After the above speech, the defensive line—which had already been made fairly close to the beach by order of Major General Osuga—was moved even closer to the beach line. Therefore, when I arrived at Iwo Jima at the end of June, there were many foxholes already on the beach, and the officers and men of Iwo Jima went around as firm believers in the Tamura Doctrine. When we read the battle instruction reports coming from Saipan, Guam, and Tinian, they closely reflected the Tamura Doctrine, but, in retrospect, at great cost. (In the battle of Peleliu, the Japanese tactical approach diverged from this doctrine.)

The Tamura Doctrine was not invented by Major General Tamura himself, but it had been the main defensive tactic used to date. It was common sense that the defender should keep a large reserve in rear areas and that once the enemy came ashore, the defender should go on the offensive with his reserves and annihilate the enemy at the beach. This idea was widespread around the world. In the Army Academy and Army War College, both of which I attended, the above approach was widely studied. Therefore, it was not surprising that Tamura insisted that the annihilation of the enemy at the beach was key.

There was one chapter, however, in the Sakusen Yomurei (Operations Manual), adopted by the army after the Nomonhan incident of 1939, which served as a warning against overreliance on meeting the enemy at the beach line.[1] Titled "Koshomen Bogo" (Defense of a Wide, Frontal Area), it read in part: "Against an overwhelming armored enemy a series of positions must be made farther away and deeper inland."

In any case, the Japanese military was overly optimistic, as seen in the comments by General Tojo that Saipan was impregnable (see chapter 2). Moreover, within the General Staff there were some who believed that thirty thousand troops could hold off an invading force. This overoptimism was seen not only regarding the Saipan campaign but also in the mainland as well. Some people said that the damage from incendiary bombs in Tokyo could be limited by water buckets used by its residents to put out the fires. We actually believed this to be true. Our inability to judge the situation clearly was appalling.

ARRIVAL OF GENERAL KURIBAYASHI

Lieutenant General Kuribayashi, accompanied by First Lieutenant (Reservist) Fujita Masayoshi, his adjutant, came to Iwo Jima by air from Kisarazu. After inspecting Iwo Jima on June 13, he told Major General Osuga and Colonel Atsuchi that he would follow the tactical approach established by the 31st Army.

The troops in the Ogasawara Islands were under the command of the 31st Army until the end of June 1944. Although the army and the navy were involved in the fighting in Saipan, Lieutenant General Obata, accompanied by Major General Tamura and Major Tsukamoto, had flown from Palau to Guam by navy plane. Obata directed the troops under his command through the communications center of the 29th Division (Dainijukyu Shidan), located on Guam. As a result, Lieutenant General Kuribayashi had to obey the policy established by the 31st Army through the end of June 1944.

I GO TO IWO JIMA

Through the kind help of the commander of the 12th Section of the Naval Staff, I was given air transportation from Kisarazu to Iwo Jima on June 29. On the morning of the 28th, I exchanged cups of water with my wife, as I was leaving the house for good. I stopped at the home of my wife's family, in Ichikawa City, located in the northwestern part of Chiba Prefecture, along the way from Tokyo to Kisarazu. I asked my wife's parents to take care of her, our daughter, and our second child, whom we were expecting in the fall 1944. "In case of my death," I told them, "please have a small funeral service for me, given the circumstances. My mother will provide some support too." I then went to an inn, the Hotel Mikasa, in Kisarazu that evening. Shortly before midnight, my brother came to visit from our hometown so we could say our final good-byes. We stayed up most of the night talking. We finally went to bed but could not sleep, realizing that this would probably be our last time together.

The weather the next day, June 29, was nice. Lieutenant Commander Nonaka Goro, commander of the Kisarazu Airfield (and the younger brother of the late Captain Nonaka Shiro, an army officer who participated in the attempted coup in 1936 by radical army officers known as the 2.26 Incident and committed suicide), saw me off. Looking out the window at the scenery of Japan as we ascended, I finally dozed off, thanks to the lull of the plane's engines and the lack of sleep the evening before.

When I woke up, we were already flying over the island of North Iwo Jima. Soon the plane started its turn over Iwo Jima. "Ah! What a tiny island," I said to myself. I noticed many damaged aircraft from the recent enemy air raids. My first impression was that the island was probably best sunk to the bottom of the Pacific.

Our plane landed near Mount Suribachi at the First Airfield. I immediately started grumbling—what a hot place the island was! What a sandy place! What a pitiful island! Major Tsukamoto was a lucky guy to have gone to a better place!

I was taken in a poor old car to the staff office located at North Village. It was a little after noon. Lieutenant Colonel Shirakata Fujie, a staff officer, and two or three other officers were having lunch. "Where is the division commander?" I asked. Someone answered, "Please have lunch first." An orderly gave me a bowl of rice with some pickles. Shirakata, who looked modest and gentle, and the others were so busy that we did not have much chance to speak. I was taken by a noncommissioned officer to Lieutenant General Kuribayashi's quarters, about 150 meters to the west of the staff office, shortly after 1:00 PM.

Lieutenant General Kuribayashi was standing in front of the island-er's home he was using as his residence. He wore a short-sleeved shirt and soldier's *chikatabi*.[2] I was meeting him for the first time. "Welcome, Major Horie!" said the general. I told him that I was to be assigned to his staff for a few days since I was unable to go to Saipan.

"I used to be the commander of the Tokyo Division [Tokyo Shi-dan]," he told me, "but as a cadet caused a fire in one of the barracks, I was fired. Soon after, I was ordered here. So, how is the situation of Japan proper?" While I was trying to answer, a sidecar came for him. "I have arranged to see the fortifications being prepared by the troops. Let's talk later. I'm sorry," he said, and off he went somewhere.

SINKING THE ISLAND IS THE BEST OPTION

I returned to the staff office and read some messages and mentally thanked the officers and men at Saipan for the brave fight they showed. Then I went to the navy headquarters on the island. I was anxious to read the navy dispatches. I talked with Rear Admiral Ichimaru Rino-suke and Commander Mase Takeji for about half an hour, mostly about what would happen to Japan after Operation *A-Go*. But these two men really had no clue about the true situation of things. They understood that things were bad, but they continued to fool themselves to some extent. On the other hand, I knew that the number of messages they were receiving in this headquarters at the front was so small that they could not see the whole situation. Commander Mase, smiling, changed the subject and said to me, "As you are a friend of ours, having stayed in the navy for more than a year, you can enjoy the privilege of ice cream that we make here. As ours is the only place that can make ice cream on this island, please do not tell anyone else about it." The ice cream tasted very good.

I told them that I had been ordered by the Imperial Japanese Head-quarters to go to Chichi Jima to make arrangements for the sea trans-portation for the Ogasawara Islands, and in particular to help fortify Iwo Jima. "I need to go to Chichi Jima and would be grateful if you could let me know if you have any air transportation to there." Both men nodded.

I came back to the staff office of the 109th Division and talked with some of the men. Most of them had arrived recently, and it was apparent that they were not familiar with the work they were to do on

Iwo Jima. However, the atmosphere of the office was completely different from that of Tokyo, particularly from that of the Convoy Escort General Fleet Headquarters, where the shadow of death was always lingering. My impression was that the office on Iwo had an easygoing atmosphere often seen in southern islands, combined with a little bit of uncertainty. Someone said that Lieutenant General Kuribayashi made too much of trivial things and was annoying. Around 5:00 PM, First Lieutenant Fujita, the general's adjutant, came to see me and said that Lieutenant General Kuribayashi wanted to have dinner with me that evening and that he would come by again when it was ready. I thanked him and then went to the adjutants' office, the ordnance office, and then into some woods behind the staff office. I was interested in the woods, whose trees were different from those on the mainland. Someone told me that was where the divisional air-raid shelter was located. It was very important for a newcomer to know about it. I had had to use the air-raid shelter at Ambina and Timor the previous year.

Just before 6:00 PM, as the sun was about to set, a senior private came to tell me that the general was awaiting me at his residence for dinner. I followed him there.

Lieutenant General Kuribayashi welcomed me, saying, "Come on in. I am sorry it is not like Edo;[3] the food here is not so good." No sooner had I said "Thank you" and begun to take off one of my boots when we heard a siren notifying us of an enemy air raid. "It is a long distance to the air-raid shelter, so let's go," said the general.

Lieutenant General Kuribayashi, First Lieutenant Fujita, the private, and I took off to the air-raid shelter. It was my first time in an air-raid shelter in Iwo Jima. I smelled sulphur. Kuribayashi, wearing the same short-sleeved shirt and soldier's *tabi* I had seen him in earlier in the day, had a walking, or riding, stick with him. He sat on a chair in the shelter and started giving instructions on some minor things. Now I understood that he really was unlike Admiral Oikawa and Lieutenant General Suzuki. I also thought that I should have tried to learn more about him before I left Tokyo.

The air raid was conducted by an unknown type of American plane, and soon we heard the "all clear" siren. Leaving the shelter in the same order as before, we returned to the general's quarters, walking between the woods and the banana grove. It had already become dark, and the temperature had cooled down a bit.

"The enemy wanted us to eat our food cold, I guess. Come in anyway, Horie," the general said.

We sat on *tatami*, or Japanese mats, in an eight-*tatami*-size room (about twelve feet by twelve). On the right was a wide room that also served as a cooking area. On the left was another eight-*tatami* room, which was Fujita's room. Following the war, I came to learn that the house belonged to Mr. Sakurai (see chapter 5), who served as the managing director of Iwo Jima Industry Co., Ltd. Some privates were cooking under the direction of First Lieutenant Fujita.

"Do you drink sake?" the general asked, adding "I only drink whiskey." I told him either was fine.

"If only Major General Nagata Tetsuzan were still alive," Kuribayashi began, "we would not have found ourselves in this present miserable situation."[4]

"Lieutenant General Suzuki Sosaku said the same thing," I told him.[5]

We poured whiskey for each other. I asked to be allowed to sit more informally, mentioning the injuries to my leg. I stretched out my left leg. "Surely," he said, and saying so, he relaxed a little bit too.

Fujita brought food in from the kitchen. I invited him to join us, and he responded that he would later. He continued bringing in the food.

Kuribayashi said, "So you were a staff officer under Lieutenant General Suzuki? One of the smartest men I have ever met. I was with him in the Army Education Administration. There were a lot of great men there, such as Nagata, Imamura Hitoshi, and Suzuki, and some others. Aizawa was insane and killed a national treasure when he assassinated Nagata, screaming 'Patriotism!' 'National Security!' and the like. These blind and stupid men did such imprudent things that we now find ourselves in this situation."

I asked Kuribayashi if he had been particularly close with the late General Nagata, because they were both from Nagano Prefecture.

"Yes," the general answered. "He was a great man. He had seen the world. He was the best disciple of General Ugaki Kazushige.[6] If there had been no fire incident at the Tokyo Division, I would not be in this godforsaken place."[7]

I told him that if I had been able to go to Saipan, I would be living the life of a warrior, somewhere between life and death.

"Fate is a funny thing," Kuribayashi said. "It is now many years ago, but I was in the United States for three years when I was a captain. I was taught how to drive by an American officer, so I bought a car. I drove around the country. I could see the close connection between the military and industry. I saw the manufacturing plants around Detroit,

too. With almost the push of a button, it seemed, all of America's industry could be mobilized for the military. Businessmen could become the
secretary of war or the secretary of the navy to handle production. In
Japan, infantry officers who came through the Military Army Academy
say that they are the main members of the Imperial Army, they exercise
great influence over all the army and the conduct of war. I don't believe
we can help. Well, are you also a staff officer who came through the
infantry, passing through the military academy?" He was passionate
about this point.

"I came from a middle school, but I used to be an infantry officer,"
I said.

"Were you? After I came back from the United States, I explained
in great detail the situation in the United States and in Europe, where I
also traveled, but no one listened." He became angrier when he spoke.
"I was also in Canada when Prince Tokugawa Iemasa was serving as
the first minister to Canada in Ottawa.[8] By the way, when I was leaving
Tokyo, General Ushiroku Jun, the vice chief of staff of the army, told me
the enemy, without fail, would come to Iwo Jima. What do you think,
Major Horie? I feel the same way. We could keep the enemy busy here,
and then the Combined Fleet could come from the mainland or Okinawa and strike him. Our role could be a great containing operation."

I spoke up and was frank. "General, we no longer have the Combined Fleet. Some naval forces still remain, but they are few and have no
power to strike. Aren't you aware of the results of Operation A-Go?"

Kuribayashi was in denial. "What are you saying, you fool? This
island is a part of Tokyo."

"Japan essentially died ten days ago," I told him. "June 19 was
when Japan died."

"Are you saying that we must just roll over and die here at the
doorstep to Tokyo? You must be drunk!" he said angrily.

"I saw the island from the sky as I was flying in today. I think the
best thing to do would be to sink Iwo Jima to the bottom of the sea. If
that is not possible, at least we should try to dynamite and sink the First
Airfield. The enemy would not be able to use the island if only Mount
Suribachi and the Motoyama area remained. If, in the future, Japan had
the chance to undertake offensive operations again, Iwo Jima would
not be necessary."

Kuribayashi called for Fujita to bring us some rice. While eating it,
in a low voice, Kuribayashi repeated, "You are drunk."

Suddenly, a siren rang again. I said to him, "Thank you for the good supper" and stood up. This time, the general put on his boots and reached for his trustworthy stick. It was about 9:30 PM, I guess. Walking with him to the air-raid shelter, I thought that I should at least try to explain in detail the real situation facing Japan, particularly about the real status of our naval power, to this expert of America and Canada, and have him prepare a proper operational strategy. But at this point we lacked faith in each other's judgment. He clearly showed that he could not depend upon a young kid like me.

I thought of the faces of Lieutenant General Suzuki, Admiral Oikawa, Rear Admiral Horie, Rear Admiral Shimamoto, and Major General Nakayama, who had been my regimental commander when I was a cadet at the 2nd Infantry Regiment, and knew that they would have certainly believed in me. I became sad and missed them.

Just before we entered the shelter, the siren sounded "all clear." We stopped in front of the staff office. I said good night to the general and told him I would report to him the following morning. I entered the staff office and went to bed in a *tatami* room inside but could not fall asleep easily, as I was kept awake by somebody's snoring. I also still felt somehow that I was a member of the 31st Army Headquarters and that if I were there, I would not feel as lonely as I did then, treated as a stranger and as someone without right judgment. I just lay there, awake.

NO CHANCE FOR JAPAN

The weather was nice the next day, June 30. Lieutenant General Kuribayashi and I went to the southern beach, where we expected that the enemy would come ashore. First Lieutenant Musashino, commander of the engineer company *(koheitai)*, ran to us and saluted. Kuribayashi prostrated himself on the beach and acted like the enemy would as he came ashore. "This beach is very wide. The enemy has to come here. There will be no alternative for him," the general said.

"If we sink the airfield, Iwo Jima would lose its value. That is my recommendation," I told him. "That is true," he acknowledged.

At this time, First Lieutenant Musashino came up and said that he was having difficulties fortifying the positions on the beach in the sand. For about two hours, Lieutenant General Kuribayashi and I went around the area by car. He would get out and ask me to lie down. He would point his stick at me like a rifle, with me acting as his target on the beaches. The instructions flew out like a machine gun's bullets:

"Stand up, Horie!" "Lie down!" "Make yourself lower!" His requests were many. I thought of Colonel Ishiguro Senkunosuke, former commander of the 2nd Infantry Regiment, and understood why his adjutants and staff officers had told me that Kuribayashi spoke too much of details. I confess, I thought that I would have the same trouble as I had had with Colonel Ishiguro, who was often inconsistent in his behavior and acted strangely. The words of Lieutenant General Kuribayashi were harsh, and he regularly spoke ill of others.

I looked at the shore of the southern beach and saw that the waves were rough. I worried about unloading ammunition and material here from the sailboats and fishing boats that would be coming from Chichi Jima. I asked the general to allow me to bring some shipping officers and men down here in the afternoon to study how to unload the ammunition and materials. Frankly speaking, I was trying to get away from him in the afternoon. I thought it would have been better for me to be in Saipan than with him here. I realized that I was going to die anyway, so it really did not matter. I returned to the divisional headquarters with the general and took lunch at the staff office.

That afternoon I went to the Shipping Branch Office. I pointed out that the office was too far from the southern beach. The men in the room and I talked about that and other things for a couple of hours. They belonged to the Army Shipping Headquarters at Hiroshima. They were particularly friendly and nice to me. The rice cakes they shared with me were very good. I told them to go to the southern beach the next morning to study the shipping situation there.

On my way back, I stopped at the Naval Headquarters. Captain Matsunaga Sadaichi, chief of staff of the 3rd Air Fleet, happened to be there. I talked with him, Rear Admiral Ichimaru, and Commander Mase for about twenty minutes. I was given a dish of ice cream again. Matsunaga was an impressive and handsome man, quite young-looking for his age. As soon as I returned to the staff office, someone suggested I should go to the hot spring located on the northern beach. I did as suggested, going with a few others. As I was getting undressed, I heard an air-raid siren and hastened to hide under a rocky ledge. There were already about forty or fifty men taking cover there, all naked.

I liked the hot springs very much. The temperature of the water was just right, and as someone who likes swimming, I really enjoyed the place. I hoped we could visit here again when there was no war and we did not have to worry about air raids.

Returning to the staff office, I started reading the dispatches. First Lieutenant Fujita came by and said that the general wished to see me at his quarters. I followed the adjutant there.

The general asked me how the hot spring was. "It's even better because it is free," he joked. "Come inside, let's eat."

Everything was the same as the previous night. Both of us started drinking whiskey and eating. The main dish was something canned, the same as the evening before. While drinking, I explained the situation of the war in the Pacific to Kuribayashi in detail. I told him that Japan could not win the war without the navy. Two years before, on June 4, 1942, the aircraft carrier *Kaga* had been sunk at Midway in an enemy air attack, and the aircraft carrier *Soryu* had been sunk by submarine.[9] On June 5, the carriers *Akagi* and *Hiryu* had been sunk in another air attack. At this point, the entire 1st Air Fleet, which had led the strikes on Pearl Harbor, was now resting at the bottom of the Pacific, and the positions of Japan and America had completely reversed. America was now on the offensive and Japan on the defensive. Then I explained to him the miserable condition of the convoy escort operations.

Every day, I told him, I had been reading about two thousand messages in the Convoy Escort General Fleet Headquarters and the General Staff. Having access to more information than most officers, I walked around the army and navy sections feeling sad and in shock. I told him about the status of each navy vessel and merchant ship and how they were being sunk day by day. I told him about all the aircraft, ammunition, armed forces, supplies, etc., that were on board these sunken ships, and many other details. Listening, the general was at first somewhat sarcastic, saying I could be a walking encyclopedia. When I began to talk about the fiftieth ship, however, the general, who was said to be one of the smartest officers and had actually received a sword from the emperor when graduating from the Army War College, came to change his expression. Looking at me, he stopped eating and drinking and just listened to me in earnest. I think I had him hooked. I went on to tell him,

It was a key point in the strategy of the Imperial Japanese Headquarters to send army troops to the various isolated islands in the Central Pacific and use the 11th Air Fleet [Daijuichi Koku Kantai] to make up for the lost carrier-based air power, during which time Ozawa's fleet would be built. However, the Combined Fleet fled Truk for Palau in February 1944 and then fled Palau for Tawi Tawi in March. Finally, it was completely defeated by the U.S. 5th Fleet in the so-called Operation *A-Go*. In other words, June 19, 1944, was the day the Combined Fleet of Japan died. But, as Lieutenant General Suzuki and Admiral Oikawa had been telling me, as long as we have been ordered to fight by the Imperial Declaration of War, we have to continue to devote our lives for the country regardless. The object now is to see how many enemy troops we can kill. If we can kill ten enemy troops per man, when we die the mathematics will tell the people of the world that we actually won the war.

I was crying by this point and had trouble speaking. Lieutenant General Kuribayashi looked depressed, too, saying, "I did not know all of this." I continued,

There are many war advocates in the army, and there are still twenty or thirty divisions intact, and so the army refuses to admit defeat. While there are not as many war advocates in the navy, they too will not admit defeat. Watching each other, as if rivals not wanting to be the one to give up, the army and navy continue this hopeless war. However, at this time, after the annihilation of our troops at Attu, Guadalcanal, Makin, and Tarawa, the Imperial Japanese Headquarters might not be able to order the island commanders to surrender their troops after Saipan. This is a difficult point for Japan, based on structural problems and customs. I, myself, am prepared to give up my life. To date, I have escaped death by a hair several times. If I were on Saipan, I would have died under Major General Iketa, and if I were on Guam, I would have died under General Obata with Major Tsukamoto. I am prepared to lose my life.

As I said this, I showed him the pack of potassium cyanide that had been given to me by Dr. Takatsuki.

First Lieutenant Fujita came in at this moment and said to me, "Major Horie, a telephone call came to the staff office from the Naval Headquarters a minute ago. An aircraft is scheduled to go to Chichi Jima tomorrow morning. It will leave here at 6:00 AM."

I thanked him and asked him to inform the navy that I would like to go on the plane. I asked the general for permission to go to Chichi Jima and told him that from there, I would like to first send to Iwo Jima the 145th Infantry Regiment, the 26th Tank Regiment, guns, and ammunition. Kuribayashi gave me permission to go and agreed with my plan.

We both remained silent for a while and were rather tired in light of our talk. It was a little after 10 PM when I finally said goodbye.

Returning to the staff office, I prepared for my departure the next day. Just about everyone was already in bed. I told the night-duty non-commissioned officer in charge to wake me up at five in the morning and that breakfast would not be necessary for me.

I was expecting the 145th Infantry Regiment to arrive the next day at Chichi Jima and knew it was going to be a busy day. Having said everything on my mind to Lieutenant General Kuribayashi, I fell asleep immediately. Nothing disturbed my sleep that night.

chapter eight

NIGHT SUPPLY OPERATIONS VIA CHICHI JIMA

**HORIE SENT TO CHICHI JIMA TO FACILITATE
EMERGENCY SUPPLIES FOR IWO JIMA**

On the morning of July 1, 1944, I was taken to Chichi Jima by a navy plane piloted by a young lieutenant. The plane flew with two bombs attached to it for antisubmarine operations, and it had to make a wheels-up landing at Chichi Jima's Susaki airfield, as the wheels did not drop down. Here again I managed to escape death. The pilot was wounded in the face when landing, but I emerged unscathed. I motored to the old Chichi Jima Fortress Headquarters, located at the main village of Omura. What a peaceful island it was, especially when compared to Iwo Jima! The scenery was absolutely beautiful! The water of Futami Harbor was pretty, too. I remembered my trip from Java to Tokyo the previous year. When our seaplane landed in the Bay of Manado in what is now northern Indonesia, Captain Yamamoto Yuji, Lieutenant Commander Tanaka Kikumatsu, Lieutenant Commander Naito Shogo, and I joked simultaneously, "I would like to retire here when I get old."

When I arrived at the old fortress headquarters, I found Lieutenant Colonel Nishikawa, who had been waiting for me. He was scheduled to go to Iwo Jima and was preparing to turn his work over to me. Major General Tachibana, commander of the 1st Mixed Brigade, was also there. First Lieutenant Nishiyotsutsuji Kimitomi, who had been working under Nishikawa, reported to me that *Noto Maru* would arrive at Chichi Jima later that day and another ship the following day.

As a result, I started work immediately. I gathered together officers from the Chichi Jima Shipping Branch (Teihakuba) and the 17th Shipping Engineering Regiment (Senpaku Kohei Daijunana Rentai), both of which belonged to the Army Shipping Headquarters at Hiroshima—First Lieutenant Nishiyotsutsuji and Major Yokota Sanichi, adjutant to Major General Tachibana—and told them the following: "Sea transshipments to Iwo Jima will begin momentarily. We may have to work without any sleep and rest. Any and all sailing boats and fishing boats will be mobilized. I hope to get your cooperation." I instructed them about unloading *Noto Maru*, which was transporting the 145th Infantry Regiment, and reloading onto smaller sailing and fishing boats.

A female clerk was still working at the old headquarters at this time. She gave me a cup of black tea. Some officials of the Ogasawara Islands Office came by to introduce themselves. A few stores were still open, selling some items. It soon became lunchtime. Major General Tachibana, Lieutenant Colonel Nishikawa, Major Yokota, several other officers, and I were seated around a table in front of the headquarters building. Tachibana was the highest-ranking officer, and he and I faced each other, as I was the newest arrival and thus a guest. The table was under some trees.

It was very surprising for me that these people were so relaxed. Tachibana talked of his favorite books about Oda Nobunaga, a Japanese general in the sixteenth century, and Kondo Isamu, another general, of the eighteenth century, and said we could win the war if we would use their tactics. Because he was speaking so seriously, I began to wonder if it were I who had gone insane. The lunch tasted good, as I was hungry. The piece of watermelon was also delicious.

COLONEL IKEDA AND CHIEF OF STAFF HORI

Noto Maru arrived that afternoon. I went to the ship to meet Colonel Ikeda Masuo, who commanded the 145th Infantry Regiment. We had become close working together in Tokyo. Suddenly a colonel appeared in front of us. He had a moustache and was wearing a staff officer's insignia. This colonel, Hori Shizuichi, was the chief of staff of our division. I remembered that he had been an instructor at the Imperial Japanese Army Academy, teaching us about railways. I arranged immediately to have the regimental flag and main force of the 145th Infantry Regiment sent to Iwo Jima by high-speed navy transport, and then I took Colonel Hori to the detached headquarters at Chichi Jima. I wanted to explain the general situation to both Colonel Hori and Lieutenant Colonel Nishikawa. Hori was a kind man and quickly befriended me, as he used to work under Lieutenant General Yokoyama Shizuo when the latter was the commanding general of the 2nd Railway Brigade (Notetsu Shireibu) in northern China. I knew Yokoyama well, as he had been a colonel and the commander of the 2nd Infantry Regiment (Hohei Daini Rentai) when I was wounded in China. As I explained the situation to these two men, Colonel Hori took some notes and was surprised by my story. Nishikawa, on the other hand, was bothered by what I said, which was apparently too pessimistic. Nishikawa responded that our Imperial Army and Navy were still strong enough to defeat the enemy and that my will must have been psychologically defeated.

That evening, a noncommissioned officer and a private took me to the officers' residence. It was a very good house. I remembered that someone said Chichi Jima had been a health resort for sick personnel in the past.

The following day, July 2, Colonel Hori and Lieutenant Colonel Nishikawa left Chichi Jima for Iwo Jima. Nishikawa seemed to be sad to leave Chichi Jima, as he had worked there for so long. In the meantime, many local residents came to see me about their evacuation, with a lot of questions and requests. The female clerk, for example, wanted to stay a while longer. They looked sad to leave the place where they had been born and had spent their lives. I sympathized with them. The girl was about seventeen or eighteen years old, and she looked happy when I told her that I would try to keep them there as long as possible if they so desired. The sea transportation of the 145th Infantry Regiment went smoothly.

EVACUATION OF ISLANDERS

I went to the Chichi Jima Naval Headquarters. I talked with Rear Admiral Mori Keikichi, Commander Kamiura Junya, a senior staff member, Lieutenant Commander Yonehara Sueo, Engineering Staff, and some others. They were all very friendly.

I was busy on July 3 with the problem of evacuating the islanders to the mainland. Many of them had come from Iwo Jima and Haha Jima by small boats to Chichi Jima, and Chichi Jima was crowded with hundreds of the extra inhabitants as a result. Most of them asked me to allow them to stay at Chichi Jima and see what happened, rather than hastening to go on to the mainland, where they had nothing and knew no one. I was very much moved by their stories and was inclined to listen to their requests.

A SERIES OF VIOLENT ENEMY AIR RAIDS

In the early morning of July 4, I was awakened by some bombs while sleeping in a mosquito net in the officers' residence. It was a total surprise attack. I could not even find my trousers for a while, which greatly bothered me. Later I found them on the mosquito net. I heard the sound of machine guns, which I hoped might be Japanese navy antiaircraft guns. It was still dark, and I was escorted to an air-raid shelter in the old Chichi Jima Fortress. Major General Tachibana was already in there. The bombing continued the whole morning. We could not do anything. A dozen or so sea fighters scrambled, but I heard they were shot down by the U.S. Navy's Grumman planes, the Hellcats. The telephones throughout the island were also down.

QUESTIONING OF AMERICAN PRISONERS OF WAR
AND STUDYING ENGLISH FROM THESE POWS

As the weather improved that afternoon, the enemy left. Lieutenant (Junior Grade) Herschel C. Connell, U.S. Navy, who had been shot down by our antiaircraft guns and had become a prisoner of war, was brought to me. According to him, Rear Admiral Clark with his task force had decided to launch raids on the Ogasawara Islands from the *Hornet* and *Enterprise* on this, the American holiday of Independence Day. He said this attack was being done ahead of the forthcoming invasion of Guam. However, it was problematic for me to catch everything he said. With difficulty, I could understand his main points when he wrote them down.

Through the above conversation, I discovered just how poor my knowledge of English was. Out of necessity I started practicing English conversation with the prisoners, who became my teachers. Thus my special English study began on the afternoon of July 4, 1944, with the help of Lieutenant Connell. Later, instructors numbers two and three came when they were captured and brought to me.[1] Finding some time during my busy life with my duties of sea transportation, cave digging, position inspections, and teaching tactics to the officers and men, I tried to improve my broken English at every opportunity. In a sense I wanted to try to forget about the gloom of the war. I was just one student, but I had three instructors. They taught me diligently. One of them became the chief instructor, and the other two became assistant instructors in turn. I studied for at least three hours every day. When the enemy air raids came, we went into the air-raid shelter and continued our English study. Many of Japanese officers and men laughed out loud at me when I got stuck on words and had trouble with pronunciation.

The information obtained from these prisoners of war gave me a general idea of U.S. strategy. As I sent the information to the General Staff in Tokyo and to Lieutenant General Kuribayashi on Iwo Jima, the vice chief of staff twice kindly sent messages of appreciation by message. Even after eleven years of English study, from the beginning of middle school through completion of the Army War College, I still could not speak coherently enough in my conversations with the first prisoner of war, or POW, I met, in July 1944. But I made progress, and when I met Captain Harold P. Smith, the senior representative of the commander, Marianas Command, aboard the USS *Dunlap* on September 3, 1945, for the surrender ceremony, my English was better than the Japanese ability of the Nisei (Japanese American) interpreter working for him. Although I received help from Imperial Japanese Navy petty officer Tamamura Fumio and Imperial Japanese Army cadet Oyama Shigeyasu, and the Nisei interpreters, I was able to make a couple of presentations for a few hours before U.S. missions visiting Chichi Jima after the war.[2]

I remember that Lieutenant Connell was a nice-looking boy from Seattle, Washington. About ten years ago, I heard, he was working in the U.S. Sixth Fleet in the Mediterranean as a lieutenant commander, but I am unaware of his whereabouts now. After World War II, when the war crimes trials began regarding atrocities that had occurred in the Central Pacific, my former instructors protected me, and the commander, Marianas Islands, provided me with exceptionally good treatment, like that received by a visiting head of state. When I returned home alive but jobless, I used my knowledge of English to survive. Later I was able to teach Japanese language and culture to American students at the University of Maryland extension program in Japan at Tachikawa Air Base and English to Japanese students at Takushoku University and some other schools in the Tokyo area. I have also been asked on occasion to write for American magazines and newspapers as a military commentator. I am amazed at how difficult it is for us humans to know what life has in store for us. Fate is a funny thing.

On July 5, a number of islanders came to my office to ask me to accelerate their evacuation. The enemy air raids the day before helped my business. They no longer wanted to stay on Chichi Jima. The lovely female clerk also wanted to be evacuated immediately. I am unsure of their whereabouts now.

LIEUTENANT COLONEL NISHI TAKEICHI, OLYMPIC HORSEMAN

Around July 18, Lieutenant Colonel Nishi Takeichi visited me at the old headquarters building. I could tell he had been shaken up as a result of the damage to the ship he had been on. I told him that I had heard of him and urged him to sit down. He looked very sad and said, "All the tanks are at the bottom of the sea now." I offered him a beer. He had won a gold medal as an equestrian jumper at the 1932 Los Angeles Olympics. He was a member of the nobility; many people used to call him "Baron Nishi."

He said to me while drinking the beer, "I was transferred to the armored forces from the cavalry and had been expecting to fight in Manchuria or China employing the maneuvering power and firepower of the tank. Now, instead, I have to go to Iwo Jima. What's more, I have no tanks now. More than twenty of them sit at the bottom of the sea."

I pointed out where the air-raid shelter was and encouraged him to drink more. I said, "I understand your situation very well. On Iwo Jima, you probably will have to put your tanks in the caves in order to use them as pillboxes. You will not be able to use the maneuvering power of the tanks out in the open."

To this, Nishi responded, "In a cave? Can you send a message to the Imperial Japanese Headquarters? If they order us to die, I don't mind dying, but at least allow us to use our tanks in the proper way."

Just then, an air-raid warning sounded. "Let's go to the shelter," I told Nishi. Suddenly some sparks flew into my office window. Nishi, with his long legs, had already stood up and was off running toward the shelter by the time I was out of the room. I decided to go back inside. I found a hole in my table and another in the floor. The sparks had come from enemy bullets. When the siren sounded "All clear," Nishi returned, and we resumed drinking beer again.

"I am aware," I told him, "that the policy of the Imperial Japanese Headquarters is to not divert troops or to transfer personnel toward some isolated island. As such, I can't forward your recommendations. Those in control there are influenced by the Hattori–Sejima line, but if you know anyone in the Imperial Japanese Headquarters you could send a message to him requesting his help." I handed him a piece of paper and a pencil.

"That is too bad," Nishi exclaimed. "I know America, as a result of my equestrian experiences. I have some friends there, too. It is all so ironic. Well, let me go to Iwo Jima, then I'll talk with Lieutenant General Kuribayashi. Thank you." Later, he went to Tokyo from Iwo Jima by air and spent about a month gathering more tanks before returning to Iwo.

In a December 18, 1944, letter to his wife, Nishi wrote: "The situation on Iwo Jima becomes more serious day by day. We do not know when the enemy will come. If everyone at home is united and works together, I can fight without too much worry. I am confident I can lead the fight here at the head of my officers and men to pay back all the blessings bestowed upon me by our country. My mind is as serene as a polished mirror. Remember: help each other and work together."[3] Judging from the contents of his letter, he did not officially raise the problem of the diversion of his troops or his own transfer after we separated; if he raised it, it was not taken up.

HANDLING THE JAPANESE PEOPLE IS RATHER DIFFICULT

On or around July 20, shortly after the resignation of the Tojo Hideki cabinet, Commander Otani and Colonel Shimamura, staff officers of the Combined Fleet, visited me out of the blue. It was about four in the afternoon. Otani stayed at the Naval Headquarters, but Shimamura stayed with me. Colonel Shimamura shared with me information regarding both the army and the navy. He was able to read all the messages from both the army and navy and could meet with many high-level people every day, just as I had been able to do when I was the army's liaison officer at the Convoy Escort General Fleet Headquarters.

After having dinner together, he said to me "In some way, I feel handling the Japanese people can be more difficult than handling the enemy." He continued, "Now, some important advisors to the emperor, headed by the former prime minister and Admiral Okada Keisuke, have been working on ending the war. However, there are rightists and leftists, as well as war advocates, etc. It is hard for the government to handle all these people. They are driven by vanity, showmanship, and power struggles. Sometimes, they cast stones at high-ranking people, destroying their homes, and even assassinating officials and doing other atrocious things. It is a big problem controlling them. At this stage, the enemy will no doubt demand 'unconditional surrender.'"

I responded, "At least I hope Japan surrenders after Germany." Japanese pride demanded at least that.

We prepared for bed that night but continued talking well into the night. Neither of us stopped the other. The next morning he left my office with Commander Otani by way of a navy car. Later I heard that he was shot down over Hong Kong. I am very sad that Japan lost another great man.

LOCATION OF THE 1ST MIXED BRIGADE HEADQUARTERS AND THE DETACHED DIVISIONAL HEADQUARTERS

After the air raids on July 4, Major General Tachibana began looking for a new location for the headquarters. Around July 10, he moved his headquarters to Tatsumidani, a valley located in the southeastern part of Chichi Jima, near Ogiura.

My own headquarters at the old Chichi Jima Fortress, located at Omura, was vulnerable from the air, and I decided to move it to the mountains in the central part of the island shortly after July 20. Our forward headquarters had about a hundred people working for it, including eleven officers. My office was composed of the office staff, a code group, communication unit, cooks, weapons experts, accountants, doctors, and a farming unit, among others. My duties were to be in charge of sea transportation, supplies, communications, liaison with the Haha Jima garrison and with the navy, and to assist the commander of the 1st Mixed Brigade in tactics.

The above was the description of the division of labor as written out on paper. However, just before my departure from Iwo Jima, Lieutenant General Kuribayashi solemnly told me, "I am unable to depend on the division commander [Tachibana] as far as tactics are concerned. You will be directly in charge of tactics yourself. If anything happens, inform me immediately. In connection with sea transportation, you will have contact with the Imperial Japanese Headquarters directly." Actually, it was hard for me to be in charge. I was only a major.

WHEN IS JAPAN GOING TO SURRENDER?

One evening, I received a telephone call from the Navy Headquarters on the island stating that Commander Kamiura was coming to visit me alone. I asked him to have supper with me in my office, since I had not yet offered him any gifts after our move here. He used to work in Rabaul as a staff officer and had had a nervous breakdown of sorts because of the enemy air raids. After a rest at his home in Japan, he was transferred to Chichi Jima.

Confidentially, Kamiura said he had not spoken to Rear Admiral Mori about the war situation but was wondering when Japan would surrender. "I think it will be as early as New Year's Day, or as late as March. What do you think?" he asked me. I replied in the same way I had to Colonel Shimamura, "I hope Japan surrenders after Germany." I said no more regarding this, as I did not want to be misunderstood. Later Kamiura was sent back to Japan by hospital ship because of another nervous breakdown.

After the war, he was brought to Guam from Japan as a war crimes witness. I was also there, and he was only about three bunks away from me at the part of the camp for witnesses. Every day he would come to me and say that the U.S. forces had planted a hidden listening device and asked me to check the ceiling. I told Shinoda Hajime and Miyazaki Isamu, both lieutenant commanders on the Naval Staff, to watch him and, if necessary, to ask the U.S. medical doctors to examine his mental condition. No sooner had I mentioned this when one morning someone cried, "Oh, Commander Kamiura!" I was surprised and went to his bed. He had died. He had hanged himself with a rope from his mosquito netting. He was a graduate of the Imperial Japanese Naval Academy. His knowledge of English was quite good. He said he had studied English and Spanish at the Tokyo School of Foreign Languages (Tokyo Gaikokugo Gakko) for two years after his graduation from the Naval Academy.[4] He had become another casualty of the war.

SHIPPING UNDER THE COVER OF DARKNESS

Because the American B-24s came to Chichi Jima during the daytime on their air raids, the loading and unloading and shipping of our ships had to be done under the cover of darkness. Whenever any transport came in to Futami Harbor, we unloaded the materials from the ships at night at Omura Pier and then dispersed them into the mountains by trucks before dawn. The next night these materials were brought back to Omura Pier by trucks and then loaded on to sailboats and fishing boats. These small fleets then proceeded on to Haha Jima. On the third night these boats went to Iwo Jima, where they were unloaded and returned to Haha Jima. We mobilized about fifty sailboats and fishing boats. It was not very difficult to unload and reload the troops, but there were many problems with unloading and reloading ammunition and food.

For the unloading and reloading work at night, I used about three thousand officers and men from the Chichi Jima Garrison, thirty trucks, and about twenty landing craft as go-betweens from the transports to Omura Pier and Ogiura Pier, across the bay. Every night, I went to Omura Pier to supervise the work. Sometimes, after midnight, I had to hit some of the junior officers for failing to direct their men. That was the first time I broke my policy of never striking my underlings. Now, twenty years after World War II, I feel sorry for having done that, but in those days, we had to work quickly. Although the workers got tired or were sleepy, we had to complete the unloading and dispersing of the materials as quickly as possible. Any delay in the departure of the transports could prove fatal, due to attacks by enemy planes and submarines, and delays in the dispersing work could lead to the materials being damaged during air raids. After midnight the workers would become tired and hungry. They would squat down and no longer move. Sometimes I made arrangements to give them food at midnight, but it was impossible to give food to all the workers. Even if I sincerely requested their cooperation, scolded them, or flattered them, they would not move an inch. Finally I would become so angry I would threaten them with a club.

Major General Tachibana would assist me at this time. He was very effective at getting them to work, as he was their commanding general, and I was only a staff member sent from Iwo Jima. These soldiers, therefore, more readily obeyed his commands. Now I feel very sorry for these soldiers. With Japan already greatly weakened and desperate, the war made us semi-insane and led us to drive the soldiers like this.

After the fall of Iwo Jima, Tachibana was promoted to lieutenant general and appointed the 109th Division commander. One hundred members of my detachment and about eighty members of the 1st Mixed Brigade helped form the new division. I came to work under him as chief of staff. He was smart and a man of action, but he was unfortunately executed by hanging in Guam after a trial as a "Class B" war criminal.[5]

SHIPPING OF TROOPS FROM CHICHI JIMA TO IWO JIMA

What was the situation with regard to the shipping of troops from the Japanese mainland to Iwo Jima via Chichi Jima? I will introduce the shipping of troops chronologically, based on what I know, below.

DATE OF ARRIVAL OF TROOPS TO CHICHI JIMA	DEPARTURE FROM CHICHI JIMA	DATE OF ARRIVAL OF TROOPS TO IWO JIMA	TROOPS
July 1, 1944	July 1 thru Oct. 30	July 1 thru Nov. 5	145th Infantry Regiment
July 1	July 1	July 1	8th Independent Antitank Battalion
	July 14	July 20	10th Independent Antitank Battalion
July 1	July 14	July 20	11th Independent Antitank Battalion

DATE OF ARRIVAL OF TROOPS TO CHICHI JIMA	DEPARTURE FROM CHICHI JIMA	DATE OF ARRIVAL OF TROOPS TO IWO JIMA	TROOPS
July 1	July 14 thru Aug. 25	July 18 thru Aug. 28	12th Independent Antitank Battalion
June 29	July 12	July 14	2nd Medium Howitzer Battalion
June 29	July 12	July 14	3rd Medium Howitzer Battalion
July 18 (tanks sank)	Aug. 29 thru Oct. 30	Aug. 30 thru Nov. 5	26th Tank Regiment
	July 11	July 18	109th Antiaircraft Artillery
Aug. 3	Aug. 10	Aug. 12	109th Radar Unit
July 1	July 16	July 16	109th Rocket-Propelled Grenades
July 1	July 16	July 16	20th Special 25-mm Machine-Gun Unit
July 1	July 18	July 18	21st Special 25-mm Machine-Gun Unit
Aug. 4	Aug. 8	Aug. 10	2nd Independent Machine-Gun Battalion
July 20 (sank but rescued)	Aug. 16 thru Aug. 24	Aug. 20 thru Aug. 16	3rd Battalion, 17th Independent Mixed Regiment

Notes:

1. Troops that arrived at Iwo Jima on the day they left Chichi Jima were shipped by navy high-speed transport.
2. Troops spending many days to get to Iwo Jima were those who stayed at Haha Jima due to the need to elude American ships or those whose ships had suffered some sort of engine problem.
3. The above chart is an overview; there may have been some other units mixed in with other troops.

IWO JIMA TROOPS STAYING AT CHICHI JIMA

Troops from such units as the 26th Tank Regiment (Sensha Daini-juroku Rentai) and the 3rd Battalion of the 17th Independent Mixed Regiment (Dokuritsu Konsei Daijunana Rentai Daisan Daitai), which had been sunk by American submarines, had to receive clothes and be reequipped. They also needed rest and medical treatment. The 26th Tank Regiment in particular had to wait for new tanks to be acquired by Lieutenant Colonel Nishi back on the mainland. Thus, there were many troops waiting at Chichi Jima who were supposed to go on to Iwo Jima under my care. This was especially true in the case of the 145th Infantry Regiment, with many personnel awaiting shipping. At times I had from 3,500 to 4,000 troops on Chichi Jima waiting to be moved.

The biggest problem I had was accommodating these men. The Chichi Jima Garrison troops had air-raid shelters for themselves. Even if these other troops dug trenches for themselves, it would be hard to expect them to be safe. One big hit by the enemy's guns or by an air raid could cause huge losses.

The tunnels on Chichi Jima helped a great deal at this time. There were five long tunnels, and most of the Iwo Jima–bound troops stayed in these tunnels. Men would sleep in these tunnels during the daytime on mats on the floors. At night these tunnels were used by trucks for the unloaded materials. We still had serious trouble, because there were no toilets in the tunnels. Many men developed diarrhea due to the unsanitary living conditions. A small number of these men became patients in the Chichi Jima Army Hospital (Chichi Jima Rikugun Byoin).

I used some of the other troops to construct a roadway in the center of Chichi Jima. It was a little more than two kilometers (one mile) long and six meters (twenty feet) wide. It was good exercise for them. Due to the shortage of food and water at Iwo Jima, we kept some of the troops behind at Chichi Jima intentionally. When the American forces invaded Iwo Jima, there were about eight hundred troops, which included some liaison members visiting my command and one hundred members of my detached office. These men, having been spared the fate that befell Iwo Jima, returned home alive after the war.

THE USE OF ANTIAIRCRAFT GUNS AGAINST GROUND TROOPS

There were 17,000 army and navy troops on Chichi Jima. Lieutenant General Kuribayashi had command of ground defense for the entire chain of the Ogasawara Islands. Major General Tachibana was in charge of the ground defense for Chichi Jima. However, Kuribayashi had put me in charge of the tactics at Chichi Jima, with the following duty assigned to me: "Major Horie will assist the 1st Mixed Brigade commander in tactics."

I often visited Rear Admiral Mori and Major General Tachibana and tried to persuade them to forget about the tactics of the 31st Army to meet the enemy on the shoreline. They listened carefully. My idea was that each person would dig his own cave position as his tomb, with no reserves waiting and no maneuvering. Each man would then "snipe" and kill ten enemy troops.

The main problem concerned diverting the antiaircraft guns and using them for a ground battle. I insisted that 90 percent of the antiaircraft guns should be put into caves and no longer used for antiaircraft battle and instead be employed against advancing enemy troops. Many people on the staff opposed my idea. The navy had a lot of 25-mm machine guns it was using as antiaircraft guns. I wanted to turn these guns over to the army and send some big army guns to Iwo Jima. However, the army argued strongly that the antiaircraft battle was more important at this stage. I felt the antiaircraft battle was wasteful and meant nothing. I told them even if the enemy planes came by the thousands they could not hurt us if we stayed in caves and tunnels. Instead we should prepare to fight the enemy's ground forces that would be advancing on us. The Naval Staff and Lieutenant Colonel Nishikawa on Iwo Jima also strongly opposed my plans, and Lieutenant General Kuribayashi was unable to make a decision. Based on the lessons learned from the battles of Saipan, Tinian, and Guam, I argued, "If the enemy tried to soften us up with air raids and naval bombardment, each exposed antiaircraft gun wouldn't last five minutes." Eventually, Kuribayashi ordered that half of the antiaircraft guns would lay down fire against the enemy ground forces.

On Chichi Jima, after dozens of attempts, I finally persuaded Rear Admiral Mori to gradually turn over some 25-mm antiaircraft guns to the army. However, unfortunately, the enemy attacked Iwo Jima before we could arrange to send the army's big guns there from Chichi Jima.

AGRICULTURAL TEAMS GROW VEGETABLES

One day, I gathered representatives of the army and navy units and explained to them the importance of being self-sufficient foodwise on Chichi Jima and stressed that we consider the local farming and fishing practices and try to allocate areas for each unit. To my surprise, Lieutenant Commander Yonehara Minoru, a representative of the navy, declared, "We get vegetables and fish from the mainland by ship, so don't worry about the navy. You can allocate both the land and sea areas to the army units." His simple generosity stemmed from the navy's custom of getting its supplies by ship, I guess. On the other hand, he may have lacked the foresight to see that Chichi Jima would soon be completely cut off by enemy submarines.

Commander Kamiura and Lieutenant Commander Yonehara subsequently went back to Japan, and Lieutenant Commanders Shinoda and Miyazaki came in their place. The vegetables grown by these agricultural teams were presented to Iwo Jima troops as a gift by the army units on Chichi Jima. The men on Iwo Jima were very pleased, but I wonder how many of the men actually received them, as there were so many soldiers and sailors on the island.

I later presented some fish and vegetables gathered by the army agricultural teams to Admiral Mori and in return received some 25-mm machine guns. Admiral Mori said he used to work for Admiral Yonai Mitsumasa; he was always talking about Admiral Yonai.[6] Mori was born in Shizuoka Prefecture, I remember, and was a good man, friendly to everyone he encountered. Sometimes he made cakes himself and would give us some. He was promoted to vice admiral in March 1945.

After World War II he was tried in Guam as a Class B war criminal. We witnesses tried to defend him, but he was sentenced to twenty years imprisonment, and later he was sent to the Australian court at Makassar (Indonesia) and was executed there by hanging. I was very sad for him.

I RETURN TO IWO JIMA TO MAKE A REPORT

On August 10, I flew to Iwo Jima to report on the situation with regard to sea transportation, defense of Chichi Jima, etc., over the past forty days to Lieutenant General Kuribayashi. I brought two bottles of water, spinach, and onions as gifts for the personnel of the 109th Divisional Headquarters. These were highly prized items in those days. When I arrived at the staff office, Colonel Hori, Lieutenant Colonel Nishikawa, and Colonel Yoshida Monzo, a new face, were there. Colonel Hori met me at the door, pulling his long moustache and smiling cheerfully. But when I got inside the mood was different. Nishikawa and Yoshida looked quite displeased. Colonel Hori introduced Yoshida, and we shook hands. Yoshida's hand was quite soft. He said to me, "I used to be an engineer, and now I am in charge of fortifications. The division commander made changes to my work without telling me. I have lost my status and self-respect. He mocks me because I am a graduate of the special course at the Army War College." When I told him that I was going to see the division commander, Nishikawa said sarcastically, "You Army War College graduates have a good time, please."[7] I sensed there was some tension between Kuribayashi and his staff officers.

When I arrived at his office, Lieutenant General Kuribayashi was sitting on the porch. He stood up and said, "Come in, I was waiting for you." He looked very happy and told me to come in and have a seat.

We went in. I proceeded to take some documents out of my briefcase and began to report about the sea transports. He said, "You have been withholding some important ammunition and equipment at Chichi Jima, like an embezzler. That's not good. For instance, you sent some 37-mm antitank guns and you kept the 47-mm antitank guns at Chichi Jima. That's a stupid thing to do." I asked him what he meant by my being an "embezzler." "You know that I would come to Iwo Jima as soon as the sea transportation is finished and die with you," I told him, adding "Anyhow, Chichi Jima is mountainous and the enemy would not be able to use tanks. I had ordered the load of 37-mm and 47-mm antitank guns sent simultaneously, but due to trouble with some of the boats the 47-mm antitank guns have probably been delayed." He was teasing, I guess. "Don't get so mad!" he said, smiling.

Lieutenant General Kuribayashi was happy about the arrival of the main power of the 145th Infantry Regiment, saying, "The regular standing troops are very good."

I explained about the remaining troops and supplies at Chichi Jima and the prospect of future sea transportation to him. He said, "The soldiers eat. So stop sending common soldiers and send mainly arms and ammunition for the time being." I told him I would do as he suggested. "I'll arrange it." Then the general invited me to eat with him that evening. After I left his quarters, I went to the Navy Headquarters. Rear Admiral Ichimaru and Commander Mase Takeji were there, as were Lieutenant Commander Okazaki Sadamu and Lieutenant Akada Kunio. Okazaki was a graduate of the Naval Engineering Academy and worked as a supply officer. Akada was a graduate of the Naval Academy at Eta Jima and served as a ground defense officer.

Akada said to me, "I'm just a baby when it comes to ground defense, so teach me, please." He was energetic. However, Okazaki said, "I am an engineer. There is nothing on this island. I would like to be transferred to some place where I could put my skills to work. Here I can't do anything." That evening, I had dinner with Lieutenant General

Kuribayashi in his quarters. It had been forty days since I had left for Chichi Jima. After we had a few glasses of whiskey, he said to me, "My staff here are all graduates of the special course of the Army War College. I am unable to rely on them. The commanders of the independent battalions are all old. They will be going downhill very soon. They are slow in every action, and I can't help being impatient with them. How goes it on Chichi Jima?"

I recalled what had happened at the staff office when I arrived there this morning and responded, "At Chichi Jima, there are many old men helping to unload and reload the ships, working after midnight. Almost all the battalion commanders are from the seventeenth- or eighteenth-class of military graduate reserve officers. It is natural that they can't control their subordinates so well. One lieutenant colonel told me, 'Soon I will go to heaven. I am already more than sixty years old. We had better not dig so many caves because we will die soon anyway.' Some of them are bent over at the back. It may be inevitable that they prefer taking it easy."[8]

"Japan has met its end," the general murmured, pouring some more whiskey for me. He worked himself like a dog. I felt that he was under a great deal of stress and was showing signs of it.

I left the general's quarters early and went by the staff office. I talked with Colonel Hori for an hour about the Army Academy days, his railway service time, and about Lieutenant General Yokoyama and then went to bed, around 10:30 PM. There were no sirens all night. The next day, I attended the morning ceremony of the divisional headquarters. All officers and men lined up, saluted Lieutenant General Kuribayashi, and then saluted facing toward the Imperial Palace. Major Komoto Kumeji, adjutant to the division commander, relayed some information to the officers and men. After he was done, Kuribayashi started scolding Colonel Hori in front of all the officers and men, saying, "You cannot fight with a beard." I fled from the spot and went to the staff office. Drinking a cup of tea, I thought of the tense situation at the headquarters.

In an old car, I went to the base of Mount Suribachi but found that it was too steep for me, partly crippled, to climb, and so I gave up. On the way back, I ran into Colonel Atsuchi by accident. He told me that the shortage of dynamite was making it difficult to construct the fortifications and asked that I make more of an effort to get some from the mainland. He also complained to me that while the navy had a lot of dynamite, the army had little of it.

I stopped at the 145th Infantry Regiment Headquarters located at Hyobyuboku and spoke with Colonel Ikeda and some of the officers and men with whom I had talked about the loss of Saipan when we met on *Noto Maru*. Colonel Ikeda and some of the others invited me to have lunch with them. I told them I had promised to stop by the 2nd Mixed Brigade Headquarters and took leave, saying that I would try to stop by later. The officers and men of the 145th Infantry Regiment saw me off with sadness in their eyes. Instinctively, I guess, we thought this might be the last time for us to meet.

I visited the 2nd Mixed Brigade Headquarters rather hurriedly. Colonel Kaido Chosaku, commanding officer of the brigade's artillery group, and Colonel Hori were there already. Major General Osuga and Colonel Hori said they had both been scolded by Lieutenant General Kuribayashi recently. I listened to these three men for about fifteen or twenty minutes, and I was startled to learn that there had been some strong differences of opinion between Kuribayashi and the other officers.

DIFFERENCES IN OPINION BETWEEN KURIBAYASHI AND HIS STAFF CONCERNING THE WAR SITUATION

I found that many officers still believed that Japan would never abandon Iwo Jima and that the Combined Fleet would come to help them without fail. For instance, Colonel Kaido asked me to send more rounds of ammunition for antiaircraft guns because they needed a lot of ammunition. I told him not to worry about the enemy aircraft, because they could not kill us if we were in the caves. Instead, they should be worried about the landing forces, and thus the antiaircraft guns should be angled downward to lay down fire on those approaching forces, who could take our lives. He replied by saying, "You are much too pessimistic over the war situation." I realized that these officers did not know the real situation of the war.

It is not a question of who was right or who was wrong. The difference of opinions had come between those who knew the results of the Operation *A-Go*, fought on June 19, and those who did not know what had happened. Unfortunately, not everyone had been told the truth.

chapter nine

DEFENSIVE OPERATIONS FROM THE CAVES

BEACH OPERATIONS OR CAVE OPERATIONS?

At 1 PM in the afternoon of August 11, Rear Admiral Ichimaru, Commander Urabe Hijiri, a staff officer of the 3rd Air Fleet, Commander Mase, and Lieutenant Akada Kunio came to our division headquarters to discuss defense tactics. Our staff office was used for the meeting room. The army was represented by Lieutenant General Kuribayashi, Colonel Hori, Lieutenant Colonel Nishikawa, Colonel Yoshida Monzo, and myself.

Commander Urabe began by conveying to us what he said was the opinion of the Naval Headquarters: "The navy will send some arms and materials to Iwo Jima. The navy wants the army to build some pillboxes around the First Airfield. The navy is ready to bring about three hundred 25-mm machine guns and the materials necessary to build pillboxes. The enemy can land only near the First Airfield, and thus if the First Airfield were defended by a lot of pillboxes in depth, Iwo Jima would be impregnable." Commander Urabe had been trained in the Army Infantry School (Rikugun Hohei Gakko); he was the foremost ground defense expert in the Imperial Navy. From his appearance I felt that he was a well-meaning gentleman.

However, I immediately opposed his argument. "I would like to know how long the coastal guns lasted at Saipan and Guam," I began. "Would you please tell me exactly how the shoreline pillboxes at Tarawa were effective? A frontal defense against hundreds of the enemy naval guns and aircraft is out of question. The past battle lessons we have received from Saipan, Guam, Tinian, etc., have taught us clearly

75

that there are no alternatives to sniping at enemy troops from hidden caves. It will be like child's play if we attempted to use the pillboxes with 25-mm machine guns against the enemy's naval gun fire. The 40-cm naval guns of the enemy alone will destroy the pillboxes without fail. How, for instance, can we prevent the enemy from landing, or can we annihilate them at the beach? How many days can we hold Iwo Jima? We, the garrison forces, must fight against the combined ground, naval, and air forces of the enemy with only ground forces. If the navy has so many guns and materials, I hope these resources can be employed for the defense of Mount Suribachi and the Motoyama area."

Although I had spoken very excitedly, when I was done, Lieutenant General Kuribayashi declared, "I agree with Major Horie."

Commander Urabe explained the atmosphere of the homeland and other problems in a sharp tone and asked the general to reconsider, saying, "In particular, I was surprised by the fact that Major Horie, who had previously been thought to be sympathetic to the navy, opposed my explanation." He smiled when he was done.

I responded, "If I had not known about the battle reports from Saipan, Guadalcanal, Guam, etc., I might have agreed with the navy without any hesitation. Now my conscience does not permit me to do so." I did not give in.

The attendees of the meeting ate an early dinner at the staff office. Urabe and I became quite cordial during the meal, but we failed to reach any compromise that evening. Upon leaving, he tapped me on my shoulder with his finger and asked that I reconsider the pillbox problem during the night.

The next morning, August 12, Lieutenant General Kuribayashi came to see me and said, "Major Horie, regarding the problem of the pillboxes, your opinion is right from the viewpoint of tactics. But the resources the navy could bring here are also important. Particularly, dynamite and cement are very valuable for what we are doing here on this island. Three hundred 25-mm machine guns are also important. What do you think about the following plan? We could build some pillboxes using 50 percent of the navy's resources and use the rest for the army."

I replied, "I have no objection to your utilizing this chance politically." I then called the navy headquarters and told Urabe that Lieutenant General Kuribayashi would like to have another meeting when convenient. Urabe, Ichimaru, and Mase came immediately by car. We all met in the staff office again.

Lieutenant General Kuribayashi started by saying, "I would like to deal with the pillbox problem in the following way. We, the army, will make pillboxes using 50 percent of the resources the navy brings. The army will then use the rest of the resources for constructing positions. How about this approach as a compromise?"

Urabe and Ichimaru nodded slightly. Nobody spoke for a while, then, Urabe stated, "Yesterday I said that the resources for three hundred pillboxes would be sent here. But on returning home I will make every effort to get resources for an additional fifty to make 350 pillboxes." Kuribayashi, Commander Urabe, and I sat together and smiled, but no one spoke again for a while, perhaps feeling each other out. We drank tea and started smoking.

I don't remember if it was I or Lieutenant General Kuribayashi who said it, but someone suggested, "The navy will deliver the resources. One hundred sixty-five pill boxes will be made at the southern beach and western beach. The rest of the resources will be used by the army. The army will furnish a one-thousand-man working party every day. Colonel Yoshida will be in charge of construction of the pillboxes."

With no objections, the proposal was accepted. The argument over the pillboxes came to an end. Later, while at Chichi Jima, I heard that the 1st Battalion of the 145th Infantry Regiment, led by Major Hara Mitsuaki, worked every day constructing the pillboxes, with the help of some other troops. Working nonstop for six months, they were able to make up to 135 pillboxes.

CAVE OPERATIONS AND RESISTING TO THE DEATH

According to Lieutenant Musashino, who returned home alive after the war, these pillboxes were all useless, as no one could stay in them under the enemy naval gunfire.

Lieutenant General Holland M. Smith, who was the commander of V Amphibious Corps, acknowledged in his memoirs, *Coral and Brass*, that the pillboxes did impact his marines, but he does not even mention the pillboxes in the front and instead discusses how his forces made it to the other side of Iwo Jima by the end of the first day.[1]

I am not saying that Commander Urabe was wrong or that the navy was wrong. A first-class officer, Major General Tamura, deputy chief of staff of the Central Pacific Fleet, defended the beaches and took offensive actions at Saipan, Tinian, and Guam. As a result, we repeatedly found that the enemy was quite happy to find our troops appearing above ground, leaving the caves, and taking the offensive, because it allowed the invading American force to use its overwhelming power. Even at night we could not move our troops, because the enemy was able to effectively illuminate the landscape. I insisted that cave operations and resisting until death were the only useful alternatives left for us, tactically speaking.

We might try to get by with the *yamato damashi* (traditional Japanese fighting spirit), or with the help of God, in some of our battles against the poorly equipped Chinese army. But in the isolated island defense in the Pacific, such psychological dimensions would not help us against superior forces like those of the Americans. Even if we could get out of the caves and charge the enemy, we would be only throwing the bodies we received from our beloved parents against the enemy's steel. This would only hasten our death, and in doing so defeat the purpose of holding out on Iwo Jima as long as possible to undertake a delaying operation to help protect the homeland.

chapter ten

SEND MORE WEAPONS AND AMMUNITION!

MY TRIP TO THE IMPERIAL JAPANESE HEADQUARTERS

On the evening of August 12, I had dinner with Lieutenant General Kuribayashi again at his residence. During the meal, I asked him to allow me to go to the Imperial Japanese Headquarters to find replacements the older battalion commanders, get more arms (particularly antitank weapons, ammunition, dynamite, and food supplies), and request an increase in ships and convoy escort vessels. The general gave me permission to leave immediately.

The next morning, I became a passenger on a navy plane bound for the mainland. I felt a little funny when I thought about how I had left Tokyo, exchanging cups of water with my wife. However, when I saw the mountains of Japan on the horizon my heart felt warm, and I was happy to be returning, if only for a short while. The human instinct to return home is strong. When I arrived at my house unexpectedly, my wife did not know what to do, but my daughter, who was two years seven months old, was very happy to see me again.

I went to the General Staff on the morning of August 14 and reported to Colonel Hattori and Major Sejima the situation on the Ogasawara Islands.

Lieutenant Colonel Itagaki Jiro, who was in charge of logistics within the 2nd Section (Operations), also listened to my report. After I finished, he said to me, "If you can find any way to implode Iwo Jima and sink it into the ocean, we at the Imperial Japanese Headquarters would like to consider it. When you return to Iwo Jima send us your estimates on how much dynamite will be required to sink it." I was quite moved, as I felt here was at least one officer who had the same idea as I. General Tojo had already left his position as chief of the Army General Staff, and General Umezu had taken over the job of chief of staff. The atmosphere had changed completely. Colonel Hattori asked me to make a presentation about Iwo Jima to the key officers of the Army Ministry and the General Staff the next morning. The talk was to begin at 10:00 AM.

After leaving the meeting, I went down to the Shipping Section and spoke with Colonel Arao, Lieutenant Colonel Miyoshi, and Lieutenant Colonel Ureshino Akihiko, whom I had not seen for a long time. Lieutenant General Suzuki, accompanied by Lieutenant Watano Tokusada, his adjutant, came into the section. I ran up to Suzuki and asked what had happened to him. He explained that he had been ordered to become the commander of the 35th Army at Leyte, Philippines, and was on his way to pay a call on the emperor. We saw tears in each other's eyes and didn't talk about the damage to the ships or the condition of the convoy escorts. We wondered which of us would die first. But, naturally, we both wanted to stay alive as long as possible. When I said farewell to him, I felt what an ironic assignment he had been given, because he did not like General Yamashita Tomoyuki. The 35th Army belonged to the 14th Area Army (Daijuyon Homengun), of which General Yamashita was in command.

The next morning, August 15, I gave a presentation about Iwo Jima and the Ogasawara Islands Force before the men in a large auditorium in the General Staff Headquarters. To my surprise, a lot of brass showed up for the talk, at least fifty officers. They came from not only the General Staff and the Army Ministry but from other organizations as well. The shocking thing for me was that the commandant and many instructors from the Army War College were also there. I thought to myself that if I had known that this opportunity would arise I would have studied harder when I was at the War College. I felt that the prestige of the War College must have declined somewhat, because the instructors now had to listen to a lecture by their worst graduate. The audience followed my talk carefully and sincerely. The atmosphere of the General Staff had changed since the enemy had taken Saipan. That is to say, no one spoke ill of the 31st Army or Major General Iketa anymore. They had learned what American forces were capable of. The War College instructors had come to listen to me about how to develop countermeasures against the American advance.

The cooperation of each section was splendid. Later, I heard that during my talk some officers had actually made phone calls to begin taking action to arrange personnel, organization, supplies, etc. I am grateful they moved so quickly.

I was also impressed because I came to feel, for the first time, that the General Staff and Army Department might finally be taking seriously the voices of the theater command and officers. They generously accepted my request for dynamite and arms. Nevertheless, they were able to provide me only one 41-type mountain artillery gun, which had been my favorite antitank weapon, given my experiences in northern China.

After my presentation, I stopped by the Ordnance Section (Heibika) of the Army Department and called on Lieutenant Colonel Oneda Noboru, with whom I had worked in the 2nd Infantry Regiment. He told me, "We can give you as many troops as needed but it was difficult to supply arms. This is the biggest problem facing our office." This was the real situation of Japan as it neared defeat.

A classmate of mine from the War College, Major Hori, who was working in the Intelligence Office, 2nd Division (Dainibu, Joho) of the General Staff, decided to give me a farewell party on the evening of August 17, with our fellow classmates. He called those who were in the Tokyo area and told me that at least ten men could attend. I was pleased with the idea and grateful to him for his thoughtfulness. I went ahead and made arrangements for a flight to Iwo Jima on August 18.

NICKNAMED THE "PESSIMISTIC STAFF OFFICER," I RETURN TO IWO JIMA

On the morning of August 16, I visited the Convoy Escort General Fleet Headquarters and the 12th Section of the Naval Staff. Everyone knew about the fate of Operation *A-Go* and that Saipan and Guam had already fallen into the hands of the enemy. To tell the truth, the atmosphere of the navy was odd. Japan was being attacked by the sea, and the weak condition of the navy, which had to deal with the enemy first, was much more serious than that of the army. I worked for the navy more than a year, and once when I had the chance to travel on a convoy escort vessel from Takao, Formosa, to Manila, in the Philippines, I saw some survivors from a ship that had been sunk. Seeing their poor condition, I realized this was like the situation of Japan as a whole. Because of this view, the officers and men at Iwo Jima and Chichi Jima had given me the unfortunate nickname *hikan sanbo*, or "pessimistic staff officer."

There were others who viewed me as a man of foresight. But this opinion was not correct. I simply saw what was happening based on the fact that I was working in hell—the convoy escort business—and came to realize the true state of Japan's situation. As General Tojo was the prime minister, all messages coming to the Foreign Ministry and the cabinet were also coming to the General Staff. So actually I was reading almost all the messages coming to the government, army, and navy.

After greeting my old navy acquaintances, I returned to the Shipping Section of the General Staff and started speaking with Lieutenant Colonel Miyoshi. A lieutenant colonel working in the Administrative Branch (Shomuka) of the General Staff yelled at me as soon as he came in, "What are you still doing here? Didn't you finish your presentation already? You should know how General Obata, who has been unable to return to Saipan, is feeling since he left the island. And you just stand around here, chatting. I dare say this to you as I was an instructor in the section next to yours at the Army Academy." He, of course, was correct. I had nothing to say in defense of myself.

After he left, Colonel Miyoshi said, "Don't worry about him. He just said such spiteful things because my section is friendly with our old comrades." I decided to call Major Hori and decline the party the following night and made arrangements to fly back to Iwo Jima the next morning.

On the morning of the 17th, when I was walking to the airplane at Kisarazu Airfield, I ran into Lieutenant Colonel Nishi. He told me that he had been able to gather twenty-three tanks and was heading back to Iwo Jima on the same plane as me. Another man was with him, Major Matoba Sueo. He had been ordered to go to Chichi Jima to replace the commander of the 308th Independent Battalion (Dokuritsu Hohei Daisanbyakuhachi Daitai). Matoba had achieved fame as a battalion commander in the 18th Division (Daijuhachi Shidan), which had attacked Singapore. At Chichi Jima, later, he became famous again because his battalion was able to dig the most caves. However, after the war, he was executed as a Class B war criminal following the trials at Guam. We all enjoyed the conversation on the plane.

When we arrived at Iwo Jima, there was a car awaiting Lieutenant Colonel Nishi from the 28th Regiment. We went to Nishi's headquarters at Maruman village and had lunch there. The lunch was prepared by Captain Matsuyama Aki, adjutant to Nishi. In the afternoon, Major Matoba and I motored to the divisional headquarters. Lieutenant General Kuribayashi appeared very much pleased when I told him about my trip to Tokyo.

As the result of my trip, almost all of the battalion commanders were to be replaced by officers thirty years younger. (One lieutenant colonel, who was sixty-two years old, was replaced by a captain who was twenty-five. So, the difference in age was thirty-seven years.) It was probably very difficult and sad for the young majors and captains to replace the older battalion commanders. These younger men did well, however, and eventually became the center of fortification, training, and combat efforts.

The Imperial Japanese Headquarters allocated more dynamite, arms, and ammunition, and the Shipping Section cooperated by sending more ships. Thus, the sea transportation between Tokyo and Chichi Jima and between Chichi Jima and Iwo Jima increased again.

The following troops were added to Iwo Jima after this.

AREA OF ORIGIN	DEPARTING HARBOR	TROOPS
Kanto, Nagano, and Niigata	Yokohama	43rd Independent 13-mm Machine-Gun Unit
Kanto	Yokohama	44th Independent 13-mm Machine-Gun Unit
Northern Honshu and Kanto	Shibaura	109th Division Howitzer Unit
Kanto	Shibaura	1st Independent Howitzer Unit

The next morning, August 18, I went to the southern beach with Lieutenant General Kuribayashi to see if we could destroy and sink the First Airfield so that the enemy had no chance to use it against Japan. After about an hour inspecting the field, he said to me, "It is impossible for us to sink this area. Could you calculate how much dynamite we would need? It is easier for us to increase the defenses. Unfortunately, there is no choice." Thus the discussion of sinking Iwo Jima came to an end.

In light of this discussion, it was all the more funny that after the war a rumor began to be widely circulated among the U.S. Marines that I had been driven from Iwo Jima to Chichi Jima due to a conflict between Lieutenant General Kuribayashi and me over the question of the sinking of Iwo Jima. Someone actually wrote about it in a book about the battle—incorrectly, of course.[1]

chapter eleven

DEFENDING IWO JIMA
TO THE DEATH

EVERYONE MUST KILL TEN ENEMY TROOPS

Lieutenant General Kuribayashi established the following plan—the Iwo Jima Garrison would place some troops around Mount Suribachi with the main strength farther inland; once the enemy began the invasion of the island, everybody would resist the enemy until the end, making his position his own tomb. Everybody was to kill ten of the enemy.

The most serious problem was how to employ the five thousand navy troops for the battle, as most of them were members of antiaircraft gun units, construction units, or radar units and did not have any training in land warfare. The special Navy Ground Units, known by the forbidding name of Nanpo Kurikusentai, under Commander Tachimi Kotaro, had in fact little training or actual experience. However, the navy did have many antiaircraft guns (about 250 antiaircraft guns in total), and if these guns could skillfully be employed in the ground battles, they would have an important effect on the battle. This was why I strongly insisted that the navy troops should be placed under the control of sector commanders and that the antiaircraft guns should be aimed at ground targets. However, it was quite difficult for the navy to understand my idea—the employment of the antiaircraft guns for ground battles.

Soon after the discussion about the pillboxes, we talked about the distribution of the navy troops. Rear Admiral Ichimaru requested that the navy troops be kept together in one place to fight, as the navy had specific traditions and wanted to die together. Lieutenant General Kuribayashi accepted his request, and it was agreed that the main strength of the navy would be placed between the East Sector and South Sector under Ichimaru's command. The navy's coastal gun units, antiaircraft gun units, and radar units were to be placed under the command of each army sector commander. Interestingly, most of the army artillery officers also opposed the diversion of the antiaircraft guns from their original functions to use in the ground battle. As the time of the enemy invasion approached, only 50 percent of the antiaircraft guns, about 150 guns, were ready for their twin duties—antiaircraft and ground battles.

FIVE SECTORS ESTABLISHED

The troops were distributed into five sectors: East, South, West, North, and Mount Suribachi. Normally, the commanders of the 2nd Mixed Brigade (Konsei Daini Ryodan) and 145th Infantry Regiment would become the sector commanders. At Iwo Jima, however, they did not become sector commanders. Breaking with tradition was a characteristic of Kuribayashi's tactics.

In the case of the Mount Suribachi sector, however, which had to fight and hold out on its own, separated from the other areas, Colonel Atsuchi was placed in control of everything. In the case of the four other sectors, the sector commanders were responsible only for lookout, coordination, and control. In actual combat, every unit and every man had to fight until the end. There was no chance to consider the use of reserve forces, change of artillery positions, or the maneuvering of troops under the cover of darkness, etc. Exposure to the enemy even for a minute meant certain death.

TOTAL JAPANESE STRENGTH—21,000 MEN

Below are the detailed figures regarding manpower, arms, ammunitions, etc., per sector. This was all the manpower available on Iwo Jima.

SOUTH SECTOR, HEADED BY IJA CAPTAIN AWATSU HOKATSU

(Army) 2nd Mixed Brigade	Major General Senda Sadatoshi
309th Independent Infantry Battalion	Captain Awatsu Hokatsu
310th Independent Infantry Battalion	Captain Iwaya Tamesaburo
1st Battalion, 145th Infantry Regiment	Major Hara Mitsuaki
109th Division Charge Company	Captain Furuta Katsunari
2nd Independent Machine- Gun Battalion	Major Kawasaki Tokio

2nd Mixed Brigade Engineer Company (main strength)	First Lieutenant Musashino Kikuso
8th Antitank (Independent) Battalion	Captain Shimizu Hajime
5th Fortress Construction Company	
109th Division Radar Unit	
20th Special 25-mm Machine-Gun Unit (Attached to the navy)	
Total Army Strength in South Sector:	4,100 men

(Navy) 27th Air Division Headquarters	Rear Admiral Ichimaru Toshinosuke
South Air Force Headquarters	Captain Inoue Samaji
South Air Force Special Navy Ground Force	Commander Tachimi Kotaro
Antiaircraft Gun Unit	Lieutenant Commander Tokiwa Teizo
Construction Force	
Coastal Gun Unit	
Total Navy Strength in South Sector:	3,000 men

EAST SECTOR, HEADED BY IJA MAJOR HAKUTA YOSHINOBU

(Army) 314th Independent Infantry Battalion	Major Hakuta Yoshinobu
311th Independent Infantry Battalion (part)	
2nd Mixed Brigade Artillery Regiment (main strength)	Colonel Kaido Chosaku
2nd Mixed Brigade Engineer Company	
3rd Battalion, 145th Infantry Regiment	
3rd Medium Howitzer Battalion	Major Kobayashi Kotaro
2nd Mixed Brigade Field Hospital	Captain (Dr.) Noguchi Iwao
26th Tank Regiment	Lieutenant Colonel Nishi Takeichi
44th Independent Antitank-Gun Unit	
12th Independent Antitank- Gun Battalion	Captain Hayauchi Masao
109th Division Rocket-Propelled Artillery Gun Battery (platoon)	
Total Army Strength in East Sector:	3,900 men

(Navy) Antiaircraft Unit	Lieutenant (Junior Grade) Ito Shigo
Total Navy Strength in East Sector:	300 men

NORTH SECTOR, HEADED BY IJA CAPTAIN SHIMOMA KAICHI

(Army) 3rd Battalion, 17th Independent Mixed Regiment	Captain Shimoma Kaichi
145th Infantry Regiment (main strength)	Colonel Ikeda Masuo
109th Division Howitzer Unit	
109th Divisional Headquarters	Lieutenant General Kuribayashi Tadamichi
109th Communication Unit	First Lieutenant Morita Toyokichi
1st Independent Howitzer Company	
Provisional Field Ordnance Unit	
Provisional Field Supply Unit	
Chichi Jima Military Police	
Iwo Jima Special Weather Unit	
2nd Mixed Brigade Pioneer Company (part)	
Disease Prevention Water Supply Unit	
Special Secret Service Unit	
Total Army Strength in North Sector:	4,200 men
(Navy) Special Navy Ground Force	Lieutenant Takahashi
Antiaircraft Unit	Ensign Iizuka Katsuo
Total Navy Strength in North Sector:	1,000 men

WEST SECTOR, HEADED BY IJA MAJOR TATSUMI SHIGEO

(Army) 311th Independent Infantry Battalion (main force)	Major Tatsumi Shigeo
12th Independent Antitank Battalion (part)	
109th Division Antiaircraft Gun Unit	
2nd Battalion, 145th Infantry Regiment (part)	
1st Independent Machine-Gun Battalion	Major Kawanami Ko
43rd Independent 13-mm Machine-Gun Unit	
2nd Medium Howitzer Battalion	Major Nakao Naosuke
21st Field Well-Digging Company	First Lieutenant Kawai Yoshio
20th Independent Howitzer Battalion	Captain Mizuashi Mitsuo
109th Division Rocket-Propelled Artillery Gun Battery (part)	
Total Army Strength in West Sector:	2,800 men

(Navy) Ogakayama Area Antiaircraft Gun Unit	Lieutenant (Junior Grade) Matsuno Ichiro
Total Navy Strength in West Sector:	300 men

MOUNT SURIBACHI SECTOR, HEADED BY COLONEL ATSUCHI KANEHIKO

(Army) 312th Independent Infantry Battalion
10th Independent Antitank-Gun Battalion
2nd Mixed Brigade Artillery (one battery)
2nd Medium Howitzer Battalion (part)
5th Fortress Construction Company (part)
2nd Mixed Brigade Engineer Company (platoon)

Total Army Strength in Mount Suribachi Sector:	1,000 men

(Navy) Antiaircraft Unit	Lieutenant (Junior Grade) Hirunuma Taro
Coastal Gun Unit	Lieutenant (Junior Grade) Hirunuma Taro

Total Navy Strength in Mount Suribachi Sector:	680 men (380 and 300)

Grand Total of Army Strength:	16,000 men
Grand Total of Navy Strength:	5,000 men

Combined Total Strength of Army and Navy:	21,000 men

TOTAL ARMS AND AMMUNITION

ARMS	NUMBER OF	AMMUNITION
Guns (larger than 75-mm)	120	100,000 rounds
Antiaircraft Gun (more than 25-mm)	300	500 rounds each
Rifles and Light Machine Guns	18,000	20,000,000 Bullets
Howitzers (80-mm and 10-mm)	130	80 per each
Howitzers (150-mm)	20	40 per each
Jet Propelling Guns	70	50 per each
Antitank Guns (47-mm)	40	100 per each
Antitank Guns (37-mm)	20	80 per each
Tanks	23	

FOOD: MORE THAN ENOUGH FOR TWO MONTHS

GENERAL KURIBAYASHI PREPARES TO FIGHT TO THE DEATH

Lieutenant General Kuribayashi was completely prepared to die should the enemy invade Iwo Jima. Moreover, he had decided he could win the battle by prolonging the American advance as long as humanly possible before he was killed. His letters to his family shed light on his thinking. In a letter to his wife, Yoshii, dated August 2, 1944, he wrote: "After my death, my belongings left behind will probably not make it back to Japan. So I will keep only those things that are absolutely necessary and send back the rest while I am still alive."[1] He continued, in the same letter: "Compared to what we are doing here, the battles in the China theater were like simple maneuvers. This island is crowded with army and navy personnel. All of them are saying that China had been easy. Everybody expects to be killed like those on Attu and Saipan. Everyone is gloomy and no one is smiling. The other night I had a dream that I returned home. At the time, you and Takako were very much pleased, but as I told them that I returned home to write my last will and that I had to go back to the battlefield, Takako looked very sad."[2]

GENERAL KURIBAYASHI'S CONCERNS ABOUT THE EVACUATION OF ISLANDERS

While most of the islanders had been evacuated during the period from July 3 to July 20, about fifty or sixty islanders remained on Chichi Jima until the end of August. Because these people had strongly insisted on staying longer, and since I had been busy with trips to Iwo Jima and Tokyo, I had not followed their situation properly.

At the end of August, I returned to Chichi Jima from my trips off-island. Soon thereafter I came down with a fever, and my health deteriorated. During this time, I received a personal message from Lieutenant General Kuribayashi. The emergency message read: "According to some rumors, some civilians have remained at Chichi Jima. Don't you know that they will encumber our forces in case of battle? Reply immediately, Kuribayashi."

I was at a loss about what to do but immediately drafted a response as follows: "To: Lieutenant General Kuribayashi, From: Major Horie. I am very sorry that my carelessness caused the delay in the evacuation of some islanders. I am certain that they can be sent back with the earliest ship. Please forgive me."

Around then, an army doctor, Captain Teraki Tadashi, examined me and declared that I was suffering from A-type paratyphus.[3] That is to say, I drew two strikes. Anyhow, Lieutenant General Kuribayashi was determined and would not change his mind.

THE FIVE VOWS AND SIX INSTRUCTIONS OF GENERAL KURIBAYASHI

Lieutenant General Kuribayashi ordered his adjutant to print five vows and six instructions and to distribute them to the officers and men on Iwo Jima. He sent me some copies and told me to print more at Chichi Jima and distribute them to the troops there.

FIVE VOWS FOR MENTAL PREPAREDNESS OF THE OFFICERS AND MEN

1. The basis of the Japanese spirit comes from the respect of God and our ancestors. We hereby make an oath to purify our mental condition and increase this spirit.

2. The growth of the Japanese spirit has come from the three-thousand-year history of our nation. We hereby make an oath to annihilate the enemy who is going to overrun this spirit, overcoming any and all difficulties.

3. The Japanese spirit will be brightened by accomplishing the Imperial instructions to the officers and men of the army and navy. We hereby make an oath to keep discipline, train ourselves, and increasingly develop our fighting spirit.

4. We are now on the front line of national defense. We must follow the operational policy. We hereby make an oath to do everything for the emperor, for the perished personnel, and for the people in the homeland.

5. We are the representatives of the people of Japan. We must be proud of our position and accomplish our responsibility. We hereby make an oath to behave, to be generous to others, and develop the Japanese spirit all over the world.

SIX INSTRUCTIONS FOR MENTAL PREPAREDNESS OF THE OFFICERS AND MEN

- We shall defend this island with all-out efforts.
- We shall overrun the enemy tanks with explosives and destroy them.
- We shall infiltrate the enemy and annihilate them.
- We shall kill the enemy with a one-shot, one-kill approach.
- We shall not die until we have each killed ten men.
- We shall harass the enemy with guerrilla tactics until the last man.

CONSTRUCTION OF CAVE POSITIONS AS TOMBS

The key point when constructing the cave positions was to make the position one that we could use to snipe at enemy forces and that could be linked by underground paths to other caves and positions. The idea of simply making foxholes was already too outdated. Everyone, including Lieutenant General Kuribayashi and his staff officers, was to make his own position, which would be like a final tomb, by himself. Because of these preparations, the forces on Iwo Jima were given the odd name of *chika heidan*, or "underground forces."

The rocks of Iwo Jima, different from those of Chichi Jima, were weak and easily broken. Moreover, they constantly released sulphur. As a result, it was difficult to dig and make caves. Using an army pick, I continued digging, and I found that an average person could not continue digging for more than ten minutes. The sulphur made breathing difficult, and we became dizzy quickly. I tried to wear my gas mask, but it was too hot to work in and thus hard for me to breathe. We dug the underground paths twenty to thirty meters (approximately sixty to ninety feet) deep. Along these underground paths we made some side rooms. The officers and men made these rooms their sleeping, eating, and resting areas. At Chichi Jima, I called these caves *mogura jinchi*, or "mole caves"

Lieutenant General Kuribayashi set up a "cave-digging discipline" and had the officers and men accomplish individual shares, a kind of quota system.

TARGET PRACTICE AND OTHER TRAINING

In training, we focused mainly on sniping, infiltration attacks at night, and antitank attacking. Victory on Iwo Jima would only be possible if we were able to kill more of the enemy than they could kill of us. The number of defenders was about twenty-one thousand men. Therefore, if the enemy were to lose more than twenty-one thousand men, the defenders, we believed, could have an opportunity to win the campaign. Of course, no one expected to return home alive. Of all the training we were engaged in, target practice and sniping were the most important. However, with ammunition supplies being of concern, the men and their officers could not practice using firing bursts with live rounds as much as they would have liked.

Our training for night infiltration attacks was based on the battle lessons learned from the Saipan Garrison. However, Colonel Nakagawa Kunio, who served as the commander of the 2nd Regiment on Peleliu, warned that this tactic should not be overestimated. Kuribayashi too wondered about the effectiveness of night infiltration attacks. He had studied alongside and interacted with American forces before, when he lived in the United States, and was hesitant to recommend this type of training, as he knew about the ability of the Americans' nighttime illumination and defense preparations. However, in the end, he ordered this training for all officers and men as a morale booster.

Iwo Jima was not like Saipan, Guam, or Morotai, which had been covered in thick vegetation and jungles. That, I believe, made it difficult for the defenders of Iwo Jima to get the results they wanted with the night infiltration attacks. Also, it seemed that U.S. forces had become aware of this tactic and anticipated it.

Antitank attacks were the second most important training, after sniping. Some officers and men chose to go to their deaths via this attack. In the battle reports sent by Lieutenant General Kuribayashi, the following information was found. "Some of the officers and men laid down among their dead comrades or wore U.S. uniforms taken from dead American Marines. Then they waited for the American tanks to advance and then exploded themselves, causing great damage to American tanks and forces."

Another side of Kuribayashi was his self-discipline, and he was unmatched when it came to saving water. He urged water conservation on everyone. He was able to get by on one cup of water for shaving and washing (mainly, he washed his eyes), and he used the remainder of the cup of water in the toilet. There were rumors that this or that officer was using too much water or that some noncommissioned officers were careless about saving water. Therefore, the water conservation shown by Lieutenant General Kuribayashi himself helped serve as a role model to influence the behavior of his officers and men.

THE STRONG WILL OF GENERAL KURIBAYASHI

I do not know exactly where he got this strong will. It might have come from the lineage of the Kuribayashi family. He used to express his opinion without reserve before his officers and men, and he often could not be stopped once he got started.

After the war, I had an opportunity to talk with Vice Admiral Kaneko Shigeji, who had been one of Kuribayashi's classmates at Nagano Middle School (Nagano Chugakko) and later became the commander in chief of the China Expeditionary Naval Force (Shina Homen Kantai). He told me that Kuribayashi had once been the leader of a strike against the school authorities. He barely escaped being expelled from school. In those days he was already good at poetry, composition, and speechmaking. He was a young literary enthusiast.

Mild-mannered types did not hold up well against his strong will, however. Colonel Hori, chief of staff, and Major General Osuga, commander of the 2nd Mixed Brigade, were relieved of their duties after their replacements in infantry tactics came. Osuga's health was bad, and he was hospitalized after his dismissal from the brigade.

chapter twelve

TWO MONTHS BEFORE THE STORM

TRANSPORTATION BECOMES MORE AND MORE DIFFICULT

On my return trip to Chichi Jima from Tokyo, I spent two or three days again on Iwo Jima before leaving for Chichi Jima. On the flight to Iwo we passed over Chichi Jima, and I noticed that American B-24s had already begun bombing that island and its neighbor Haha Jima from Saipan. Now even at night we had to be prepared for the enemy's air raids on our ships at Futami Harbor. There were now not only enemy submarines in the waters between Iwo Jima and Chichi Jima but also enemy surface ships. The navigation of sailboats and fishing boats became extremely difficult, and many times they were forced to stop partway at Haha Jima.

The conditions for these sailors had become as dangerous as they had been for the big transport ships that had navigated along the coast of New Guinea a year ago. Now, navigation between the homeland to Chichi Jima could only be carried out by high-speed destroyers or navy high-speed transports. Japan had lost all of its high-speed merchant ships, and had only transports that could reach speeds of seven or eight knots. The faces of the newly arriving troops looked pale with worry and tension.

As mentioned earlier, in the beginning of September 1944, I was suffering from type-A paratyphoid fever and was hospitalized in the Chichi Jima Army Hospital. The hospital buildings had been dispersed into the forested areas in the hills. Chichi Jima itself was only about twelve square miles, and we had to be prepared for enemy bombing at any time. I had a high fever of more than forty-one degrees Celsius, which continued for more than seven days. I actually thought I would go to heaven as a result of being killed by the enemy's bombing of the island.

Thanks to many good doctors, including the hospital's head, Lieutenant Colonel Shibata Kan, and the kind help and courage of Sergeant Hasegawa Shigeo and his men in carrying me to the air-raid shelter five or six times a day, I was able to leave the hospital after about a month. During my hospitalization I was able to carry out my duties through First Lieutenant Nishiyotsutsuji.

DESPERATE SHORTAGE OF FOOD AT IWO JIMA

There were about 17,000 army and navy troops at Chichi Jima, or about 15 percent fewer than at Iwo Jima. Unlike Iwo Jima, however, there was enough water, and we had plenty of vegetables. The officers and men made charcoal, too. The islanders who were drafted by the army as agricultural teams made great contributions. First Lieutenant Kosuga Tadaaki, second adjutant to Major General Tachibana, was a graduate of an agricultural high school, and he directed not only the farming but also the honeybee cultivation. As a result, we were able to send many items to Iwo Jima, including water. In those days the empty bottles were very valuable. These bottles were filled with water and were presented to Iwo Jima troops. The notice, "This bottle must be returned to Chichi Jima," was put on each bottle so that it could be reused.

Charcoal was also sent to Iwo Jima for heating in caves, as the temperatures dropped on Iwo Jima in the winter. I regarded the above gifts as private ones, leaving it up to the individual units to decide to make contributions and not seek to influence or otherwise control them. Each unit probably did things differently, so someone receiving an item might have been lucky and others not receiving one might have been unlucky.

I gave priority in shipping to arms, ammunitions, explosives, and personnel through the end of October, with the second priority going to food. I did not interfere with the planning for food, which was handled by First Lieutenant Tase Shunichi. Frankly speaking, I had approved Tase's recommendations without checking them carefully. In the middle of November, I received an urgent message from Iwo Jima telling us that the shortage of food there was serious. It said that the first priority should now be given to food. Afterwards, the focus of my efforts became food supply. When U.S. forces landed on Iwo Jima the following year in the second half of February, the Japanese defenders already had a two-month supply of food built up.

AIR TRANSPORTATION BETWEEN IWO JIMA AND THE MAINLAND

Until the end of October 1944, many air transport missions were conducted between Iwo Jima and Kisarazu, near Tokyo. As the 3rd Air Fleet (Daisan Koku Kantai) Headquarters, the senior headquarters of Rear Admiral Ichimaru's 27th Air Division (Dainijunana Koku Sentai), was located at Kisarazu, much close liaison took place. Runways would be repaired between enemy air strikes. This construction work was no small feat. The army was completely dependent on the navy for its air transportation. The navy helped the army a great deal in this respect.

The Army Ministry used to send newspapers, and the General Staff used to send some whiskey to the division headquarters. Passengers would often purchase vegetables and other things in the Kisarazu area and bring them to Iwo Jima as well. The army and navy urged their troops to write home.

OUTSTANDING ARMY OFFICERS WERE SENT TO IWO JIMA

In November, Lieutenant Colonel Shirakata Tokuji was transferred to Hachijo Jima Garrison (Hachijo Jima Shubitai), south of the Izu Peninsula near Tokyo, and in his place came Lieutenant Colonel Nakane Kanetsuji, from the Oshima Island Garrison (Oshima Shubitai). He arrived on November 6, 1944. Nakane was a *kendo,* or Japanese fencing, expert, holding the rank of fifth grade (of eight). He was called a "god of infantry tactics" and was the top graduate of the Army Infantry School. He received the emperor's award at the graduation ceremony.

On December 20, Major Yamanouchi Yasutake was assigned to the 109th Division. His father (Yasutsugu) hailed from Tosa (modern-day Kochi Prefecture, in the southern Shikoku area) and was a cavalry officer who had become a major general in the Imperial Japanese Army. Like his father, Major Yamanouchi was commissioned as a cavalry officer, in 1935 (one year senior to me), and later was transferred to the armored forces. His story was somewhat tragic in that he was ordered to Iwo Jima right after graduating from the Army War College. (In a contrast of fates, Major Fujiwara Kan, who had come to Iwo Jima as the commander of the 3rd Battalion, 17th Mixed Regiment [Daijunana Rentai Daisan Daitai], went back to Tokyo in November in order to enter the War College.) On December 27, on his way to Iwo Jima, Yamanouchi stopped at Chichi Jima because his aircraft had to make an emergency landing. He stayed at my quarters that evening, and we talked through the night. He looked sad and pitiful. The next morning we parted, wishing each other well. This was the first and last time I met him.

On December 30, Colonel Hori was transferred to the 2nd Mixed Brigade, and Colonel Takaishi Tadashi arrived as his replacement. Colonel Takaishi also was an authority on infantry tactics. I received from him a letter written with a calligraphy brush. I knew that he was a good writer and a modest man. Around this time Major General Osuga was transferred to the headquarters of the 109th Division, and Major General Senda Sadasue came from the Sendai Reserve Officers Academy (Sendai Yobishikan Gakko).

As a result, by the end of 1944 three authorities in infantry tactics—Major General Senda, Colonel Takaishi, and Lieutenant Colonel Nakane—were in place on Iwo Jima. I know that while the dispatch of these talented officers was done at the wishes of Kuribayashi, the final selection of these men was made by the Army Ministry, and it was a truly wise decision.

"SONG OF IWO JIMA"

The officers and men at Iwo Jima composed a poem called the "Song of Iwo Jima" (Iwo Jima no Uta).[1] Singing this song, they waited for the enemy's invasion. The lyrics were sent to the mainland, and it was sung toward the end of the battle by the Japanese people at midnight on March 17, 1945, and was broadcast throughout Japan and to Chichi Jima and Iwo Jima as the remaining fighters at Iwo Jima were making their banzai charges.

IWO JIMA ON THE EVE OF THE ENEMY'S ASSAULT

The enemy's assault was approaching daily. The uncertainty of the officers and men increased day by day. I would like to introduce the situation there at the time through the following three letters.

In a December 18, 1944, letter to his wife, the Baroness Takeko, Lieutenant Colonel Nishi told her and his family:

> I sympathize with you because I imagine Tokyo is very cold now. This place is just like a winter resort. If we stay in our caves we do not feel cold. We have no braziers, but we do not actually need them. We are now nervous because the enemy's bombers visit us almost every day and night. The biggest trouble is the shortage of sleep caused by the bombing. In order to avoid this additional stress, we are concentrating our energies on cave digging and in expanding our underground living areas. As soon as we can complete these underground rooms we should be able to get enough sleep. Even B-29s could not do anything to these rooms. We are

going to dig about twenty meters deep and make underground paths. Then, we may not have to worry about the enemy's one-ton bombs.[2]

On the same date, Lieutenant Colonel Nakane told his wife:

The enemy's air raids come more than ten times a day. Also the enemy's task forces struck the island two times. There was no damage. Everybody is hearty, and you don't have to worry about me. The beans brought from our house were planted and now the bean plants have grown. Harvest time is approaching. The squashes and eggplants are very good. Luckily I could have two harvests this year. The trouble is that the quantity of them is small. These vegetables are valuable because we produced them by our own sweat. We have saved enough water so I could have a bath yesterday. Everyone was happy. We can also get some fish as whenever the enemy makes an air raid, a lot of fish are killed by the bombs and end up on the beach. Sometimes we find mackerel and sharks. The enemy air raids come regularly, almost every day. So if they do not come we tend to miss them. The enemy task forces attacked us on November 11 and December 11. Now we are in a stronger position and are the soldiers of the gods. We are gladly waiting for the American devils to come.

A couple of weeks before the start of the battle, in a letter dated February 3, 1945, Lieutenant General Kuribayashi wrote to his wife, Yoshii:

How is the evacuation from Tokyo to the rural areas going? Do you want to stick it out in Tokyo? The enemy's air raids will increase so I think you had better evacuate from Tokyo while you still can. The enemy dropped some incendiary bombs and some napalm bombs here recently. They can make a sea of fire. Despite these violent air raids, I am still healthy. I am trying to get some fresh vegetables, and I have a small farm for myself. This place is not good for one's health, however, and we have many sick troops. Almost everyone gets sick at least once, but fortunately I have not suffered from any disease yet.

This was the final letter from Kuribayashi to reach his family.[3]

chapter thirteen

FAREWELL, EVERYONE, ON CHICHI JIMA

U.S. LANDING PREPARATIONS

On February 13, 1945, I received a phone call from the Chichi Jima Special Naval Base Headquarters. According to the base, a patrol plane of the Japanese navy had found about 170 enemy vessels moving northward eighty miles west of Saipan. I was asked if I thought they were headed to Iwo Jima or Okinawa. I responded that I believed there was about a 60 percent chance they were headed to Okinawa, because Okinawa had a higher strategic value, and only a 40 percent chance they were headed for Iwo Jima.

On February 16, Task Force 58 raided the Kanto area of Honshu, the main island of Japan, and the Ogasawara Islands in general. U.S. forces also started bombarding Iwo Jima with naval gunfire. According to messages coming in from Iwo Jima, there were some enemy destroyers anchored about 1,500 meters offshore, and they were shelling the island nonstop. Behind them were some cruisers, and farther behind them were some battleships, and these vessels, with several hundred guns firing, looked like a distant mountain range. Lieutenant General Kuribayashi, by radio, ordered all officers and men on Iwo Jima to go to their defensive posts, and in messages to the respective garrison headquarters on Chichi Jima and Haha Jima told them to take care of their own defense of the islands, wishing us good luck.[1]

I thought that the men on Iwo Jima would meet the same fate as those who had defended Saipan, and I felt very sad. As someone who had been unable to reach Saipan in time to defend it due to the delays I experienced (see chapter 3) and had been unable to join up with General Obata and the 31st Army in Palau, I felt ashamed I could not par-

Horie (in army uniform) with his relatives, including sister Koko (far left, back row), brother Yoshioki (middle, back row), mother (far left, front row), and grandmother (second from left, front row), ca. 1936. (Courtesy of the Horie family)

Horie as a second lieutenant, 1936. (Courtesy of the Horie family)

Horie (center) with unidentified fellow second lieutenants, 1936. (Courtesy of the Horie family)

Horie (first row, center) as an instructor at the Army Officer Candidate School, Ichigaya, Tokyo, spring 1937. (Courtesy of the Horie family)

Wedding photo of Horie's sister, Koko, and her husband, an officer in the Imperial Japanese Army. Major Horie is in the middle row, third from right. (Courtesy of the Horie family)

The Imperial Japanese Army Academy, Ichigaya, Tokyo, ca. 1907.

Horie (last row, second from left) in his class graduation photo at the Army War College, Ichigaya, Tokyo, November 1942. (Courtesy of the Horie family)

U.S.-Japanese meeting making final arrangements for the surrender ceremony, aboard the USS *Dunlap,* September 3, 1945. Horie, second from the left, has his head turned away from the camera. (Courtesy of the U.S. Navy)

Japanese general Tachibana signing instrument of surrender for the Ogasawara (Bonin) Islands during the ceremony aboard the USS *Dunlap,* September 3, 1945. Horie is immediately behind Tachibana, to his right. (Courtesy of the U.S. Navy)

Horie with his wife, Sumiko, infant son, Yoshibumi, and daughters Yoshiko (left) and Reiko (right), 1952. (Courtesy of the Horie family)

Horie making a speech about international affairs entitled "Our National Security" before the Sowa chapter (Koga, Ibaraki Prefecture) of the Lions Club, ca. 1980. (Courtesy of the Horie family)

Colonel James H. Tinsley Jr., USMC (Ret.), with sword given to his father by Major Horie. (Courtesy of Robert D. Eldridge)

ticipate in the battle. I did, however, fulfill my duties on Chichi Jima. I relayed messages coming from Chichi Jima to the Imperial Japanese Headquarters in Tokyo. Also, expecting that the enemy would invade Chichi Jima as well, I was actively preparing for combat.

Two U.S. prisoners of war, a marine captain pilot and a navy ensign copilot, were brought to me. As my command of the English language had improved somewhat, I was able to get some information from these two prisoners, who had flown from the carrier *Hornet*. I reported the information obtained from them to Tokyo and Iwo Jima. The information indicated that the main landing forces attacking Iwo Jima were the 3rd, 4th, and 5th Marine divisions. Also, I learned that the enemy would not be landing on any other islands in the Bonins and would launch an even bigger operation against Okinawa next month. My seniors at Iwo Jima and Tokyo were very happy to get my urgent messages. Furthermore, the prisoners told me that the seizure of Iwo Jima would be completed in about a week, then some army forces would come to Iwo Jima to relieve the marines, and the landing craft would be assigned to Okinawa.

They were worry free. They joked and hummed songs to themselves. They told me that as soon as the U.S. forces landed on Kyushu the war would be over, and they could return home. They said if they did return home, they would be treated as heroes and be promoted. They felt their accumulated earnings would all be paid at once and they could use the money for their honeymoons. They even wanted to teach me to dance. One prisoner, the ensign, told me his father had died when he was young, and his mother, who worked as a hairdresser, had sent him to college. He said he would like to get married as soon as he got home to please his mother. Nothing had ever surprised me as much as the psychology of the prisoners of war from a democratic country. It was diametrically opposite from that of Japanese troops.

On February 17 and 18, the enemy bombardment of Iwo Jima continued, and there seemed to be an increase in the number of vessels participating. According to the news issued by the Imperial Japanese Headquarters, Vice Admiral Mitscher's Task Force 58 raided Japan proper on the 17th.

THE ENEMY LANDINGS BEGIN

At about 9:00 AM, February 19, 1945, the enemy began its invasion of Iwo Jima, with hundreds of landing craft under the protection of fierce naval gunfire and air strikes.

As anticipated, the invading forces landed on the south beach, and then, based on conventional practice, occupied some beachheads. They moved in tanks and artillery and exploited the results. The garrison forces on Iwo did not initially try to oppose the landing forces. The Iwo Jima commander had prohibited any counterattacks. This was one of the key tactics of Lieutenant General Kuribayashi. He was implementing a battle plan based on lessons that had been learned from the warriors who had made the ultimate sacrifice at Saipan, Tinian, and Guam.[2] He was determined to follow through with the plan. Counterattacking meant nothing more than exposing our guns and falling victim to the tremendous naval bombardment of the enemy waiting offshore.

Not counterattacking was the key to the defense of Iwo Jima and the reason why the battle achieved as much as it did.

GENERAL KURIBAYASHI'S BATTLE CONDUCT

The words "calm," "bold," "philosophically mature," and "prudent" do not even begin to describe Kuribayashi's greatness. These qualities were seen in the following attitude and actions he took. Shortly after the enemy's landing, he began reporting to Tokyo about the battle and his subordinates' distinguished service. He also made arrangements to collect money from the officers and men and donate it to the National Treasury. He was intent on having all matters taken care of prior to his own impending death.

In the afternoon of the first day of the invasion, he sent a message to Tokyo stating that Second Lieutenant Nakamura Kenichi, platoon commander of the 8th Independent Antitank-Gun Battalion (Dokuritsu Sokushaho Daihachi Daitai), had destroyed more than twenty enemy tanks before he was killed in action, and he wrote a letter of commendation for Nakamura's bravery in action. He requested a two-rank promotion (from second lieutenant to captain) for Nakamura. Later, he wrote a commendation for distinguished service for Captain Hayakawa Masao, commander of the 12th Independent Antitank Battalion (Dokuritsu Sokushaho Daijuni Daitai), Captain Shimizu Hajime, commander of the 8th Independent Antitank-Gun Battalion, and Captain Furuta Katsuya, commander of the 109th Storm Company (Totsugeki Chutai), and requested two-rank promotions for all of them. Twice he wrote letters of commendation for the 145th Infantry Regiment and the troops as a whole. He also warned Tokyo not to overestimate the value of night infiltration attacks and informed officials there that the 37-mm gun was not particularly effective against the enemy's M-4 tanks.

Kuribayashi's staff was able to collect a total of about 125,000 yen from the men in the various units. After learning this figure, he reported that this amount was to be donated to the National Treasury. Then each unit burned the money in its possession.

Lieutenant General Kuribayashi never asked for reinforcements. His only complaint was that he had to commit many of his troops to the expansion work of the No. 2 and No. 3 airfields by orders of Tokyo, which he felt was not only a waste of time and labor but were done at the expense of other important fortifications.

BLOODY BATTLE

The enemy landed with the 4th Marine Division on the right (as seen from the sea), the 5th Marine Division on the left, and 3rd Marine Division in reserve. The 5th Marine Division attacked Mount Suribachi, and the 4th Marines advanced onto the Motoyama plateau. As both divisions suffered heavy losses, the commander of V Corps committed the 3rd Marine Division against the Japanese East and North Sectors.

Although the marines suffered heavy casualties, they expanded their area of control, committing additional artillery and tanks while more than one hundred fighters flew over the island and about five hundred naval guns offshore fired to protect the landing forces.

The dead and wounded of the Japanese garrison forces were left exposed to the fire, but the remains of the dead U.S. Marines were picked up, and the wounded were evacuated to hospital ships.

Until about February 26, desperate fighting took place around Mount Suribachi, Jinetsugahara, Minami Village, Ishikiriba, Byobuyama, etc. As the garrison forces were not allowed to expose themselves or mobilize in any large numbers, the defenders fought individual and hopeless battles, resisting to the death.

After landing, U.S. forces focused on using the 5th Marine Division to attack Mount Suribachi. Colonel Atsuchi and about a thousand army and 680 navy officers and men continued to hold out. The enemy finally came with flamethrowers to burn out or burn up the defenders in the caves. The summit of Mount Suribachi was held against several attacks. On February 22, Atsuchi sent the following message to General Kuribayashi: "In addition to a growing number of casualties and enemy air-sea-land attacks, we are facing the enemy's flamethrowers. If we stay here, we will only die as we are. We would like to break out for a final banzai charge."

In response, Lieutenant General Kuribayashi replied to him with the following irate message: "I had expected the First Airfield would fall to the enemy. But, why is it that Mount Suribachi could fall within only three days?" In this exchange, we can see how the general had determined to have his officers and men stay in their positions as their tombs and fight until the death. On March 8, when Major General Senda, commander of the 2nd Mixed Brigade, sent a message to Kuribayashi stating that he would like to head out for a banzai charge, the general immediately ordered Senda through the radio to keep his positions until the last moment. (In fact, Senda disobeyed this order.)

Lieutenant General Kuribayashi was well aware that there were many people who wanted to take the easy way out through a banzai charge but that if that happened he would not be able to inflict heavy casualties on the Americans and prolong the battle for as long as he had expected. Everyone therefore, he used to say, had to be patient and calm and stay in his position as long as possible.

On February 26, Lieutenant General Kuribayashi sent the following message about the casualties of the Iwo Jima Garrison and of the enemy: "Our losses: the frontline troops have lost 30 percent on average. The losses have been large among the officers, about two-thirds. Most of the machine guns are destroyed. Sixty percent of the big guns have been destroyed. The enemy's losses: Casualties, about 13,000 officers and men. Two hundred ten tanks destroyed or stranded. Sixty aircraft shot down. Two battleships, nine destroyers, and three landing craft sunk. More than thirty landing craft burned."[3]

REPORTS OF DESPERATE FIGHTING

Even after February 27, the officers and men continued to bravely resist, staying in the caves around Tamanayama, Motoyama, Osakayama, Man Village, Kita Village, and Hyoryuboka. U.S. forces, committing their tanks and artillery and using newly landed Army Air Forces, moved little by little, tearing up the ground, and gradually tightening their ring. At this point they began calling for Japanese forces to surrender.

In the following pages, we will look at the battle situation through messages sent out.

(1) TANSAN[4] (109TH DIVISION STAFF OFFICE) MESSAGE NO. 306
0750H, MARCH 4, 1945, IWO JIMA (VIA CHICHI JIMA)
TO VICE CHIEF OF STAFF, IJA

The enemy has finally arrived at some parts of Motoyama Airfield (No. 2 Airfield) and North Airfield (No. 3 Airfield). Thus, our organized resistance has come to have some gaps. In addition, the enemy's attacks against other defensive positions have increased.[5]

Our forces are making every effort to annihilate the enemy but we have already lost most of our guns and tanks, and two-thirds of our officers. We may have some difficulties in future fighting. Particularly, now, as our headquarters and communication center are exposed to the enemy's forward positions, we are afraid of a possibility of interruption of messages between our headquarters and Tokyo. Of course, each strongpoint may be able to hold off for several more days. Even if these strongpoints are broken through by the enemy, our survivors may be able to continue to fight on their own for sometime later. Anyhow, from the fact that the enemy has almost achieved their main purpose to occupy this island we are very sorry that we could not have better defended this island. Now, I, Kuribayashi, believe that the enemy fighters would invade Japan proper from this island. Our country would be placed under the enemy plane wings. I am very sorry because I could imagine the disastrous scenes in our Imperial land. However, I comfort myself a little, seeing my officers and men die without any regret after struggling on—in land battle against the overwhelming enemy with many tanks, exposing them to the indescribable bombardments. Although I am just before death, I calmly pray to God for a good future for my mother country. Upon the big change of battle situation, considering the communications interruption, I, here, apologize to my seniors and fellow members that my power was too small to stop the enemy's invasion.

I remember an old war story: Although Generals Mune and Taira, officers, men, and their families were all killed when they met the Mongolian invasion, resulting in losing Iki and Tsushima islands between Honshu and Korea, the Japanese army was able to win the battle at Tatara Beach in Kyushu, making our country, blessed by the gods, safe. Believing that my mother country should never go to ruin, my soul will always battle the enemy and defend the Imperial land forever. Please examine our battle instructions and opinions sent through messages. If they are found to be good to use to modify our military tactics and training, I would be pleased if they are used. Chichi Jima and Haha Jima Garrisons will be strong and be able to utilize the terrain. But I suggest that the 109th Divisional Headquarters be reestablished on Chichi Jima, and place a brigade headquarters on Haha Jima. At last I hereby thank my senior and fellow members again for their kind help during my life. I add here that we could get along with our navy until the last moment. Goodbye, Kuribayashi.

(2) TANSAN MESSAGE NO. 329

2300H, MARCH 5, 1945, IWO JIMA (VIA CHICHI JIMA)

TO VICE CHIEF OF STAFF, IJA

The fatal blows came upon us from air and sea. Against this small island the enemy employed heavy naval gunfire with two battle-ships, five heavy cruisers, ten light cruisers, and forty destroyers. The enemy used at least four hundred naval guns on the above ships. It is impossible to describe how bad the gunfire was for us. The enemy aimed at our important areas and positions through expert targeting and the use of observation planes. The enemy was able to continue even at night. Until now, about 300,000 rounds have probably been fired. Most of our beach positions, main posi-tions, and many facilities were destroyed due to this firing. The air superiority of the enemy is absolute and decisive, and one day there were more than 1,600 sorties. From dawn to dusk there is no gap in the sorties or a lack of aircraft in the sky. There are always 100–230 fighters, and they can strafe or bomb any target at any time. During the daytime, they not only can pin our troops down but the enemy ground forces can also infiltrate through our weak points using their tanks as spearheads under air protection. Our forces cannot employ any countermethods under these circum-stances, losing gradually any and all guns. We are forced to fight the enemy with only our rifles and hand grenades. This might be sound like a grievance, but it is a fact that I dare report to you.

(3) TANSAN MESSAGE NO. 430

1000H, MARCH 17, 1945, IWO JIMA (VIA CHICHI JIMA)

TO VICE CHIEF OF STAFF, IJA

The enemy troops in the North Sector have been attacking our strongpoints since this morning. Their spearheads are tanks. The enemy troops now are attacking with flamethrowers against our divisional headquarters and naval headquarters. Close and des-perate fighting is taking place there. To date the enemy's casualties have mounted to 33,000 men. Our present strength at this time was about five hundred troops in the northern sector and about five hundred troops in the eastern sector.

(4) TANSAN REPORT NO. 427

1725H, MARCH 18, 1945, IWO JIMA (VIA CHICHI JIMA)

TO CHIEF OF STAFF, IJA

The battle is approaching the end. Since the enemy's landing, the bravery of the officers and men under my command would make even the gods weep. In particular, I am pleased that our troops have continued to resist the enemy at sea, in the air, and on land. Despite being overwhelmed by material superiority we have fought with little more than our empty hands. However, I have lost my men one after another in this vicious fighting, and I am very sorry that I have let the enemy occupy even one part of Japanese territory. There is no more ammunition and no more water. All survivors must now go out for a banzai charge. As I think of my debt of gratitude to my country I have no regrets. Unless this island is retaken, Japan will never be safe, I believe. I sincerely hope my soul will be a spearhead for the future renewed attack. Praying to God for the final victory and safety of our mother country, let me say "goodbye." About Chichi Jima and Haha Jima Garrisons, although I believe they would hold their islands firmly against any enemy attempts, I hope you do them a favor. At least let them read some of my poor poems.

> *Without any ammunition,*
> *It is very sad for me to leave this world,*
> *Failing to achieve my important duty for the mother country.*
> *I would not want to rot in the fields,*
> *Unless I know my soul will take vengeance.*
> *I would like to take up arms,*
> *Even if I were to be born seven times.*
> *I worry about what would happen to the future of Japan,*
> *When weeds would grow up on this island.*

GENERAL ATTACK ORDER

Kuribayashi issued the following general order to the surviving warriors at 5:50 AM on March 17:

The battle is coming to the final phase. Our garrison will make a general attack against the enemy tonight. The starting time will be at one minute after midnight, March 18. Each unit will go out of its present position against the facing enemy. Everyone will fight until the end individually. I will be always at the head of our troops. Lieutenant General Kuribayashi

The Imperial Japanese Headquarters made arrangements to broadcast the Iwo Jima song around Japan through NHK (Nihon Hoso

Kyokai) radio, starting at one minute after midnight on March 18, to show the gratefulness of the people of Japan to the surviving fighters.[6]

On the morning of March 17, I sent the following message to Lieutenant General Kuribayashi. "Being unable to follow you, my heart is saddened. Major Horie." I lacked spirit at this point and could only feel sorry for not being with the general and everyone on Iwo Jima.

LAST MESSAGES FROM IWO JIMA

During the night of March 17, I was ordered by Tokyo to communicate with Iwo Jima in order to notify Lieutenant General Kuribayashi that he had been promoted to the rank of full general, effective that same day. I wanted to reach the general before it was too late. But unfortunately, there was no answer. I ordered my radiomen to continue calling Iwo Jima on March 18 and again on each successive day. I did so expecting a miracle. But the radio on Iwo Jima never answered.

By 8:00 AM on March 23, I had given up trying to reach the Iwo Jima radio station. While I was preparing to take out my horse to go on an inspection of our defensive positions, one of my radiomen ran toward me and called to me, while catching his breath, "Major Horie! Iwo Jima answered!" I canceled my plans to inspect the defenses and told the radioman to send the promotion news to Iwo Jima immediately. I then went to the Chichi Jima radio station. However, the radiomen on Iwo Jima were too busy trying to send the accumulated messages to us for forwarding to Tokyo and were not at this point ready to receive any of our messages. The messages from Iwo kept coming one after the other. I could not stop weeping as I thought of the radioman who was hurrying to send the last messages just before his death.

After the war, I heard from one of the survivors that the radioman had not received any of our messages, because the codebooks had already been burned.

Some of the messages we received from Iwo Jima after March 23 included:

1. Situation at 12:00 AM, March 21, 1945
    (a) Left the division headquarters at one minute after midnight on March 18. Gathered all the survivors of the 145th Infantry Regiment, South Sector, North Sector, East Sector, and West Sector, at the western area of Kita Village. We are still fighting. The strength under my command now is about four hundred.

(b) The enemy placed a siege on us on March 18 and 19 and attacked us with tanks and flamethrowers. Using explosives, they attempted to reach the entrances of our shelter.

2. Situation at 1 PM, March 21
   (a) We are still fighting as of March 20 and 21.
   (b) The distance between the enemy's front line and our shelter is about 200–300 meters. Some tanks have been attacking us.
   (c) The enemy has called on us to surrender through a loudspeaker but we have just laughed and paid no attention.

Using Nisei, Koreans who had given up or were captured, and Japanese prisoners of war, American forces announced, "Lieutenant General Kuribayashi, don't you think that it is a shame to make your soldiers hold out this long? Surrender them, please. . . . We have good fresh water here. We will treat your wounds as well."

3. Situation at 9:10 AM, March 22
   The remaining officers and men of the navy headquarters joined us in our shelter on March 16 and remain with us.
4. Situation at 10:00 AM, March 22
   Lieutenant General Kuribayashi and his men are still fighting. We have fought for five days without any food or water. However, our fighting spirit is still running high. We are going to continue fighting bravely to the end.

Around 5:00 PM on March 23, our radio crackled and caught the following message from a radioman on Iwo Jima: "All officers and men of Chichi Jima, farewell."

After that, there was silence. I wept again.

I cried a lot during that time. I have never cried due to a scolding or even out of frustration with my duties. But I could not stop weeping when I read the farewell message from this radioman, whose last minutes I describe in the beginning of chapter 1. Tears, tears, and more tears came out. It was not only I who cried. The others gathered in the room of the Chichi Jima radio station kept crying too, thinking that their comrades on Iwo Jima had finally met their fate. Corporal Kawajiri Hiroyuki and Cadets Oyama Shigeyasu and Hiroishi Hajime of the Code Unit wept as well. I hoped for a second miracle and ordered the chief of the radio station to intercept any and all messages on a twenty-four-hour basis for the next three days, every thirty minutes for the following three days, and every hour for the three days after that. However, no more messages came from Iwo Jima.

THE LAST MOMENTS OF GENERAL KURIBAYASHI

Regarding the last moments of the general, I have heard many stories from many sources, including some U.S. marines. Former major Komoto Kumeji, who served as the senior adjutant to General Kuribayashi and flew to Tokyo on February 3 on official duty just before American forces invaded and missed the battle on Iwo Jima, recently sent me a letter that addressed this question. According to him, various interviews were obtained about the last moments of the general from the survivors of the battle after the war. The main part of his letter is as follows.

> Lieutenant General Kuribayashi was very strict in military discipline. He was punctual and was a man of action. But he was also warmhearted. He always inspected every corner of the island and remembered the terrain. He guided the troops on their formations and construction of fortifications and shared with the troops cigarettes he carried in his pocket that he had been given by the emperor. He washed his face and brushed his teeth all with just one cup of water. The officers and men of the division headquarters produced some vegetables and sent them to the kitchen. The leaves of the sweet potato grew throughout the year. The general liked to eat the boiled leaves, putting some soy sauce on them. Regarding the general's last moments, many stories have been told by various survivors. It seems that in fact he died on March 27. According to one sergeant who was always with him, the general was wounded in his leg when he participated in an attack and was unable to walk anymore. On the morning of March 27, he committed suicide along with Colonel Takaishi, chief of staff, and Lieutenant Colonel Nakane, operations staff officer. This seems to be the truth about his last moments.

In this chapter, I have tried to discuss objectively the circumstances concerning the Iwo Jima campaign. In the next chapter, I will use eyewitness and vivid accounts regarding the actual fighting from some survivors.

chapter fourteen

OUR CAVE BECAME A SEA OF FIRE
First Lieutenant Musashino Kikuzo's Story

This chapter and the following two are drawn from the diaries and notes of the battle and immediate postwar period by three survivors who were captured by U.S. marines: Lieutenant Musashino Kikuzo, First Lieutenant Yamazaki Takeshi, and Seaman First Class Koizumi Tadayoshi.[1]

Recollections of Lieutenant Musashino Kikuzo
Commanding Officer of the Engineer Company, 2nd Mixed Brigade

HEAVY CASUALTIES EMERGE FROM A SERIES OF BANZAI CHARGES
During the night of February 15–16, 1945, enemy vessels enveloped Iwo Jima with several rings and began their brutal air strikes and naval bombardment. Hundreds of aircraft filled the sky, and many more naval guns shook this small island. Vessels on the horizon line looked just like big mountain ranges.

The enemy started landing on February 19. Soon, a series of desperate battles developed at Minami Village and Jinetsugahara. First Lieutenant Matsuo Hideyoshi and the 135 pillboxes he had helped construct there had been completely destroyed by the preinvasion bombardment four days before the landing. They were completely useless. The enemy troops around Jinetsugahara and Chidori Village were pinned down for two days by our fire.

Lieutenant General Kuribayashi had ordered us to get in close to the enemy in order to avoid the bombardment. Captain Nakagome Yukihiko's troops and Lieutenant Taki Jiro's troops at Jinetsugahara participated in a series of close battles, and most of them were annihilated on February 22, having been mostly run over by tanks.

At noon on February 23, the Mount Suribachi Sector troops, commanded by Colonel Atsuchi, were hit by general attacks of the enemy, and in response they launched a banzai charge. At night, the colorful flares of the enemy illuminated every tree and piece of grass just as if it was during daytime.

On February 23, all of our defense positions located south of Minami Village were destroyed by the enemy, and the First Airfield became a large tank-assembly area. Our defenders, whose positions were destroyed, went out for banzai charges into the enemy in succession, screaming a battle cry. Of course, no one returned. After the enemy landed, twenty to thirty infiltration teams went toward the enemy, but with little success. None of them returned either.

On the evening of February 23, the enemy assaulted the defense positions at Minami Village commanded by Captain Awatsu Katsutaro with some tanks. The caves were destroyed by the enemy's explosives. Enemy troops accompanied by some tanks advanced, using flamethrowers, while naval gunfire and air strikes supported them. The antitank trenches and foxholes that our forces had prepared were useless against the enemy. Thus, our defense plan to stop the advance of the enemy around Minami Village became hopeless.

The air-sea-land cooperation of the enemy before us was too overwhelming for me to describe, while our own situation was beyond hope. Five companies of Japanese navy troops had been alongside Captain Awatsu's battalion (with every company commanded by an army officer) at an area of Minami Village plateau. They were overrun in ten minutes, and the survivors headed north. By the evening of February 23, one-third of Iwo Jima had fallen into the enemy's hands. Our telephone lines were cut everywhere, and there was no way to repair them. The work of the messengers became very important, but many were killed themselves on their way to or from their duties, carrying the wounded.

My air-raid shelter had been strongly constructed. There were eleven entrances to it. The shelter had been linked with defense positions, and they were well camouflaged. I was proud of my shelter and positions, saying that they were the strongest on Iwo Jima. The trenches between the positions had a zigzag shape. The enemy troops who met the serious resistance in front of my positions bypassed us and advanced toward Tamanayama positions, where the 2nd Mixed Brigade command post was located. The enemy troops, having many tanks ahead, attacked Tamanayama, under the protection of air strikes and naval bombardment. The garrison forces of Tamanayama resisted desperately, and there were many casualties on both sides. The main forces of the battery of brigade artillery at the western plateau of Tamanayama under the command of First Lieutenant Hirota Satoshi, one machinegun battalion located around Byobu-Iwa under the command of Major Kawasaki Tokio, and the brigade reserve (with a strength of about one infantry battalion) defending Tamanayama under the command of Major Anso Kenro had been killed in action by March 6. Major General Senda, commander of the 2nd Mixed Brigade, seeing the battle situation, decided to make a banzai charge on March 7.

On March 8, Senda reported by radio to Lieutenant General Kuribayashi radio that he wanted to go out for a banzai charge with his men. Kuribayashi immediately told him to "cancel your banzai charge." But Senda had already made up his mind, and he ignored the above order. That day, he issued the following order to the surviving troops under his command.

2ND MIXED BRIGADE GENERAL ATTACK ORDER

The enemy has been advancing on us. The brigade will go out of its present position at 6 PM, March 9, attack the enemy, and advance toward Mount Suribachi. Major Anso's troops will be on the right, First Lieutenant Musashino's troops will be in the center, and Lieutenant Akagi Mamoru's troops (including First Lieutenant Soma Hiroshi's company) will be on the left front. Every unit will advance toward Mount Suribachi. Each howitzer gun, rocket, etc., will start firing at 6 PM and protect the advance of the frontline troops. I will be at the head of our forces. On a final note, officers should suggest to the wounded personnel who cannot partake in the advance to Mount Suribachi that they commit suicide in front of their commander before the commencement of the banzai charge. Major General Senda.

HAND GRENADES GIVEN TO THE WOUNDED

Officers understood the instructions of Major General Senda. But it was very hard for them to suggest to their wounded subordinates that they commit suicide in front of them, because these subordinates had worked for them just like their children or younger brothers for a long time. Finally, the officers agreed not to tell the wounded subordinates about the suicide request but simply to inform them about their departure for the general attack, to explain to them that they would not be able to see them anymore, and to give one hand grenade to every wounded person. When they received the hand grenades, tears came out, which we could see through the candlelight. I felt more sorry for them than for the healthy soldiers. In the shelter there was no longer any rice or water, nor could anyone go out to get water.[2] The only things left were the wounded and their belongings and an equal number of grenades.

As I stood outside the shelter, I faced toward the shrine, Miyachigoku Jingu, in my hometown of Kyushu, Japan, and prayed to the gods to extend their help for the wounded personnel.

BANZAI CHARGE OF THE 2ND MIXED BRIGADE BEGINS

At 6 PM that day (March 9), the firing by both Japanese and U.S. forces was intense. The enemy set up barbed wire, loudspeakers, and some wires, which we called "piano lines," on the ground strengthening their defense line. If anyone touched the wires, a flame would shoot out. Flares made things brighter at night than they were during the day and preceded the firing of hundreds of machine guns. Our troops dug under the barbed wires using scoops and were able to advance against the enemy, but we suffered heavy casualties, and there was no control over the troops. It seemed that most of Major General Senda's troops were killed around the line between Byobu-Iwa and Minami Village.

This general attack was over at dawn of March 10, leaving several hundred corpses, including Major General Senda's. He had put one white band, on which a rising sun had been marked, on his head and wore socks and cloth gaiters. He had his sword on his waist and a hand grenade in this hand. He had advanced ahead of the right frontline troops. He is said to have been killed in action at the southern corner of Byobu-Iwa. When he issued his order of the general attack on the evening of March 8, he had been dressed the same. After he read the order, he asked the officers to drink a cup of water as a toast. Then he said, "Many thanks for your efforts. Let's see each other again at Yasukuni Shrine."

GUERRILLA ACTIVITIES BY THE DISGUISED REMNANTS

The general attack of the 2nd Mixed Brigade was over at dawn on March 10. However, there were many stragglers left without any commanders around Jinetsugahara. They were moving about without any semblance of order or direction. Gunfire was heard nonstop throughout the day and night. The area south of Minami Village was covered by hundreds of enemy tents. The only thing we could see clearly was the sky. The terrain had been completely changed. There were many shell holes. The former flat fields had become hilly. We did not recognize where we were. At night thousands of stars shined in the sky peacefully. During the daytime we hid in caves, and at night we wandered in the battlefields, aimlessly, without hope.

Two of my subordinates came with me to Jinetsugahara. We stayed quiet. Indeed, none of us had the spirit to talk anyway. If I sat on the ground, they sat, and if I walked, they followed me. We had nothing but the water in our canteens. They were killed by the enemy's fire on the night of March 13, after which I moved around alone. On the evening of March 14, I met a soldier named Kurata and knew then that we were in front of my old air-raid shelter. When I removed the stone door of the entrance, I heard some Japanese talking inside. I said the password, "Nogi," and someone inside replied with the answer, "Togo."[3] As I entered the shelter, I found First Lieutenant Soma, Dr. Benitani Seizo, First Lieutenant Kawai Yoshio, Warrant Officer Masuko Ichita, Master Sergeant Takano Masao, and about eighty army and navy personnel. Lieutenant Soma had been in charge of them, but after I arrived, I took over the command. None of them, or I, for that matter, were in good health. Every night several teams consisting of a few people went into the enemy positions to get water and food. Each time some were killed, and thus the population in the shelter decreased night by night.

For some reason, this shelter had been bypassed by the enemy, and Kita Village became full of enemy troops. The men under my command maintained order and were well behaved. They had already been doing well on their own when I arrived.

Ah! Iwo Jima. Seventy years ago, you became a part of Japanese territory, but what purpose have you served? You just became a place for the lives of thirty thousand people to be taken. What an island of tragedy you are!

I watched the battle closely. It would be only a few days more before all the Japanese forces would be defeated. Later, I learned from one of the stragglers of the 145th Infantry Regiment that the regimental flag had been burned by order of Colonel Ikeda, regimental commander, on the evening of March 17 as the survivors of the regiment went out for their banzai charge.

LIEUTENANT GENERAL KURIBAYASHI'S GENERAL ATTACK ORDER

The battle of the whole island entered the last phase on March 17. General Kuribayashi issued the general attack order on that day. He gathered about eight hundred men, consisting of the survivors of 145th Infantry Regiment, Major Hakuta Yoshinobu's battalion, Major Oka Wazo's troops, etc., including naval personnel.

Just before issuing the general attack order, I heard, he had been his old self, reciting some poems. He told the officers that the men could not fight on an empty stomach and should finish the remaining food and water before departing on the banzai charge. In the evening of the 17th, one of the survivors said, General Kuribayashi and the other men left the caves and advanced toward the No. 3 Airfield. Most of them, including the general, died heroically before dawn on March 18.

The general had anticipated this situation well before the outbreak of the war. Shortly after he arrived at Iwo Jima, he told me, "The Japanese war planners do not seem to have paid any mind to the real situation in the United States. Even though I have tried to explain it to them, they do not understand. No matter how partially one looks at things, Japan could never win against the United States."

TELL THIS DISASTROUS STATUS TO THE JAPANESE PEOPLE
During the banzai charge, Major Yoshida, in charge of fortifications, was ordered by the general to stay alive and find a way to get to Japan and tell the people of Japan the disastrous situation that befell Iwo Jima.

Receiving these orders, Yoshida joined the stragglers and looked for a chance to get off the island. In the middle of May, he and a naval engineer tried to get in one of the American airplanes parked at the No. 3 Airfield and fly to Japan. However, before taking off, he was discovered by the enemy and shot to death.[4] It was not only Major Yoshida who tried and failed to get off the island. Many others tried to leave Iwo as well. Dozens of rafts were found crashed up against the shore on the eastern coast. Many men had attempted to leave using these rafts made of logs, but no one seems to have succeeded. In order to avoid the careful watch of the enemy, these men got into the rafts in bad weather and drowned or otherwise met their fates.

THE BATTLE CONTINUES AFTER THE BANZAI CHARGE
OF GENERAL KURIBAYASHI
I believe that there were at least three thousand officers and men alive even after the death of General Kuribayashi. Every unit had been disbanded and the movements disorganized. The individuals came together and formed new groups, however, and fought the enemy without anyone being in command.

By April 19, my group had grown to about 220 or 230 men. Although I was the group's commander, I myself did not even know the exact number of men in my group, because it changed every night.

OUR CAVE BECAME A SEA OF FIRE ON APRIL 19

On April 19, as soon as a U.S. marine approaching our shelter was shot to death, the enemy came to the entrance of our cave and poured aviation fuel into it. Then the enemy used some flamethrowers to ignite it. Our shelter suddenly became a sea of fire, with explosions. There was no chance to escape; about 150 men died almost instantly.

I don't know how human beings can do something like this to one another. It is inhumane and without compassion. I am at a loss for words in describing the situation. The oxygen was sucked out of the cave, and the men were crying in pain, screaming to be killed. About sixty or seventy men, who were in another part of the cave at the time digging to make an additional shelter, were burned and injured but somehow managed to survive.

DETERMINED TO DIE

On April 21, while waiting in the additional shelter, we decided to go out for our banzai charge. I made the following speech: "We have done our best for more than a year in the defense of this island. But now it is all over. Your distinguished service will remain forever in the annals of Japanese history. The day before yesterday, 150 of our group were killed. I believe that now the enemy is going to try to finish us off. We might not be able to live much longer. We had better go out and die in the fresh air. We would not wish to face the enemy looking like we do, but we cannot do anything else at present. So, let's go out for the banzai charge and free ourselves. You are free to act on your own, but our final destination is the Kita Village if we make it. Good luck. I will be the commander until I leave the cave, but once we are outside, you are all to act on your own. However, I do have one final command right now. Anyone who might survive should tell the people of Japan about the tragedy that befell us on this island." With this, we did three banzai cheers in honor of the emperor and prayed for the happiness and luck of the people of Japan.

First Lieutenant Kawai, Dr. Benitani, and five more soldiers who did not agree with me about launching the banzai charge remained behind in the shelter.

LEAVING THE CAVE

Around 10 PM on April 21, First Lieutenant Taki and I left the cave first. In front of the cave were hundreds of the enemy tents, and above the cave was an enemy airfield.

I knew that Warrant Officer Masuko and Master Sergeant Takano had come out after us, but I did not see them when I turned around. When about ten men had emerged from the cave, the enemy started firing. A lot of our men were probably killed at the entrance to the cave. Taki and I walked toward the eastern coast. On the way we met about ten Japanese soldiers. They did not know about the fates of their comrades. It was dawn by the time we arrived at the shoreline, and so we sought a cave to wait in, as we could no longer walk around in the open. We entered a cave and waited until night. Takano came to our area too with about five or six soldiers. When dawn came they hid themselves behind a rock, but they were discovered by the enemy and were shot and killed. Masuko seems to have been killed right after he stepped out of the cave. He was fifty-three years old. Takano was thirty. Masuko was good at composition, and he used to be a grammar school teacher when he was younger. He was a man of good character. He liked sake very much. So even now when I drink sake at home, I first offer a cup to Masuko's soul at the altar in my home. Takano was born at Kanda in Tokyo and used to run a taxi service. He could drive a car by himself. He was very good in penmanship and was obedient to his parents.

It seems that Captain Otsuka Keichiro and First Lieutenant Watanabe Hiroshi were alive until to the middle of May. They were heavily wounded in the banzai charge of the 2nd Mixed Brigade and were evacuated to an air-raid shelter. In the middle of May, they bid farewell to the other personnel in the cave and left it. They reportedly told some of them that they would kill themselves after washing at the beach on the east coast, but no one saw them after they left the cave.

Otsuka came from the Kanto Garrison in Manchuria as the commanding officer of the Independent Engineer Company and was a respectable man. Lieutenant Watanabe was one of my platoon commanders. He was a graduate of Tokyo University and used to be a high-ranking official in the Imperial Forest Bureau. Lieutenant Kawai and Dr. Benitani held out until June 21, when they committed suicide with four soldiers.

First Lieutenant Asada Shinji (an engineer) was a bright example of Japanese tradition. Heavily wounded in a banzai charge at Mount Suribachi at noon on March 12, he continued to live until May 12. In the meantime, the marines called on him to surrender several times, but on May 13 he left the following letter addressed to Admiral Raymond A. Spruance, who was in overall command of the Iwo Jima operations, and committed suicide together with Sergeant Kameda Shunsuke (an engineer) and several other soldiers.

> 13 May 1945
> Admiral Spruance, United States Navy,
> Thank you very much for your kindness. We gratefully received the cigarettes and canned stuffs you left for us. We are sorry that we cannot accept your call for surrender due to the traditional custom of the old Japanese samurai. We do not have any more water and food. At 4:00 AM, May 13, we will commit suicide and go to Heaven.
> First Lieutenant Asada Shinji, Imperial Japanese Army

I heard about the above letter from a soldier while I was wandering around the battlefield.

1,500 STRAGGLERS

Lieutenant Taki and I continued a cave life at a plateau on the east coast. The enemy placed an explosive in our cave, and we suffered from yellow phosphorous. I wanted to kill myself using a hand grenade, but Taki persuaded me not to do so. The enemy began searching for Japanese survivors, following the trails of the footwear of the Japanese troops. The Americans would explode the cave entrances where they found evidence of Japanese troops. I guess the enemy thought that the Japanese survivors might be suffocated by blocking these entrances. However, the Japanese troops made exits using scoops or shovels that they had with them.

By the middle of May 1945, I think there were still more than 1,500 Japanese stragglers. There were no more systematic battles, however. Individual troops simply continued searching for food and water. Everyone worried only about himself. Those kinds of days and nights went on and on. During the day, the stragglers hid in the grass, near the bottom of trees, or in the crevices of rocks, and at night they became thieves and burglars, stealing from the American supplies. Everyone took care of his bodily needs like animals, and the place became disgustingly dirty, not fit for humans. We had to crawl around in this filth, for if we didn't we would get spotted by the enemy. If we stood up and walked, our footprints would be visible, so we crawled around like two-year-old babies. After April 21, Taki and I moved around together. There was no one commanding us. Taki would often say, "Let's die together. Let's not get separated." He had become so sad and desperate.

WANDERING ABOUT LOOKING FOR FOOD AND WATER

Around this time, whenever we went to the place where we expected to find water, we ran into four or five other stragglers. We were all in the same boat. We were looking for food and water. We could hear the sound of gunfire all around the island at night. The guerrilla-stragglers must have been caught by the enemy and shot at. The number of Japanese troops rapidly declined. We all continued to crawl around, and when we saw one another, we immediately knew the other was a Japanese soldier. When we met, everybody would talk about his own hard life, and the hours would pass quickly. Then everyone would start again on his hopeless wandering. Some would go west, others would go east. Still others would go forward, and others back in the other direction. When asked where they were going, no one knew. I felt particularly sad on moonlit nights. Looking at the moon, I would think how old my son must be now or of my wife's face.

One night, under the dim moonlight, Taki and I, hiding ourselves behind a rock, were sinking into deep thoughts. By chance, we found two big green cabbages. They were about one foot high. Probably some troops had grown them. We ate them up. They were a gift of the gods. They tasted wonderful. We thought that we could last four or five more days, thanks to them. Suddenly two men approached us—Lieutenant Soma and one more soldier. We embraced each other, wept with joy, and laughed. We had thought that the others had died.

Lieutenant Soma said that now the Imperial Japanese Headquarters would commit any and all aircraft and naval vessels plus a budget of seventy billion yen to launch a counterattack to take Iwo Jima. As we were already on the island, we would help lead the counterattack. "I have the fifth degree in Kendo, after all," he added.[5]

Soon after his story finished, he and his fellow man went to a cave, but they were unfortunately buried alive by the enemy's explosives.

Major Maeda Kazuo, an artillery battalion commander, was reportedly still alive until the second half of May 1945.[6] One night, Taki and I went to his big shelter, located north of Tamanayama. There were some Japanese machine guns at the entrance of the cave, and they fired anytime they heard the sound of footsteps. As we could not get into the cave, I never got to see him. He and his men ended up committing suicide around the end of May. Major Maeda was a graduate of the forty-seventh class of the Army Academy and hailed from the Kanto Garrison in Manchuria. He served under Colonel Kaido. He was a likeable person and was well respected by his men. His artillery battalion inflicted heavy losses on the enemy at Jinetsugahara, but he did not speak about his own battlefield exploits and instead spoke about the distinguished service of others.

THE 2ND MIXED BRIGADE'S CAVE WAS FILLED
WITH THE SMELL OF THE DEAD

During the night of June 8–9, Taki and I walked to the old brigade cave. We decided to stay there overnight. We wept, remembering the face of the late General Senda.

We walked to his former command post. The whole cave and hallways were filled with corpses. Hundreds of dead bodies still kept their shape, in a variety of poses. The cave had served as a field hospital for the severely wounded during the fighting, and as a result there were many dead in there. There was no food after the brigade left on its banzai charge, and so the wounded died of hunger right where they had been left. Black hair was still growing from some of the dead. The heads of the dead were all facing east, the traditional direction for those who are dead. Perhaps they instinctively laid in that direction before they died. There were thousands of big black flies. Every time you drew a breath, several would fly into your mouth.

The wounded had probably thought of their country and probably cheered "banzai" for the emperor before passing on. It seems they devoted themselves for the country, even forgetting their wives and children and other loved ones. War, I think, is first and foremost a struggle between the privileged classes of each country. The officers and men actually fighting were there basically just to serve them. I believe that all the Japanese people should pray for the souls of all those lost.

BECOMING A PRISONER OF THE AMERICAN MILITARY

Taki and I stayed in this cave three nights with these corpses. On the evening of June 11, we left the cave, after saluting the corpses. We decided to try to leave the island by raft. We passed through the enemy tent area but were unable to find water or food.

Taki suggested we go to a cave where he thought we could get some dried bread. To reach the cave we had to pass under the enemy's barbed wire. We were without food and had no choice. We crawled toward the barbed wire but soon drew enemy machine-gun fire. The firing ceased after about thirty minutes. Taki was about ten meters away. He let out a cry. I crawled over to him. He had been hit in the head several times and was bleeding profusely. He was soon dead. I wept and regretted that I had not been killed with him, but it was too dangerous to stay there with his body. I left for the eastern coast. I was scared to death to be alone.

On June 12, I hid myself under a rock at the east coast. I had no sword or hand grenades anymore. I did not even have a helmet. I made up my mind the next day to starve myself to death. There were some banana trees in a small valley. I lay under a rock covered by these trees. I could not even move an inch anymore; it was just like dreaming. On June 16, on the verge of dying, I noticed a dog scratching the ground. I saw about six or seven U.S. soldiers directing their rifles at me. I closed my eyes. They wrapped me in a blanket and brought me to a field hospital.

Contrary to my expectations, the Americans treated me very kindly. They gave me not only medical treatment but much nutritious food. They gave me several injections a day. As their treatment was good, even serious patients recovered quickly. I am so grateful to them.

In Chidori Village, they had constructed a cemetery for 4,800 Americans and one for the 23,000 Japanese killed. There were 1,019 Japanese army and navy personnel (ranked major and below) taken prisoner by the U.S. military.[7]

chapter fifteen

THE MOST UNFORTUNATE BATTLE
First Lieutenant Yamazaki
Takeshi's Story

This story, by First Lieutenant Yamazaki Takeshi, is in letter form.

Letter to the Widow of Lieutenant Colonel Nishi Takeichi from a Survivor, Former First Lieutenant Yamazaki Takeshi
26th Tank Regiment

THE MOST UNFORTUNATE BATTLE

In older times, our ancestors said, "Bushido—the way of the samurai—is to die." These words look beautiful, but I think that they are too easily used.

For both the survivors as well as those who died there, Iwo Jima was the worst of battles, I think. Thoughtless words like "Bushido is to die" cannot really be applied to Iwo Jima. Modern war does not allow such easygoing words to exist; death is too violent and widespread.

When I remember your husband, I am not able to control my tears. I do not weep because of his death, for he was the regimental commander, and he died performing his duty. The reason why I find myself crying is that the battlefield was bad, beyond description. We lost count of who died, how they died, where they died, when they died. They just died where they were. I wish it could have been a battlefield of samurai, like the above phrase about Bushido, but it was not. It is very sad for me to write these things to you.

But it is true that Iwo Jima was different from other battlefields. In other battles, soldiers gave medical treatment to the wounded personnel, told warmhearted stories, wrote their wills, saw friends,

121

etc. I even wonder if grass and trees will ever grow again on Iwo Jima.

Our troops had been well trained and performed their duties very well. Let me write about some battle situations. On March 8, Shikauchi Takashi's company took the guns out of the cave and put them in exposed positions. As a result, all of the company's personnel were annihilated. The members of Company No. 1, a tank company commanded by Captain Suzuki Toshio, were killed on March 9 near Nidan-Iwa. On the same day, Captain Saito Norio's tank company left the north coast to launch strikes, but all the tanks were destroyed. A bullet penetrated Saito's shoulder, and, injured, he came to the regimental headquarters. In addition to Saito, several other officers came to Lieutenant Colonel Nishi's command post that day, including Captain Katayama Seiji, Captain Nishimura Isanaka (who, five days before the enemy landed, had made an emergency landing on Iwo Jima on his way from Marcus Island to Japan proper), 2nd Lieutenant Yamashita Ichiro, myself, Captain Suzuki, and First Lieutenant Otani Masaya. From March 10 on, without tanks, we fought an infantry battle.

One day, as I could not go back to my company, I stayed at the regimental headquarters. Lieutenant Otani was then in the process of interrogating an American prisoner of war. A navy engineering officer came in our headquarters around the same time. He was examining a bazooka. Under his care, I fired it for the first time in my life. After this, I was able to fire it against enemy tanks and machine-gun nests every day. Shortly thereafter, Captain Katayama and Lieutenant Otani were killed in action.

I went to the command post every day to receive the regimental orders. The cave was about three hundred meters long. There were three levels, which were filled with wounded personnel. The only lamp was in the regimental commander's room. About fifty blankets were hung up at the bends in the cave to protect against the enemy's flamethrowers. Unfortunately, the entrance of the cave was discovered by the Americans, and the enemy used explosives and a flamethrower. Lieutenant Colonel Nishi suffered burns to his eyes during this attack, but he had no trouble walking. After this, his adjutant was always with him.

The following day, probably the same day of Lieutenant General Kuribayashi's banzai charge, our regiment decided to break out of the cave and head north. We took a lot of time for saying farewell to the wounded personnel. We left them three days' worth of bread, eight hand grenades, and two pistols. Unfortunately, we did not have any water to give them.

We left the cave around 8 PM, I think. I led the advanced-guard company. After exiting the cave, we immediately drew a volley of fire from the plateau on the left, and I was wounded on my right thigh. Although Dr. Kawashima Shintaro was alongside me, he did not see my wound and moved onward. I continued walking, with great difficulty, and crawling north by myself.

I arrived at a cave where Captain Suzuki was. I was happy to see him. I slept and slept for two days and two nights. He woke me up and gave me two rice balls. We could not stay there anymore. He and I left the cave and again began walking north in the dark. I was unable to walk and had lost sight of him. I became alone again. My sword became my walking stick. Only the blade was left, I having lost the scabbard. The blade sank deep into the ground each time, and it was hard for me to pull it out. Finally I threw it away. I still had four hand grenades with me. Where and when should I use these to kill myself, I thought? I preferred to die naturally, in the rain.

Dawn finally came. I saw a man ahead of me and shouted to him. Fortunately, he was a Japanese soldier. He helped me into a cave. I don't really remember anything else, just staring at a light deep in a cave. Someone put some sake in my mouth from a lunch-box-type container. Everyone was drinking sake, which had been found in the cave. The person who had shared it with me was First Lieutenant Matsui, one of my classmates. He carried me to his bed. I stayed there for four days. As a result, I became better.

While laying down, I could hear many conversations. What happened to the regimental headquarters? Where was Lieutenant Colonel Suzuki? Many people came in and out. Matsui was under the command of Major Sakoda Fumio, so I heard about the major's last moments as well as of Suzuki's. Matsui and I moved caves twice after that. Lieutenant Yokoyama Yoshio, commander of the 109th Division's rocket-gun company, was with us too, I think. In the last cave we stayed at, I heard about the details of Lieutenant Colonel Nishi's death. I also learned about the death of Lieutenant General Kuribayashi. One staff officer tried to get out of Iwo Jima by raft. These things were not very interesting for me, because I could not move at all. I was absentmindedly watching those who still could move.

chapter sixteen

COME OUT!
Seaman First Class Koizumi Tadayoshi's Story

Recollections of Former Seaman First Class Koizumi Tadayoshi
Hinode Gun Position, East Sector

SENT TO IWO JIMA EXPERIENCING HEAVY AIR RAIDS

I was drafted by the navy on July 13, 1944, and given basic training at the Nagai site of the Yokosuka Naval Gun-Firing School (Yokosuka Hojutsu Gakko).[1]

On October 20 that year, my classmates in the above school, a hundred of us seamen, left Yokosuka for Iwo Jima under the command of Ensign Kato Fumio by a high-speed naval ship. A bad storm had just passed the day before, and the sky was now clear and the day beautiful. Joined by another high-speed naval ship filled with army troops, we left the Hemi Pier of Yokosuka, expecting never to return again. We arrived at the Minami Pier area, which was in the southeastern part of the island near Mount Suribachi, on Iwo Jima shortly after 8 AM on October 23.

There were no trees at all near the area we landed. There was only a long sand beach as far as we could see up to the First Airfield. The sun was much stronger than in the mainland, even though it was already toward the end of October, and without trees there was no shade. The island is small. It is only approximately six kilometers east to west and four kilometers north to south. We were taken to the Tamanayama waiting area, between the two airfields, temporarily, and placed under the command of Captain Inoue Samaji, Iwo Jima Naval Garrison commander.

Since it was our first day there, we set up our tents. While we were doing this, around 3 PM that same day, the air-raid sirens rang out, and

124

moments later numerous shells began exploding. Subsequently, we saw a B-29 bomber, which we had heard so much about on the mainland, coming toward us, its gray body shining in the sky at a height of about eight thousand meters.

We did not yet know the geography of the island, so someone who had spent some time on Iwo took us to an air-raid shelter. The shelter was a tunnel in the sandlike ground and was quite fragile. Nobody spoke in the shelter. Some of our bombers went up to intercept the B-29. There were no planes left on the airfield, as the Zeros had scrambled as well. The bombs dropped by the B-29 were loud and shook the tunnel and us, causing the tunnel dirt to fall in on us and down our shirt collars. When the air raid finished, we immediately went outside and were surprised to see the number of holes in the airfield. After releasing its bombs, the B-29 flew away. Some of our Zero fighters pursued it, but it was only our planes that were shot down, to my regret.

After the air-raid siren was turned off, the island got quiet again. I had gotten thirsty by this point. There were many sulphur springs but no drinking water to be had anywhere. Fortunately, I had some canned pineapple I brought from the mainland with me; I shared it with my friends Sato Hajime and Masuda Minoru and some others. I will never forget the taste of the pineapple juice that day.

We stayed at Tamanayama for about two or three days. During this time, we were being assigned to the respective naval gun positions to which we would be attached. Some were sent to Suribachi, others to the north. Those whom had known one another in the mainland and helped each other along the way were now being split up and sent on their respective assignments to help defend the island. My own assignment was decided; I was sent to the Naval Garrison Headquarters. Our headquarters building was located on a small hill, with the First Airfield to our west, Mount Suribachi to our south, and the Minami Pier, where we first landed, to our east.

The headquarters was in the home of one of the islanders, who had since been evacuated to the mainland. It was more like a shack, but for a house it was one of the better dwellings on Iwo. There was a field hospital nearby. Everyone on the island hoped for water, but little rain fell. It was particularly tough on someone like me who loved to gulp water when he drank. I was introduced to the officer in charge and told to become the deputy. I was also placed in charge of land defense around the gun position, as well to be an aide of Ensign Kato, who had brought us down to Iwo.

B-29s and B-24s raided the island every day around 3 PM. They usually made their raids in formations of about thirty planes, at eight to ten thousand meters. They bombed our airfields only and then left. Our antiaircraft guns made every effort to shoot them down, but while the smoke enveloped the planes, no rounds actually reached them. I started to envy the way the planes kept their tight formation and left unharmed. When the raids first started, I manned my guns but gradually became used to the raids and, powerless, just watched them afterward.

ASSIGNED TO THE HINODE GUN POSITION IN THE EAST SECTOR

On December 1, 1944, Ensign Kato and I were assigned to the Hinode gun position in the East Sector. When we went to the position, I found that it was located on a cliff and that those there had been using 25-mm antiaircraft guns. Ensign Kato became the gun position commander. Looking out to sea on the eastern shore, I saw several dark objects. Looking southward, I could see the airfields one after the other. The sea was calm, and it was a pleasant day. Shortly after this, we began to be shelled from ships that had been on the horizon. It was my first time to experience shelling from the sea. The enemy's shells landed indiscriminately. We sought shelter in a pillbox and waited it out. Following Ensign Kato, we took a narrow road and made it to the Hinode gun position. We had walked for quite a while but did not run into anyone else along the way. However, we did see several small houses in the woods that we walked through. According to some people, I heard there were as many as 33,000 men on this small island. I was much encouraged by this.

There were already some men at the Hinode gun position when we arrived. They welcomed me when I arrived. The sun rose directly in front of us every morning, and it was actually a pleasant place to be. Ensign Kato was in charge of fifty men. The gun position was located on a cliff, and we had ten different 25-mm gun placements. We were to help defend the Kamiyama twelve-centimeter antiaircraft guns, and I was to be located at the tenth gun emplacement. Our closest air-raid shelter was about a hundred meters away. We spent the days in tents pitched in the shade of the woods.

The tents were good for collecting water when it rained. Water was collected in drums and saved as drinking water. It could not be used without permission. There were so many flies. Since we ate outdoors, we had to constantly shoo the flies away with handheld fans. Meals were made by Petty Officer Komatsuzaki Chuzaemon every day. In the morning we had drills, and in the afternoons we constantly dug tunnels. We had no time off. One time, someone yelled that some Lockheeds were approaching. We ran and barely were able to get to our gun positions in time. The plane came in low. Ten guns in our position fired simultaneously at the four planes approaching. Our number one problem was the air raids that took place during meal preparation times. In order not to draw enemy fire, Komatsuzaki had to extinguish the cooking fire. The resulting rice often turned out imperfect, but it never tasted bad.

My work involved the running of the gun position, and so I was usually never far from the telephone in our command tent. One time, however, an enemy plane came out of nowhere and began firing at me. I ran back and forth between a sand embankment and a papaya tree, but the plane just continued to shoot all around me. The papaya tree eventually fell to the ground, all shot up. I will never forget the smoke and dirt flying up from the bullets that were coming after me. I found later that a bullet had gone through a pocket on my trousers, but I myself was spared.

The Hinode gun position seems to have been on the ideal route for the enemy planes when they approached and flew over the island. Aircraft-carrier planes, Lockheeds, and fighters all came in low from the east and bombed the island so hard it seemed like it would lift up. There were almost no times when they came in from behind us, across the island. We shot at them with all we had as if we were not going to let them through our antiaircraft wall of fire.

Beginning in December 1944, the air raids by the enemy increased dramatically. They came two or three times in the morning, afternoon, and at night. I do not drink alcohol or smoke, but I do like sweet things, including sweet beans preserved in sake and candy. As I had not taken a bath since I arrived at Iwo Jima, one day I went down to the beach and washed my body with seawater, including some sulphur.

During the daytime, we had little time to relax, as we had to stand guard at our antiair defenses, but the evenings were relatively quiet for us at the Hinode gun position. I often looked at the good-luck charms that I had been given before coming to Iwo Jima, which included pictures of my parents, an amulet worn next to my skin, and a small round mirror given to me by my mother. In the picture, my father was looking at me as if to give me courage, and my mother as if to provide me with a smile. One day, to my surprise, I found that the mirror had been broken. I do not know when or how it broke. It felt ominous, and I put the broken mirror in an ammunition box. Many people used to use the ammunition boxes as their desks for letter writing. The boxes were also used to send military mail back to the mainland.

I was twenty-four years old at this time, a zealous sailor, among the youngest there. However, I did not forget to write to my family. My father had been killed in action in northern China in 1937, but I still had my mother and younger brothers and younger sisters at home. I would find time almost every day to write a note to them on a postcard and send it off to them. Even if it was just one sentence, it provided them with a sense of security and relief that I was okay. If the post-cards stopped arriving, they would know that the situation had gotten worse, so I made sure that I wrote every day. My ammunition box had been penetrated by an enemy machine-gun bullet during an air raid, and I ended up, one day, writing a long letter using some pieces of stationery that had bullet holes in it. What I wrote was essentially the same thing every time, as most things, such as dates, weather, features of the island, and places, were considered military secrets. There were no shops or anything to buy here, so I did not need my pay and sent it all to my mother when the war situation became worse. After the war, my mother told me that she could guess how serious the war situation on Iwo Jima had become when she saw the stationery with a bullet hole in it and that I had sent her all my money.

From the middle of December 1944, the enemy's air raids became worse, with one or two planes bombing us constantly. As one was bombing us from above, a second one was appearing over the water approaching us. It was a real war of nerves. From this point, the con-nections with the mainland began to wane. Before long, it was the first of the new year. The only planes we saw in the sky were those of the enemy. We longed for some with the Rising Sun mark to appear but they never came. It was excruciatingly sad. Through the rumor mill, we heard that planes had been sent on at least three occasions to help us but that every time they had been shot down by enemy planes waiting for them. We became very discouraged with that news when it reached us. There were three or four Zero fighters on our airfield, and we all hoped that more would be sent.

Iwo Jima had become an isolated island in the middle of the Pacific Ocean by this point. Every day, we had to try to fight off the enemy planes and avoid the naval shelling while defending the island. Time passed quickly by, and upon entering February the enemy's air raids and naval shelling became even worse. Submarines operating around the island began sinking more vessels. Submarines would sometimes operate about three kilometers from our gun position. One day a small white wave appeared just this side of a long, thin island that was located about four kilometers from us. We believed it was a submarine and fired our 25-mm guns at it at once. When it turned out to be a whale, we all let out a big laugh.

The lack of rain still continued to be a problem. On February 15, which was otherwise a quiet day under a beautiful blue sky, we got word from one of our reconnaissance planes that a large fleet was heading from the south in a northerly direction. This was the start of a true emergency situation. I had the feeling that the U.S. military was going to launch an invasion of our island. Everyone had a serious expression on his face, like it was absolutely necessary to win. We became extremely busy at this point, checking our 25-mm guns, moving the water and food storage drums inside the cave, reinforcing the entrance to the cave with dirt, and camouflaging the entrance to it with tree branches so as not to be spotted by the enemy. We finished our preparations to be ready to fight and stood guard.

Even though the sun was beginning to set, we still did not see any of the ships of the enemy's fleet, only the red sun off in the horizon. The island was quiet. Those not on guard duty were all inside the cave anxiously waiting, having trouble sleeping. The cave was about 1.5 meters wide, two meters tall, and about thirty meters long. Sulphur bubbled from the hot springs in the cave, making it like a sauna in there.

THE ENEMY'S NAVAL SHELLING BEGINS

When night turned to dawn on the morning of the 16th, I looked at the sea from the entrance of the cave. About four kilometers from shore, many warships were anchoring and arranging their guns against Iwo Jima. We could see many enemy personnel walking on the decks of the vessels. There were submarines moving back and forth in between them and the shore. Hundreds of the landing craft were also covering the sea. It appeared as if they were ready to launch an invasion. However, like the quiet before the storm, neither the Americans nor we had even fired yet.

The enemy's naval guns begin firing when their carrier-based aircraft started raiding the island. There was no stop to their rapid firing. We waited and watched the enemy until they approached. The entrance of the shelter was in a rather high location, so we could see everything, but we were also easy to spot as well. Ensign Kato, with a stern face, watched from the camouflaged entrance of the shelter, as did I and my comrades.

The enemy's naval gunfire against the southern beach was beyond description. Since we were some two kilometers from there, our gun position was for the most part unaffected. The landing craft were in a line, several deep, approaching with the tops of the waves splashing off of them. When quite a few enemy forces landed, our machine guns, which had been quiet until then, let loose and fired on them all together.[2] Moreover, several guns firing a new type of rocket shot at the enemy on the beach, who had nowhere to hide. As soon as we fired, however, the enemy discovered our positions, and their planes immediately dropped out of the sky and began their strikes on us. We were soon in the middle of an air, sea, and land battle. Several of us left the shelter and took up our positions at the guns and fired at aircraft that were attempting to hit us. It was quite different from trying to hit carrier planes that flew in from the sea.

Enemy planes enveloped the island. It was probably lucky that there were none of our planes around. It was like when we were cooking our meals, trying to shoo away the flies. Each of the gun positions were attacked from the air. We used our guns to help try to shoot down some of these planes that came to attack us. We were being struck from right to left and were busy turning and firing the gun. I was not sure where the other gun positions were but could tell by the path of the attacking aircraft. We were hit by hostile fire several times, but fortunately no one was injured or killed. We had complete confidence against the enemy's planes. However, we could tell how rapid their guns were by the sounds of the rounds hitting the ground around us and the smoke and sand flying about. Since our 25-mm guns were firing much slower, this was a big cause for concern. Out at sea, we could see none of our own ships; all the warships were those of the enemy, and they continued their relentless firing. In this engagement, the enemy was unable to realize success and gradually began to pull back. Iwo Jima returned to being quiet again. It was a victory for us.

However, the enemy seemed to have learned nothing and tried once again to make a landing a second time on February 19. While we were waking up and waiting for dawn, we could see that the number of planes and ships had grown as compared to the last time, and we knew that this was the beginning of the real battle of Iwo Jima. We immediately assumed our combat positions.

At 8:00 in the morning, a large warship, which appeared to be the flagship and was right in front of our position, launched its first round as a signal. Immediately the others began with the rapid firing. The first shells flew over us and hit our rear areas, falling like rain. This time, the shelling covered the whole island. Bombers, probably from Saipan, joined the fight along with landing craft and amphibious tanks. The United States was very well prepared with equipment. There were only two places the enemy could land on beaches—those on the southern and western shores. There were no other places, besides these two, where U.S. forces could land. The enemy landed on the southern shore. The sea was calm that day and the weather advantageous.

The bombardment continued for about two to three hours. We could see their rounds flying right over us. The sounds of their firing and the explosions as well as of our guns were deafening. I think the enemy started landing around 10 AM. Some of our army troops began firing against the marines and their landing craft with machine guns and howitzers. At this time, enemy planes were concentrated over the landing area, and since they flew over us as they prepared for their strikes, it was easy for us to shoot at them without getting too tired. The marines began advancing behind tanks up the steep incline, made up of volcanic ash. They entered the minefield and were met by our mortars and other fire. The enemy was no doubt surprised. When the enemy front line advanced about three hundred meters ashore, any and all Japanese weapons concentrated firing on the enemy. Many tanks broke down, and marines were pinned down. But the enemy continued to land more men and tanks. It took two to three hours for the enemy to land its forces.

Our antiaircraft gun position at Hinode continued to combat the enemy's planes that were there supporting the landing. As with the shelling we experienced from the sea, while our position was hit a few times, no one was injured.

Each of our positions was well dug in and thus not easily visible from the sea. However, they were visible from the air, as there was no grass or trees around them, which had been cleared away. When we were spotted from the air, the bombers would lower their elevation and drop drums filled with napalm and set them alight. Fortunately they fell away from our gun positions, and we were unhurt, but they burned a lot of black smoke for some time.

Our Hinode gun position was close to the enemy's landing area. It seemed that they were trying to destroy everything in front of their advancing forces. Around the time that the sun was setting to the west, an unbelievably large shell landed from the southern beaches. Fortunately it fell about a hundred meters from us, hitting the side of a cliff, but it was as if a gun of one of our own forces had mistakenly shot at us. The enemy's planes left the area when it got dark. There was still some sporadic fighting on land. The first day of the vicious fighting at the Hinode gun position thus ended.

I DO RECONNAISSANCE OF THE ENEMY

When it was dusk, I was surprised to see the tremendous number of the empty cartridges scattered around my gun. We had been firing the gun dreamily. Meanwhile, most of the enemy aircraft left, although a few rounds of naval gunfire were being continued. The enemy vessels were exchanging signals by light, relaying something to each other. The warships continued firing even at night, two or three rounds at a time.

Around this time, I heard that the line between where we once had been at the Naval Headquarters and the First Airfield and the western shore had fallen into enemy hands. If this was true, that meant the island was now divided in two, with our forces on Mount Suribachi cut off from us. The enemy constantly fired flares into the sky, and the night turned into day. At this point, a strange thought came over me. I had believed that in wartime it did not matter if it was night or day, but at night the enemy did not employ planes for the most part and was not very active. I thought it was very unusual to be this quiet. We quickly cleaned the guns, left some guards outside, and went into our shelter. The entrance had been entirely transformed during the day, and we actually had trouble finding it. The cave was uncomfortable, with its heat and sulphur odor, but the only other choice was to sleep outside and risk being spotted by the searchlights and having our site bombed. As we were doing all this, our location was struck again. Our telephone lines were torn to shreds, and we were cut off from all communications.

Since we were without knowledge of what the enemy was up to, Ensign Kato ordered me to take three men and reconnoiter the enemy around the southern coast. We four members said goodbye to Ensign Kato and the others, exchanging cups of water. We left the shelter one by one between the enemy's searchlights and crawled along the ground. The landscape of the island had completely changed. The tree grove that had been nearby was now reduced to a pile of dirt. Small hills had been flattened. Everything was different, and we had difficulty finding our whereabouts. We occasionally heard shots over our heads. Eventually we arrived near the southern dock area. We were unable to find where our Naval Headquarters was.

The illumination flares did not stop. One time we saw a man standing in a foxhole. He was an enemy sentry. When I looked at him under the searchlight, I knew that he was a tall black man. He was mumbling and fingering the trigger of his automatic rifle. Although we had some hand grenades that we could have used on him, we decided to bypass him, as our duty was to conduct reconnaissance. The enemy was very busy landing war materials in the southern beach area.

Fortunately, we were not spotted by the enemy and continued to conduct our surveillance before returning. The warships continued firing, which made it worrisome, but the sentry did not see us. We decided to hurry back by detouring.

About halfway back, it seemed as if a searchlight was following us. As soon as it turned directly on us, an explosion occurred, knocking me temporarily unconscious. When I came to, I was in an Imperial Army shelter, and there were many soldiers around us. Our forces had carried us into the shelter. This was the first time that someone who had taken shrapnel in his back from the Hinode gun position had been injured. We told the men from the army the enemy's positions and shook hands with them to thank them for rescuing us. We loaded our wounded comrade on a stretcher and carried him with us. There was no road or path to speak of on this volcanic rocky terrain, but we finally made it to the shelter of the army doctor and left our comrade under his medical care. We felt bad that we were unable to provide him with care ourselves, and it was a sad farewell.

During the time that we were away from our own shelter, the landscape had again changed, and we were unable to find the entrance to it. We called for Ensign Kato while walking and finally made it to the cave. We apologized to him for our casualty and reported the enemy's position and doings. During this time, the relentless shelling of the U.S. Navy's ships continued.

CLOSE ATTACKS ON THE ENEMY TANKS

The next day, February 20, enemy air strikes and naval gunfire became more intense than the day before. It was as if the enemy was challenging our will to fight. The entrance to our shelter was partially buried by an explosion. We had to dig our way out like moles. We got out and took our positions.

When I turned and looked back at the entrance to the shelter and the landscape around, I could not help but be impressed by the explosive might of the naval gunfire during just one night. There were pieces of shells and the aftermath of their explosions all over the place. Although they were just pieces, I could see large sections of the shells among them and figured out that while they were in great quantity, they seemed to be of slipshod quality.

The enemy's aircraft continued to strike our position like the day before. However, the naval guns were going over our head, seemingly to concentrate on the central part of the island. We could hear the sound of small arms and machine guns near the second airfield. We were in a location lower than the airfield, and the gunfire was flying over our heads. However, we still did not see any of the enemy close up. All we had to protect us was our 25-mm machine gun. We threw aside our cumbersome helmets, and with our backs to the enemy's warships we began firing at the carrier planes, shooting a few down. We did not see any of our own planes again this day, as well. Moreover, we were bombed like we had never been bombed before. Some bombs exploded about sixty or seventy meters overhead, and the fragments rained down on us like the legs of an octopus. We called this an octopus bomb. We got hit by it three times, but fortunately our gun was not damaged, nor were we injured.

Around 4 PM, a large warship came in close and began to fire. The sailors on the U.S. ship were so close we could almost touch them. We immediately directed our fire at them and the warship. Until that point, our gun position had been unknown to them. They immediately lowered their guns and began firing all together at us. We hid behind the ordnance area of the number ten gun. Dirt came crashing down on us. Due to the extreme concentration of fire, we were ordered to retreat and dove into our shelters with the shells following after us. We somehow managed to all get into the shelter, having dug out the entrance to get into it, but by doing so we now gave away the location of our shelter to the enemy. At that point, the warship began pummeling us, eventually collapsing the entranceway and burying us inside.

The shelter was extremely hot with the sulphur and heat from the island. The steam became our only source of water. We put cans in cracks along the wall to collect water that slowly ran off the sides of the walls. We waited until the evening to go outside and check the gun. However, the warship had completely destroyed the gun position, and we just stood there and stared. There was still no sight of enemy soldiers. However, we could hear the sounds of small-arms fire and machine guns, and occasionally a stray round would fly near us and time bombs would go off. Moreover, illumination flares were dropping constantly, making the Tamanayama area appear as if it were in daylight.

Compared to the daytime, it looked as if we had been able to push the enemy back. Nevertheless, we were forced to stay in the shelter until one night we began close-in operations against the enemy tanks using antitank mines and Molotov cocktails. We crept into the enemy's area. I was in the Tamanayama area and found an enemy tank. I watched it closely for a while, and eventually someone came out of the tank. I was glad when this happened and used a tree branch to place a mine under the tank and covered it with dirt and began to head back. However, in my rush to return, I had stood up too high, and the enemy saw me and fired his rifle at me. I froze, and then the tank shot its flamethrower at me. My legs were partially hit. Because I was far enough away, I was able to sneak away in the dark. I was lucky that the American forces preferred not to fight at night.

LEAVING THE SHELTER AND BECOMING ISOLATED

I lost track of what the date or even the day was, but one night when it was completely dark we received an order from headquarters to depart the Hinode gun position and assemble immediately at the headquarters.

None of us from Hinode knew the geography of the island or even where the location of the headquarters had been. Of course, no one knew where the new headquarters, stood up in the middle of the battle, was. We decided to follow orders, however, and make our way to wherever the headquarters was. We disposed of our personal belongings and, weaponless, took leave of the shelter, where we had become used to staying. Along the way, we had to be careful to avoid the searchlights of the warships and the illumination flares sent up by the enemy. Flares were being dropped well up to the north as well.

From the eastern side of the island, we walked in groups of four or five in a northerly direction. As we had never been far from the gun position, we were unfamiliar with the island and were like blind men leading the blind. We walked in the shadows created by the enemy's flares, along the crevices of the hills and rocks, and right under an enemy sentry standing on a cliff. We were hurrying to the cave housing the headquarters and at one point lost sight of the group that had the orders and directions to the cave. Six or seven of us got separated and wandered right into the enemy's area. We saw some of our soldiers lying bleeding, injured or dead, in foxholes or in crevices in the rocks and changed direction. However, we ended up hitting a trip wire, and machine guns opened up on us. We were trapped and could not move.

The machine gun eventually stopped firing, and we were able to move again. We saw numerous bodies piled up on each other from what appears to have been a strike on one of our shelters. None of them had guns. Probably U.S. troops took them all. On top of the remnants of the shelter, someone yelled down to tell us that the area we were in was dangerous—we were in the middle of a minefield and could see some of the exposed mines. It was likely one of our own minefields, but somehow our forces got caught in the middle of it and were killed. I was surprised to see in the distance a pole with a light, which was on. Along the way, we triggered another trip wire and were shot at by machine guns on several occasions, but eventually we made it to the northern sector and what appeared to be the cave of the headquarters.

We had been reduced to six people during the course of our wanderings. Imperial Navy lieutenant (junior grade) Ito Shigoichi, the new commander of the Kamiyama gun position, had joined us. The shelter was sixty to seventy meters deep, but it was hot on the inside, so we did not go too far in. It was quite wide, and there were holes in the wall like bunks, for sleeping. In addition to the entranceway we came in from, there was another entrance toward the middle of the cave, and later we discovered there was another one farther in. There was not really anything in the middle of cave, but there was food and water for cooking. We ate for the first time in a long time. At this point, the island was almost completely overrun by the enemy. The entranceway was camouflaged with rocks piled up, and we did not go out during the daytime. Every evening we went out to look for our comrades, but we ended up hitting the trip wires and causing the enemy to fire machine guns at us. In the end, we did not locate any of our own troops. The longer we went without weapons, the more we desired the automatic rifles of our enemy. We continued to go out at night, wandering around looking for food and weapons to steal from the enemy. We began the life of troops defeated and alone.

Before long, a big new road was built in front of our camouflaged shelter, as were structures for the enemy. A pillbox of sorts was made right in front of the enemy's sleeping area, and our movements became even more restricted. However, we desperately needed green vegetables, and one very dark evening we struck out to find some, but we turned up empty. Before long it was April and then May. We decided it would be better to make a break for the ocean and try our luck there than it would be to die in the cave. In order to create a raft, we needed wire or rope to tie together the wood. Every night, we went out looking for some, but the six of us were unable to find any to make our great escape. Sometimes someone would come back carrying some of the enemy's dynamite, mistakenly thinking they had picked up some fruit.

The enemy fired at the island in a way suggesting that it was looking for crevices and hideouts. The vibrations really shook us. Shells from the warships landed close to the entranceway to the shelter. Speakers from the ships also played the melody from the Japanese fable "Sakura, Sakura" in an attempt to draw out stragglers. One day, we went out looking for wires using the light of the stars and found two new telephone cables of the enemy. We drew in the one on the left, which was quite heavy. We pulled on the other one too but did not notice that it was attached to the top of one of the enemy's structures. We rushed back to our shelter. Perhaps we were discovered that time, because around 10:00 AM the next day we heard some sounds around the entranceway toward the middle of the shelter, and before long someone came in holding a metal hand lamp. Someone else entered as well. We hid deeper in the cave, holding grenades that we were going to use on them. When they looked in our direction we threw the grenades at them, but they did not have any affect. They threw down their lamp but ran off with their rifles. We ended up having only three grenades left.

Shortly after this, we heard some noises near the entranceway we were at and then saw some light come into the cave. We heard some English being spoken and then saw an automatic rifle being thrust in. We were in one of the passageways of the cave and not in any direct danger, but we all looked at each other as if it were the end. We were tired, underfed, and underweight by this point.

WE ARE GOING TO PUT SUFFOCATION GAS IN YOUR CAVE

Because of the lack of medicine and the heat in the cave, my legs, which had been hit by the flamethrower, were swelling up. I was in such pain and could not even put socks or shoes on, and my feet were a mess. I began thinking it might be worth ending it at this point. I was going to take one of my comrade's grenades and go back into the cave and blow myself up. Lieutenant Ito, aware of what I was thinking, told me not to. About twenty minutes later, the sound of automatic rifles stopped, and some speakers that had been placed by the entranceway began to call out in Japanese with a strange accent, "Korosanai, detekoi" (We won't kill you, come out). We had absolutely no desire to step out and instead were prepared to die within the cave.

The message on the speaker continued for a while, as did some rifle fire. When it became lunchtime, the enemy used a prisoner of war or a Japanese American to call out to us again, this time in perfect Japanese: "We are going to get some lunch. Please think about whether you will come out or not in the meantime." Shortly after that, I looked outside, and my eyes hurt from the brightness of the sun. About a hundred meters away, there was a huge enemy encampment. Since we could not move around during the day, we decided to make a break for the sea that night. Just then, there was the sound of some footsteps by the entranceway. In Japanese we were told that the enemy was going to put some suffocation gas into the cave, and shortly after that some red, smoky powder appeared. We knew it was dangerous, but we headed to the entrance near the center of the tunnel. Fortunately, there was good ventilation, and we were not affected by this red smoke. Thanks to this episode, we learned that some of the steam from the cave would escape from this hole.

It seemed that the enemy left, because it got quiet again. We could not let our guard down. We were nervous and tension filled as we waited for the evening to come. Around 10 PM, we left the cave to head toward the coast to make our break for the open sea. Occasionally a flare would go up, but it seemed more like fireworks. We made it to the beach. We had to hurry to make a raft, gathering branches and logs and anything we could to make it. We succeeded in actually making a rough one. The six of us pushed it into the Pacific, but the waves pushed us back, and the raft ended up breaking into pieces. Back up on the beach, we gave up our hope to escape from the island. Drenched to the skin, and without any hope or options left, I picked up a comrade's grenade and headed to the remnants of a pillbox and went inside it to kill myself. Low and behold, inside was Lieutenant (Senior Grade) Itabashi by himself. We cried tears of joy when we met. The sun was rising by this point, and the worst was about to happen. Several enemy soldiers were coming our way, talking noisily, and perhaps following our footsteps. They threw some rocks into the pillbox and called to us, but we did not understand what they were saying. They seemed like they were going to charge in. A grenade preceded them but hit a rock before it landed inside and exploded. Before I knew it, Itabashi had pulled out a pistol and killed himself, at the same time the grenade went off. The date was May 17.

I am not sure what the enemy soldiers thought, but they left in any case. I buried Lieutenant Itabashi in the pillbox and left there that evening. Lieutenant Ito saw me struggling with my bad legs and loaned me his shoulder to lean on. We went into a crevice that was the size of about one *tatami* (less than one meter by two meters). The other four went into a hole across from us. It was actually quite good. Although it was in the morning, we sang military songs. While the other four could not see, Lieutenant Ito and I were able to see the enemy's tents right below us. Lieutenant Ito unsuccessfully tried to stop them from singing. Before long, we heard the footsteps of enemy soldiers. Three grenades were thrown into the hole across from us, and we could no longer hear the singing of the military tunes. At the same time, we had not noticed that there was a hole in our cave, and Lieutenant Ito was shot by an enemy soldier.

WE WON'T KILL YOU, SO COME OUT!

I could no longer walk at all, and so I tried to pull out the safety of the hand grenade I had picked up at the beach, but it was rusty, and I broke a tooth struggling to pull it out. A lot of enemy soldiers had gathered about three meters away.

One of them was firing into the ground yelling "Detekoi, korosanai!" Although I was a defeated enemy straggler, I still had the pride and traditional Japanese spirit of Yamato-damashii. However, I no longer had any weapons, only one rusty hand grenade in my right hand. I could not fight or even respond. With my legs bad, I was just leaning against the rock wall. One of the enemy soldiers picked me up and carried me to his tent area. My life as a member of the Japanese military ended this day, May 18, 1945.

The Americans immediately tended to my legs and gave me what was probably a bottle of vitamins, full of red pills. I was placed in a fenced-in area for prisoners of war. It was about fifty meters long by fifty meters wide. There were machine guns at each corner. There were two tents for us to sleep in. There were twenty-two prisoners. When I arrived, someone asked me if I came from Minami Iwo Jima or Kita Iwo Jima. He may have been joking, but I was incensed as a fellow Japanese. There was a nice superior there who calmed me down. I settled down to life as a prisoner of war, a POW. I heard that the total number of Japanese prisoners taken up to then had been about a thousand. Two ships had already taken most of the prisoners somewhere. We were the last group, and a ship was coming in about two or three days to pick us up. Every evening, we lined up for roll call. Because we sometimes moved, the counting got fouled up, and the U.S. soldiers had to recount.

We thought it was funny to confuse them, and the U.S. soldiers started laughing too.

I heard that the first prisoners had been shackled day and night, and so their movements had been restricted. Fortunately, we were not chained at all, but we were under constant guard. We had no hopes or desires at this time. One evening at the end of May, we heard a sound we had long waited for: the engine sounds of our planes approaching over the island. Two planes dropped bombs but were met by anti-aircraft fire. One crashed near the shore, and the other one, grossly disfigured, crashed into Mount Suribachi. Subsequently, I think it was the morning of June 1, about 1,700 B-29s and B-24s flew over Iwo Jima heading northward to bomb Tokyo.

Seeing this endless line of enemy planes flying above us, I prayed for the safety of our homeland. Shortly after noon, the enemy planes began returning. Some had been hit by the antiaircraft fire over Tokyo, and there were white parachutes falling from the sky. The planes kept going until they crashed into the ocean. Other planes came in and landed, having flown on just one of their four engines. Many other planes were similarly damaged. I could see that the antiaircraft forces of our military had fought bravely. One day an enemy officer visited us at the POW camp and said, "We won the war by the number of our weapons, but we lost to your fighting spirit."

We left Iwo Jima several days later. I think it was June 3. The remaining twenty-three of us departed Iwo Jima by ship and were taken to Guam. We were placed into the hold in the lower part of the ship. As we were leaving, we thought about the faces of all of our comrades who had died on Iwo and cried for them. During the three months we fought on Iwo, we had held out hope that the 4th Fleet was on its way to help, as we had been told to expect. We had clearly been too optimistic that this would happen. The enemy had been able to do as he pleased, and now we had turned over Iwo Jima, which was called the entrance to Japan, to the enemy without the least resistance.

FROM GUAM TO HAWAII

It was the island of Guam where we finally arrived. Looking at the island from the sea, it was unlike Iwo Jima and did not appear to have been the site of a fierce battle at all. It was covered in a lush green. We were placed in a POW camp when we arrived. We were separated from the other prisoners, placed deep within the POW camp, because we POWs from Iwo Jima were seen as more dangerous than those from other campaigns, as we had caused about thirty thousand American deaths and casualties. As a matter of fact, we did not fear dying, and given the chance we probably would have tried to kill more American personnel if we could have. So, placing us in special confinement was probably a wise move on the Americans' part.

We maintained this feeling for the rest of our time on Guam. At the end of June, we were taken by ship from Guam to Hawaii. We were closely watched by armed guards on the ship, but by this point, it did not matter anymore. The scenery of Pearl Harbor was breathtaking. It did not look at all like a naval base. The entrance was narrow, but the harbor was wide. The green mountains looked down on Pearl Harbor, and the harbor was a beautiful blue. We could see all the way to the bottom. Honolulu looked just like a postcard. We were in awe as we looked for the first time at the United States. I thought of the brave men of the Japanese navy who had led the attacks on Pearl Harbor, and especially of the nine who failed to return.[3] Wherever we looked, there were countless battleships, cruisers, submarines, and aircraft carriers docked in the harbor. Unlike our forces on Iwo Jima, the United States had an infinite abundance of power and a strong resolve. This fact was made very clear to us this day.

As soon as we landed in Hawaii and went ashore, we were separated by our branch—army and navy. After being lined up and greeted, we were put into a camp that was so large we could not even count how many Japanese prisoners were there. We were given some medical shots and were allowed to relax. After a while, we were questioned. We were asked about the names of the commanders of Japanese bases and about the paper-balloon bombs that had been sent from Japan and which had struck terror in the hearts of Americans.[4] We all gave false answers to the questions, using names of already deceased comrades, for example. We lived as we did, not knowing if there was a tomorrow, and spent our days like this. I was surprised one day to see a very good photo of a Hitachi manufacturing plant taken from the sky by a U.S. plane.

FROM HAWAII TO SAN FRANCISCO AND THEN ON TO TEXAS

We moved again around the end of July 1945. Our POW group grew to 138 when we were joined by prisoners of war from Saipan, Tinian, Guam, and Peleliu. Among them was an IJA colonel. Around this time, we began to enjoy ourselves. The crew members of the ship were friendly, and we exchanged things with each other. They gave us chewing gum and chocolate, and we gave them pictures of Mount Fuji. Someone painted Mount Fuji on a loincloth, which was very much liked by many people. In the beginning of August, we passed under the famous Golden Gate Bridge and landed in San Francisco. There was a Japanese ship that had a bright Red Cross mark on it, but according to the crew of our ship, it apparently had carried weapons. I felt like I was hearing about some of the inside stories of the war. I heard the news of the end of the war on August 15 when I was at a prisoner-of-war camp in San Francisco.

The American newspapers were filled that day with pictures of the emperor and the U.S. president on the front page. There was some playful teasing between the Caucasian troops and the Nisei troops, but even though the Nisei were Americans, I felt proud that there were some people of Japanese blood in America. Nevertheless, we could not believe the war had ended. What did this mean, if in fact the war had ended? I felt very sad and worried about my mother, brothers, and sisters.

After about one month in San Francisco we were moved to another POW camp by train through the Rockies to Camp Huntsville, Texas, on the Gulf of Mexico. There had been German prisoners in the camp before us. Someone had written, "Let's wait another twenty years," in typical German fashion.

There was a big movie theater, as well as a fire department and a large hall in this large camp. Large barracks with heaters were lined up, but the only ones there were us, 138 POWs. The camp commander had once lived in Yokohama for three years. Despite being Caucasian, he spoke good Japanese and addressed us very modestly when we arrived at this camp. In his greetings to us, he said, "I imagine you wish to know about us Americans. Well, we wish to learn about you and your feelings, too. Let's all try to get along here."

We asked him to give us some work. He told us that there had been requests from the town to have the POWs do work in town, but that he refused them, telling us that he did not think Japanese should have to do that type of labor. We were able to work around the camp freely, but that simply meant cutting the grass and other gardening around our building. There were some who went to the mess hall on kitchen police (KP) duty. One day I said something in English, and after that they thought I could speak English and put me to work cleaning in the commander's office and the officers' residence. I have to admit there was some fun amid the loneliness.

The camp commander organized a ticket system, and with these tickets every prisoner could buy chocolate, cigarettes, beer, Coca Cola, stationery, etc. Thanks to donations from the outside, we had all new equipment to play baseball, boxing, and tennis, among other sports. There was even a piano. We were authorized to write letters, but none of the Japanese prisoners wrote any. I am sure that if there had been prisoners from other countries, they surely would have happily written letters. Our education had made us as we were. Every week, Captain Chapel would give us a talk about the Bible.[5] As Christmas approached, we decorated our hall and the Americans did theirs. Among the beautiful Christmas decorations were ornaments that on careful inspection said "Made in Japan." It made me miss Japan all the more. At the same time, I was proud to see Japanese products had made it this far. We were invited to celebrate Christmas with the Americans.

As New Year's approached, we asked the camp commander to buy some Japanese rice, miso, and soy sauce for us. He kindly agreed to our request and had the rice and soy sauce flown in from Hawaii (he was not able to get the miso). Even though we had been enemies, I was so impressed with his kindness. After a while, the prisoners themselves undertook guard duty at the front gate. Anyone entering the camp was to leave his weapon with us and pick it up upon leaving. All of this was unheard of in Japan. I am particularly thankful to First Lieutenant Buckstar in this camp for his special treatment toward me. He taught me much about treating one another with respect.[6]

RETURN TO OUR BELOVED JAPAN

In the middle of January 1946, authorities in Washington, D.C., decided to return us to Japan. We were to travel by air to Hawaii and thus could only carry a certain amount of belongings with us, but due to problems with arranging air transportation we ended up going to Seattle by train. We crossed the Rocky Mountains, arriving at the Pacific Ocean. We traveled through the Great Plains one day and saw hundreds and hundreds of B-29s and B-24s that had returned from the war. The scenery of the snow-covered Rocky Mountains was enough to make us feel better after more than half a year as POWs.

We boarded a thirty-thousand-ton ship, USS *General William Wiegel*, in Seattle.[7] Eating on board with the crew, we arrived at the port of Uraga, located about thirty kilometers southwest of Yokohama, February 23. We had never thought we would have the chance to see Japan again.

After arriving in Japan, I was astonished to see that the prices of commodities had gone up so high and that so many cities had been destroyed by the U.S. bombing raids. I could see how the people of Japan had suffered during (and after) the war.

On February 26, wearing a new navy uniform given to me by the Uraga Naval Demobilization Branch and carrying a knapsack with my clothes and belongings from America, I returned to Mito City, which had been destroyed by the bombing. In the evening, I found a small shack made of galvanized steel plates where my house used to be, in a vast, burned field.

My mother had prayed for Japan's victory and my success, but the horror of the war had turned her once-black hair white. She could not speak and only cried with joy when she saw me. She looked at me up and down two or three times to see if I was real, then she and I wept, embracing each other. When I heard from her that Mito City had been bombed on August 2, I had to regret that Japan had not stopped the war earlier despite all of the bombing raids on the country.

I said a silent prayer for all those heroes who had died on behalf of the country and who are now resting in Yasukuni.

chapter seventeen

WARRIORS REMEMBERED

In connection with the Iwo Jima campaign, there are many warriors to be remembered. Let me describe some of those who stand out in my memory. Since Lieutenant General Kuribayashi appears throughout this book, I will not discuss him in this chapter.

COLONEL IKEDA MASUO, COMMANDER, 145TH INFANTRY REGIMENT

Shortly after the beginning of the Saipan campaign, Colonel Ikeda and I were in close contact regarding the plan to retake Saipan, but we had actually met years before. In 1937, when the 14th Division was engaged in operations along the Keikan Railway in northern China, he was a lieutenant colonel and serving as the senior adjutant for the division. I was still a second lieutenant and serving as the commander of the signal unit for the 2nd Infantry Regiment of the 14th Division. At the time, Second Lieutenant Kikuchi Mitsuaki, assistant adjutant to the 2nd Infantry Regiment commander, used to go to the divisional headquarters to receive orders every day.

One day, near Hotei City, Lieutenant Kikuchi had gone to another unit to report on something, and I was sent to the divisional headquarters, located on a small plateau, in his place. Lieutenant General Dohihara Kenji, divisional commander, Colonel Sano Tadayoshi, chief of staff, Lieutenant Colonel Yazaki Kanju, operations staff, and Captain Mizumachi Katsushiro, intelligence staff, were all there directing the fighting. Lieutenant Colonel Ikeda soon started the roll call of the order receivers in a small forest near the plateau.

When I answered "present" as the order-receiving officer of the 2nd Infantry Regiment, Ikeda asked me, "What happened to Lieutenant Kikuchi?" I answered, "Since Kikuchi had been sent to another unit on business, I came here in his place." To this, Ikeda yelled, "Only Adjutant Kikuchi can do this job. Go back to your regiment and send Kikuchi immediately!" I was displeased and said, "I am a regular officer and senior to Kikuchi. I am working in the operational section, so I believe I am able to handle this responsibility." Ikeda immediately responded very angrily, moving his small moustache, "I am afraid that mistakes can be caused by a man who is not in the right position."

Being quite embarrassed, I finally went to Captain Mizumachi, whom I had met once, to get his help. Mizumachi said he would talk to Ikeda. With his help, I was permitted to receive the divisional orders. At that time, I noticed the fact that a captain staff officer was much more powerful than a lieutenant colonel serving as an adjutant.

Six years later, in the summer of 1943, I was on a train from Hiroshima bound for Tokyo. I was a captain then, and a staff officer. By chance, Colonel Ikeda and his wife were sitting beside me. As I knew their daughter had married Captain Tozaka Susumu, one of my classmates at the Army Academy, I greeted him and told them that I was friends with Tozaka, their new son-in-law. When I told them about the story in northern China, Ikeda said, "Very sorry. It was my fault for being so rude." Thus, when he and I began to work together on the plans to retake Saipan, we had become quite friendly.

The 145th Infantry Regiment was a regular unit on active duty, consisting of young people from Kagoshima Prefecture. It was indeed one of Lieutenant General Kuribayashi's prized units. Its battle service record was excellent, and Kuribayashi issued two letters of commendation. I remember Colonel Ikeda's message from Iwo Jima: "We have just burned our regimental flag. Regiment Commander." It was March 7, 1945, I think. My heart was full of deep emotion when I read it.

THE SIDECAR DRIVER FOR THE 145TH INFANTRY REGIMENT

For about ten days from when I joined the Saipan-retaking project to the time of my departure for Iwo Jima, the sidecar driver of the 145th Infantry Regiment drove me between the Imperial Japanese Army Headquarters at Ichigaya, the Convoy Escort Fleet Headquarters at Kasumigaseki, Yokohama Harbor, Shibaura Army Shipment Branch, and other places. He was a loyal and righteous man. Anyhow, he was a typical Satsuma-Hayato (a samurai of the old Kagoshima region). I visited the 145th Infantry Regimental Headquarters at Hyoryuboku twice. In both cases he came up to speak with me. I am sorry that I do not remember his name, nor do I know what became of him.

MAJOR ANDO, BATTALION COMMANDER, 145TH INFANTRY REGIMENT

I spoke with forty or fifty officers of the 145th Infantry Regiment aboard *Noto-Maru,* at Chichi Jima, and at Hyoryuboku at Iwo Jima. Major Ando was particularly amiable.[1] He regretted very much that his regiment had been unable to go to the Sunda Archipelago with the main power of the parent division, the 46th, due to the lack of shipping. From messages issued by the 145th Infantry Regiment and from stories of some survivors, Ando was said to be very brave, and his battalion inflicted heavy casualties on the enemy.

CAPTAIN OKA, IJN, CONVOY ESCORT STAFF

Captain Oka was sitting next to me in the office of the Convoy Escort Fleet Headquarters. He was a carefree naval gunner and had a special character, different from that of Captain Oi Atsushi, who was a more scholarly type. When relaxing, he used to tell dirty stories and tried to lighten things up in the dark atmosphere of the staff office.

He was assigned to our office two months after I had arrived, but since we sat next to one another and he was so amiable, we soon became drinking buddies and used to go to the Shinbashi area of Tokyo to drink. On days Japan lost many ships, we would drink until at least 11 PM. Although I suggested we go "dutch," he often paid the whole tab, saying, "My pay is bigger than yours." He did not have any children, I guess. Whenever he got drunk, he would vent his frustration that the level of Japanese technology was so low. "The enemy can fight during the night or in the fog using their radar systems, while we Japanese depend only on our bodies inherited from our parents and the Yamato-damashii [Japanese spirit]," he would say. Tears came down from his face when he spoke of Japanese crews, sailors, and troops aboard the ships who had to die due to handicaps in technology.

After the war, I heard the following story from some engineers. "The big obstacle in the development of Japanese technology," they said in unison, "was Yamato-damashii," a national identity that was easily enraged and easily cooled. From 1937, every warship had a radar system, but many ship captains had it removed or disconnected, saying such equipment should not be used.[2] Yamato-damashii was believed able to replace technology, as long as one kept his patience and believed. In fact, when the Japanese navy was forced to use radar in the fog in the Attu and Kiska operations, it resulted in great success.

On August 4, 1944, the Convoy *Matsu* (Pine Tree) operation, consisting of two transports (Nos. 4 and 132) and the destroyer *Matsu*, reached Futami Harbor, Chichi Jima, carrying the 1st Independent Machine-Gun Battalion. I brought a lot of Chichi Jima–grown watermelon by car to Captain Oka, who was with the convoy. He had two or three more officers with him, and we sat up on the deck of the ship having some soft drinks. The biggest watermelon was offered for us, and the others were given to the sailors.

I asked Captain Oka to take a letter addressed to my wife that I passed to him, which included about two hundred yen in cash. I hoped one of the typists working at the Convoy Escort Fleet Headquarters, who lived near my house, could take it to her. He gladly accepted it. Symbolic of how serious the war situation was at the time, he did not tell any dirty jokes. While we were still talking, the warning siren suddenly sounded. He and I looked at each, and his face turned pale.

I told him to be careful, and he said he thought they should be able to get out of the harbor safely. "I will take care of that letter," he added. It was around one o'clock in the afternoon. I ran to my car and told my driver to go to the nearest air-raid shelter. But very soon thereafter the siren rang again, and the warning was over. The *Matsu* left Futami Harbor accompanying the two transports. Watching them, I prayed for their safe return. About twenty minutes later, the warning siren rang again, as sixty or seventy U.S. carrier-based aircraft assaulted Chichi Jima. I worried about Captain Oka's party. Around 2 PM, several American ships started firing on Chichi Jima. The naval gunfire continued for about an hour. After the enemy left, I motored to the naval headquarters to see the messages. One read, "We are going to attack the enemy fleet. *Matsu* Commander." This was the last one issued by the *Matsu*. Captain Oka devoted himself until the end for the Ogasawara Garrison.

FIRST LIEUTENANT KAWAI YOSHIO, COMMANDER, 21ST WELL-DRILLING COMPANY

It was probably the middle part of July 1944 when First Lieutenant Kawai visited me at the Chichi Jima detached headquarters. I discussed the problem of well drilling with him, a young respectable man, for about twenty or thirty minutes. Our talks expanded to other things as well. It was clear that he was well educated and well mannered, unlike me.

According to some survivors, Kawai was still alive until the end of May 1945, wandering from cave to cave with a military doctor, First Lieutenant Benitani Seizo, of Musashino's engineering unit. As they encircled him, the Americans called on him to surrender, but he was unable to break with Japanese custom and killed himself instead (slitting his wrist with his sword.) He was a man's man, I believe.

CAPTAIN IWAYA TAMESABURO, COMMANDER, 310TH INDEPENDENT INFANTRY BATTALION

I do not remember when Captain Iwaya arrived at Iwo Jima or whether or not he went to Iwo Jima via Chichi Jima. However, I do recall that he was a close friend of the commanders of the 304th and 308th independent Infantry Battalions at Chichi Jima. I met him several times. He was a sincere person and told me about his battalion. He also asked me about the battle lessons from Saipan and Guam. He fought with the survivors of the 109th Divisional Headquarters and the 145th Infantry Regiment in the North Sector until the end. He seems to have been good to his friends.

MAJOR TOMIYAMA MASASHI, MEDICAL DOCTOR, 109TH DIVISIONAL HEADQUARTERS

On July 1, 1944, when I arrived at Chichi Jima, Dr. Tomiyama was not in his office during the day. That night he came to my quarters with a car. Introducing himself as a doctor, of a rank corresponding to someone graduating from the forty-fifth class of the Army Academy (three years ahead of me), he asked me if I could go up to the office for a drink with him and Lieutenant Colonel Nishikawa before he headed off to Iwo Jima the next day. I thanked him for his kindness and went with him. Soon, Nishikawa came to the office as well. The doctor had already prepared a lot of beer and sake. Saying, "Tonight may be the last chance to drink," he drank quite a bit. Nishikawa and I drank a lot too.

At first we talked about the general situation of the world, the future of Japan, etc. But soon our conversation turned to field sanitation. Then Dr. Tomiyama said, "If I survive and have the chance to return home, I would like to retire from the army and open an obstetric-gynecologic hospital. Please introduce your wives and other future patients to my clinic."

We continued talking for about three hours. This was the first and last time we had the chance to drink and talk together. Afterward, I wondered if he had been transferred to Japan proper. Last year (1964), when I checked the list of the dead on Iwo Jima provided by the Ministry of Health and Welfare's Repatriation Division (Hikiage Engokyoku), I found his name. I quietly prayed for his happiness in the other world.

LIEUTENANT COLONEL NISHIKAWA HAJIME, INTELLIGENCE STAFF

Lieutenant Colonel Nishikawa Hajime was a graduate of the thirty-seventh class of the Army Academy and finished the special course of the War College. He served on the staff of Major General Osuga, commander of the Chichi Jima Fortress, before departing for Iwo Jima. I replaced him upon my arrival at Chichi Jima.

For the first two days after I arrived, he and I were always together. We talked and drank, including at the get-together with Dr. Tomiyama. As Lieutenant General Kuribayashi believed strongly in the tactics taught by the graduates of the War College, graduates of the special courses usually did not participate in the discussions about tactics. However, Nishikawa was not like the others and was not afraid to speak up. Particularly in connection with the use of antiaircraft guns, he sharply disagreed with me. Eventually he sought the aid of Commander Mase of the navy, and Colonel Kaido, the commanding officer of the artillery brigade. My opinion was that we should not worry so much about fighting off the enemy aircraft and instead place the antiaircraft guns in caves and aim them at formations of enemy tanks and ground troops. He dismissed my opinion, saying that "only artillerists can understand how artillery should be used."

I stayed on Iwo Jima for only a short time, but the arguments between Nishikawa and me were quite serious. However, we did not take the disagreements personally. He even confided that he missed the more peaceful life at Chichi Jima and, because he suffered from piles, hoped I would replace him on Chichi Jima as soon as my work providing sea transportation was over.

FIRST LIEUTENANT MORITA TOYOKICHI, SIGNAL COMMANDER, 109TH DIVISION

The signal company of the 109th Division came to Chichi Jima in September 1944. Its arrival was right after my return to Chichi Jima from my trip to Iwo Jima (and then back and forth to Tokyo). First Lieutenant Morita stayed at Chichi Jima for a while. As some of his subordinates were on Chichi Jima, he was able to justify his being there.

He came by to visit almost every day. He asked that I help his headquarters at Chichi Jima, because Chichi Jima was the center of the divisional operation area. I told him that I agreed it made sense from the perspective of radio communications but that because the signal company is just like a part of the divisional headquarters and with the main power of the divisional headquarters now at Iwo Jima, I believed he should first go to Iwo Jima and speak with Lieutenant Colonel Nishikawa and Colonel Hori, the chief of staff. Upon going to Iwo Jima he sent me word that he was having difficulties, as the telephone lines were constantly being cut by the enemy air raids.

After the beginning of the enemy's preinvasion shelling, the telephone lines were rendered unusable, and they had to rely on about fifty wireless radios and orderlies for liaison purposes. What's more, because the divisional headquarters reported that it took an orderly eight hours to move one kilometer during the evenings, I believe it was very difficult for communication to take place.

At the beginning of March 1945, the No. 1 radio (the largest one at Iwo Jima, which could directly communicate with Tokyo) was destroyed. Then, Iwo Jima used the No. 3 and No. 5 radios. (The No. 3 radio could communicate with Chichi Jima. The No. 5 radio began to be used around the middle part of March 1945.) At the end of the Iwo Jima operation, the biggest trouble for the communication unit was that there was little time between burning the codebooks, breaking the radios, and joining the banzai charge. I can only imagine Lieutenant Morita's face at this point.

FIRST LIEUTENANT FUJITA MASAYOSHI, ADJUTANT TO GENERAL KURIBAYASHI

Fujita, a modern youth, wearing glasses, was liked by Lieutenant General Kuribayashi. He had been picked up by the general in the Tokyo Division before they came to Iwo Jima. He was a well-educated boy from a good family and a graduate of Aoyama Gakuin University.

Lieutenant General Kuribayashi and I dined alone together five times. Each time Fujita saw to the cooking and carried the food and drinks. Although I told him to sit with us, he used to demur, saying "Yes, a little later," and instead concentrated on getting the food served. It was some time in December 1944, I recall, that he suddenly came to my office at Chichi Jima. He came there for personnel-related matters of the 1st Mixed Brigade. During his stay of two or three days, I took extra-good care of him, treating him like a VIP, in order to repay him for his kindness at Iwo Jima. The fresh vegetables and well water, as well as the chance to take a bath, pleased him very much. To my regret, whenever he was in the bath, the air-raid siren used to ring, making it necessary for him to get out of the bath. He wanted his general to also be able to experience the bath, taste the fresh vegetables, and drink the well water.

In those days the supply of food at Iwo Jima was low. (There was enough for twenty-five days in the middle part of December.) I hoped to increase the level to about a two-month supply through sea transports at night. If I could do that, I wanted to go to Iwo Jima myself. Then, I could join Fujita and Lieutenant General Kuribayashi at supper again, I told him. When I said I thought the enemy might go to Okinawa and the Chinese mainland, he responded, "Lieutenant General Kuribayashi says the enemy will come to Iwo Jima without fail." Most of the staff officers and adjutants were rather cool toward the general, but Fujita adored him, and they were quite close.

SADAOKA NOBUYOSHI, WHO FOLLOWED GENERAL KURIBAYASHI

Sadaoka was a middle-aged man from Kochi Prefecture in Shikoku who had worked, I heard, for Lieutenant General Kuribayashi as a tailor when the latter was the chief of staff of the Southern China Army in Canton, China, and again for him in Tokyo, while the general was the commander of the Tokyo Division. It was around the end of August 1944 when he suddenly appeared at my headquarters on Chichi Jima and said to me, "I came here as a civilian to work for Lieutenant General Kuribayashi. I would like to be sent to Iwo Jima." I asked him how he had gotten to Chichi Jima. He told me that he had waited for a sea transport for a week at Shibaura Harbor in Tokyo and finally was able to board one coming here. I asked him why he had come to such a dangerous area. "I want to work for Lieutenant General Kuribayashi." I responded that as a civilian he could find work on the mainland of Japan, but he pleaded to be sent to Iwo Jima. I was moved by his sincerity but told him, "I doubt you could reach Iwo Jima. I don't want you to get killed on the way there. Wait for a while. I will ask Lieutenant General Kuribayashi by radio what to do about you."

I sent a message to the general about this problem. His answer was to persuade him to return to Japan proper. In connection with this case, I was moved once again by the greatness of the general, and I was surprised by the close relationship between these two persons.

REAR ADMIRAL ICHIMARU RINOSUKE, 27TH AIR DIVISION

Ichimaru Rinosuke was a graduate of the forty-first class of the Naval Academy, I am told, which would have corresponded to the twenty-sixth class of the Army Academy. He was one of the best pilots the Japanese navy had. According to his widow, Ichimaru had helped establish the Navy Pilot Training School at Oppama, in Yokosuka, Kanagawa Prefecture, and for five years had been the first department chief of the school. He liked to write poems, thirty-one-syllable Japanese odes *(tanka)* and seventeen-syllable verses *(haiku)* but was otherwise a taciturn and sober person. In the army-navy conferences, which I attended only twice, he did not speak except in rare cases, and his answers were a brief and formal "yes" or "no."

I visited his headquarters several times. He had his staff do the talking, and he did not say much. But he was not unsociable by any means. To begin with, despite having been sent from Kisarazu as the commander of the Naval Air Force, he had no planes and was forced to fight a ground battle. How sad he must have been. Furthermore, the number of officers and men under his direct command was very small, and antiaircraft gun units, radar units, and construction units had composed the main naval power. In the second army-navy meeting I attended, when the distribution of army and navy strength was being discussed, I had proposed that naval personnel should be distributed equally to each sector. The admiral answered, however, "The navy has its own traditions, and we would like to die together at the same place, so I wish the army would allow the main part of navy personnel to fight and die together between Tamanayama and the southern beach." He had a clear humanism about him, as seen in these words. I found myself keeping quiet, and General Kuribayashi approved his wishes. As a result, the main power of the navy was to be concentrated between the South Sector and the East Sector.

According to messages from Lieutenant General Kuribayashi, the admiral moved to Kuribayashi's shelter with his staff on March 16, 1945, and joined the banzai charge. According to a survivor, Ichimaru was separated from army and navy officers after the charge. With a sergeant of the 109th Division Signal Company, Ichimaru exploded some grenades in the middle of a concentration of enemy trucks near the southern beach. Afterward, he gathered some of the surviving navy personnel and continued fighting. I do not know about his last moments.[3]

COMMANDER MASE TAKEJI, NAVAL SENIOR STAFF

Mase Takeji entered the Naval Academy from the fourth grade of Hiroshima Middle School. He was a graduate of the fifty-seventh Naval Academy class. When I visited the naval headquarters on Iwo Jima first, it was he who gave me the ice cream, mischievously saying, "Don't tell anybody else." At that time, there was only one ice-cream-making machine on Iwo Jima. He was tight-lipped and used to make others speak before he would answer.

I once was having dinner with him in the army staff room when Commander Urabe came from Kisarazu, and the army and navy had our heated discussion over tactics. I also met him five or six more times at his headquarters and talked for twenty or thirty minutes every time, eating ice cream.

LIEUTENANT COMMANDER OKAZAKI SADAMU, NAVAL SUPPLY STAFF

I stayed for several days on Iwo Jima in August 1944. I met Lieutenant Commander Okazaki Sadamu every day during this time. He later visited Chichi Jima, and we had dinner with the other navy personnel at the Chichi Jima naval headquarters. He repeated many times that he was not suited for the supply staff's job, as he was a graduate of the Naval Engineering Academy. He said, "I would like to have a plane or warship. Then, I could utilize my techniques. Now my job is mainly to distribute dynamite and ammunitions. How dreadful." He was quite passionate about his other skills, however.

During the fighting on Iwo Jima, he entered Lieutenant General Kuribayashi's cave with Rear Admiral Ichimaru on March 16 and joined the banzai charge the next day, but I do not know what happened to him after that.

LIEUTENANT COMMANDER AKADA KUNIO, GROUND BATTLE STAFF

In August 1944, I went to Iwo Jima again and met Lieutenant Commander Akada Kunio for the first time. He was a young man, still a navy lieutenant at the time, and full of fighting spirit.

He constantly asked me about ground tactics, saying, "As the military training given at my middle school and the ground tactics taught at the Naval Academy were lacking, please teach me." When I told him that tactical ideas in ship battles are quite different from those on land and that naval weaponry is quite different from that of the army, he responded, "That is my point." His determination to learn about the army was quite clear.

I said, "Unlike the army, the navy is rich and has many weapons. How to use them will affect your value to the battle as well as the effec-

tiveness of the delaying actions of the Iwo Jima Garrison as a whole."
Again, he declared, "That's my point," the determination clear on his
face. He and Lieutenant Commander Okazaki were friendly, but their
thinking and attitudes were very much in contrast. I mentioned that I
thought the effects of the battle would be greater if the navy were to
transfer one hundred antiaircraft guns to the army for a ground battle.
He shook his head and said, "But, it, but . . . ," and sighed, finally saying, "What an interesting idea you have."

When Commander Urabe and I had our heated exchange, Akada
did not say anything, but he later approached me and told me he was
very much surprised at the large difference in thinking between the
army and the navy. I felt quite attached to him and came to see him like
a younger brother.

He entered Lieutenant General Kuribayashi's cave on March 16
with Rear Admiral Ichimaru, but it is unclear what happened to him
afterward.

COLONEL TAKAISHI TADASHI, CHIEF OF STAFF, 109TH DIVISION
A graduate of the thirtieth class of the Army Academy, Takaishi Tadashi
was an infantry officer and a graduate of the special course of the War
College. Since he arrived at Iwo Jima at the end of December 1944, I did
not directly meet him. Every day, we exchanged messages, so I came to
know his character. In the middle of January 1945, I injured my right
leg, having fallen from my horse. He immediately sent a letter of sympathy. He had written it by hand with a brush, and his penmanship and
his way with words were quite wonderful. To my regret, I subsequently
misplaced the letter.

He was an expert on infantry tactics. Together with Lieutenant
Colonel Nakane, operations staff, he was of great help to Lieutenant
General Kuribayashi, I heard. He was courageous even after the banzai
charge, and it seems that he committed suicide using his pistol with
Lieutenant General Kuribayashi and Lieutenant Colonel Nakane at the
entrance to a cave on the morning of March 27.

LIEUTENANT COLONEL NAKANE KANEJI, OPERATIONS STAFF
Nakane Kaneji was a graduate of Toyohashi Middle School, in Aichi
Prefecture, and then of the thirty-fifth class of the Army Academy. He
was first assigned to the 18th Infantry Regiment in Toyohashi. He is
said to have walked quite a distance every day when attending the
middle school and was very obedient to his parents. He received a pres-

ent from the emperor upon graduation from the Infantry School. Later he finished the special course of the War College. He was bold and was called the "god of infantry tactics." He achieved the fifth degree in Japanese fencing *(kendo)*. I was told by one survivor that from the time of the enemy's landing to his eventual suicide, Nakane was always calm and was the pillar of morale for the divisional headquarters.

He departed mainland Japan for Iwo Jima on November 6, 1944. He left two daughters, a nine-year-old and nine-month-old. I could tell from reading, after the war, the letters he sent to his wife from Iwo Jima that he was not only obedient to his parents but also very kind to his wife and children.

MAJOR YOSHIDA MONZO, FORTIFICATION STAFF

A graduate of the forty-third Army Academy class, Major Yoshida Monzo also finished the special course of the War College. He directed fortifications and was vigorous in executing his duties. He was unafraid to air his complaints. Once he was angry at Lieutenant General Kuribayashi because the general corrected the defensive positions that Yoshida had made. For a while, he had also served on the staff of an army air force in Japan proper and argued quite forcefully that the army should send aircraft to the No. 2 and No. 3 airfields on Iwo Jima. Around March 10, 1945, I read the following message originating from Iwo Jima: "We had expected many aircraft would be sent to Iwo Jima. Our men exerted much effort into expanding the airfields, all in vain." The frustration in his message to Tokyo was on par with his ability to complain.

There is a rumor that during the banzai charge on March 17, Lieutenant General Kuribayashi ordered Yoshida to save himself and try to make it to the mainland to report on the situation in Iwo Jima and that until the end of May or so he sought to leave Iwo Jima by raft. Failing, he and a navy lieutenant snuck onto the runway and got into an American airplane and tried to fly off to the mainland, but they were shot and killed before they could take off.

MAJOR YAMANOUCHI YASUTAKE, INTELLIGENCE STAFF

Major Yamanouchi Yasutake was a cavalry officer and graduate of the forty-seventh class of the Army Academy. He was ordered to Iwo Jima right after his graduation from the War College at the end of December 1944. Due to a problem with his aircraft, he landed on Chichi Jima and stayed with me one night at my headquarters before going on to Iwo Jima.

He seemed to be a boy from a good family but seemed rather piti-ful. I often still think of him.

LIEUTENANT COLONEL NISHI TAKEICHI, COMMANDER, 26TH TANK REGIMENT

Nishi Takeichi was a graduate of the 36th class of the Army Academy, and he was so famous as an Olympic horse rider that even children knew of him.

I met Nishi for the first time when he visited me at the Chichi Jima detached headquarters after the ship carrying his tanks and regiment was sunk. Of course, I already knew his name. I was impressed when we met by the following two things I saw in his posture. When I saw him I was impressed that he seemed to be both a tough man yet an aristocratic gentleman, with long legs. These two contrasting qualities blended harmoniously in Nishi. During our talks he confessed that he was a heavy drinker and told me how much he drank in Hokkaido and Manchuria. So I knew that, however rude I was in thinking it, I had been correct in seeing that he had a tough—or better said, rough—side.

In the middle of August 1944, when I was getting on an airplane at Kisarazu Airfield headed for Iwo Jima on my way back following the trip to Tokyo, I ran into him by chance. He was returning to Iwo Jima after spending a month in Tokyo gathering tanks in Japan proper. We became close on the plane ride. When we arrived at Iwo Jima, we went to his headquarters to have lunch. I talked to him one last time after that when we met on the road on Iwo Jima.

According to a story told to his family by a survivor of the battle, his attitude during the fighting was magnificent. He eventually com-mitted suicide on the coast somewhere, facing Tokyo. I am not sure whether the story that the U.S. Marines called to him and personally asked him to surrender is true or not. On the other hand, everyone in that battle, whether he was a general, a private, or a lieutenant colonel, is a hero and should be missed. Thus, Nishi alone should not be taken up. However, being a world-class equestrian, it is no doubt that he is missed.

Last year (1964), during the Olympic games held in Tokyo, some Americans visited Nishi's family and talked about his life and times.

COLONEL HORI SHIZUICHI, FORMER CHIEF OF STAFF, 109TH DIVISION

Hori was a graduate of the twenty-ninth class of the Army Academy and mainly worked with railways. He finished the special course of the

War College. He was good at listening to others carefully and taking notes. He was modest, but he did seem proud of his big moustache.

They had seemed to be close at one point, and I am not sure why the relationship between Lieutenant General Kuribayashi and him became bad. When I went to Iwo Jima the second time in August 1944, relations between them had reached their lowest point. Both of them had their strong points, but they just were not getting along. This is true of any family, any military command (including in U.S. military commands), especially when they live together, eat together, and work together for twenty-four hours a day on an isolated island. Relations become either very good or very bad in that sort of situation. Hori was eventually replaced, on December 30, by Colonel Takaishi and was sadly transferred to the 2nd Mixed Brigade Headquarters.

It is said that he was either killed during the brigade's banzai charge on the morning of March 9 or that he continued to live until May in caves. I myself found him to be a friendly, kind, and gentle man. However, his story was, it is true, somewhat tragic.

COLONEL ATSUCHI KANEHIKO, COMMANDER, MOUNT SURIBACHI SECTOR

In the spring of 1944, Colonel Atsuchi Kanehiko was ordered to be in charge of the defense of Iwo Jima with about a thousand army troops. Under the command of Major General Osuga, then Chichi Jima Fortress commander, Atsuchi made his defensive positions a little farther in from the beaches. In May 1944, after the visit made by Lieutenant General Obata Hideyoshi, 31st Army commander, and Major General Tamura Yoshitomi, assistant chief of staff to the commander in chief, Central Pacific Fleet, Colonel Atsuchi had to move his defensive positions to comply with their instructions. Then, by order of Lieutenant General Kuribayashi, he had to move the defensive lines again, this time inland. As a result, he lost the trust of his subordinates. However, he was ordered to be in charge of the Mount Suribachi Sector, so it can be said he was given a good place to die as a soldier.

Atsuchi was born in Kagoshima Prefecture and had an unyielding spirit. I remember he told me to get more dynamite.

MAJOR GENERAL OSUGA KOTAU, COMMANDER, 2ND MIXED BRIGADE

A graduate of the twenty-seventh class of the Army Academy, Osuga Kotau was an artillery officer. He finished the War College too and was a conservative gentleman. He was a typical officer, who listened to his subordinates and approved their plans. He was a good contrast to Lieutenant General Kuribayashi, who liked to make decisions himself and lead the way. Kuribayashi recognized this and used to say that his style had been learned when he studied with the U.S. Army. Osuga was particularly friendly with Colonel Kaido, artillery commander, and Colonel Hori. I visited his headquarters twice, and by coincidence all three of them were there together having tea both times.

In December 1944, Osuga was replaced by Major General Senda Sadasue, commandant of the Sendai Reserve Officers Academy. Osuga was transferred to Lieutenant General Kuribayashi's headquarters but was hospitalized in the field hospital due to illness. Once it was rumored that he had been flown back to Japan by air before the enemy landed. But it seems that in fact he died during the fighting when he was still in the field hospital.

chapter eighteen

TRAGIC ISLAND, IWO JIMA

PROTECTING THE WAR CRIMINALS

In the end, the enemy did not come to Chichi Jima. It was very sad for me that so many of my senior and fellow members of the Japanese armed forces were killed on Iwo Jima. I could not do anything from Chichi Jima. The war was over on August 15, 1945. Frankly, I was satisfied that Japan at least waited to surrender after Germany. However, I did have mixed feelings. Some readers might be surprised, but Japan could have continued the war for a long time without naval and air power. However, I don't want to overstress this point: as the war had ended without any hostile invasion of the mainland, arrogant and shortsighted people in Japan might start saying that Japan was in fact never defeated.

On September 3, 1945, we signed the local instrument of surrender aboard USS *Dunlap*, off Chichi Jima. The next day, we began preparing for the evacuation of our troops and repair work on the roads, docks, and airfield, etc. That day I threw the potassium cyanide I had acquired in 1944 into the sea. The issue I most worried about was the problem of the abuse of American prisoners by some of the officers and other men. Although there were no perpetrators from my detached head-quarters, some suspects were found in other army and navy units. All senior members were confined, and I was ordered to be the regular representative of the Japanese army and navy by the U.S. occupation forces. Fortunately, both out of necessity and in light of the fact that I had had a chance to study English with the American prisoners, who were very good at teaching (see chapter 8), I had little trouble negotiating in English with the U.S. forces. Moreover, the prisoners who taught me English protected me from the war crimes trials. No one called me the "pessimistic staff officer" any more.

After six months, when about 17,000 army and navy personnel had been evacuated to the Japanese mainland, a tank landing ship (LST) lay at Omura Pier to take twenty-five war criminal suspects and forty-five witnesses to Guam for war crimes trials. The ship left Chichi Jima on April 6, 1946, with its seventy Japanese passengers, heading for Guam.

All of the suspects and witnesses (including myself) were without the protection of the Japanese government and were at the mercy of our former enemy. After our landing in Guam, other suspects and witnesses arrived from Truk, Wake, and other places, to make a total number of sixty-three suspects and sixty-three witnesses. The suspects were placed in solitary cells inside the stockade, surrounded by barbed wire, and the sixty-three witnesses were put in three tents outside the stockade. I was ordered to be in charge of the witness camp and was sometimes asked to be a witness or interpreter.

The only task left for us sixty-three witnesses was to speak in defense of the suspects. The American investigation had been able to contact thousands of people related to the respective cases, and much evidence and documentation had been gathered. I myself translated several hundred petitions, but to my regret, they were not very effective. Thinking about the war criminals and their families, I had to be disappointed by the tragedy deriving from the failure to teach international law in the schools and colleges and the general tendency in Japan to mistreat the individual. I was also sad about the loss of Japan's sovereignty as a result of the Allied occupation.

YESTERDAY'S ENEMY ON IWO JIMA IS TODAY'S FRIEND

By October 1946, the Guam war crimes trials, conducted by the Commander, Marianas Command, were over. I was sent to Uraga, near Yokohama, with the other sixty-two witnesses and was demobilized there. As someone with no property and only a partially crippled body with which to make my way, I had to find work.

I immediately went to General Headquarters, Supreme Commander, Allied Powers (SCAP, GHQ), to see Major Robert Shaffer, who had served as the executive officer, 1st Battalion, U.S. Marine Corps occupation forces, Chichi Jima. I asked him if he could find a job for me in GHQ. He called a "Captain B——," the labor officer, and asked him to come to his office with the GHQ employee roster. When Captain B—— came to his office, Major Shaffer asked him to find a job for "this friend from the battlefield." Captain B—— responded, "All important positions in GHQ have been occupied by Nisei (Japanese Americans), and there is no vacancy for Major Horie. However, there are four positions for interpreters at Tachikawa Air Base." As Tachikawa Air Base is in a somewhat inconvenient location, being outside of Tokyo, I asked them to give me a night to think it over and went home. My wife said, "There are many former officers living on sales of their own medals and clothes. There is no other choice but this job." The next morning, I went to GHQ again, and, with Major Shaffer's recommendation, I went to Tachikawa Air Base to take the interpreter's job. At the time, there were about seven thousand American and six thousand Japanese working there.

My supervisor was Lieutenant Colonel George L. Huffman, who was a year older than I. We shared many tales of war and became quite close. He had served in the European theater as a pilot. When I mentioned Iwo Jima, he asked me if I had known Lieutenant General Kuribayashi. I was surprised and said that I used to be on his staff. After that, we talked exclusively about the Iwo Jima campaign. During our talk, he whispered to a beautiful typist sitting near him. As I was leaving, he handed me a "mess pass" that the typist had prepared at his request, saying, "This is our present to yesterday's enemy and today's friend." Also, he told me, I would be authorized to have transportation. The base motor pool had been given the word. He shook my hand warmly. In those days, the food situation was bad, but I was lucky enough to be able to eat for three years in the American military's dining hall and to have a car take me to and from work. I was promoted from interpreter to supervisor, to office manager, and then to advisor. In those days there were only four slots for advisors at Tachikawa Air Base. He introduced me to Brigadier General John P. Doyle, commanding general of the base, then to Colonel William R. Morgan, 6100th Air Wing commander. Doyle, Morgan, and I often met to talk about Iwo Jima. I still thank the souls of the perished personnel on Iwo Jima, because I believe their help has brought about the kind treatment I received at Tachikawa Air Base by these American officers.

In those days, Tachikawa Air Base was growing, and I was able to help out some 430 families by seeing to the hiring of fifty-one former regular army and navy officers and members of the bereaved families at the base. This was my small way of repaying the help of the perished personnel of Iwo Jima.

After the armistice was signed on the Korean Peninsula in the summer of 1953, Iwo Jima came under the command of Tachikawa Air Base. Brigadier General Doyle's successor, Major General Paul E. Ruestow, made plans to go to Iwo Jima and bring me with him. However, due to difficulties in my getting a passport and the fear that something might happen to me, the trip was canceled.[1] Instead, the Air Force's commander on Iwo Jima still stops by to see me when he comes to Tachikawa Air Base.

SHARING ROCKS FROM IWO JIMA WITH THE BEREAVED FAMILIES

As I had become friendly with Major General Ruestow, deputy commander Brigadier General William T. Hudnell, Colonel Herbert Sears, the chief of Information Services and Personnel, and Major Garold B. Ritchie, Colonel Sears's assistant, I submitted the following suggestions regarding Iwo Jima, which they accepted: (1) retrieve rocks from Iwo Jima and distribute them to bereaved families in place of their loved one's remains; (2) employ Lieutenant General Kuribayashi's son Taro at Tachikawa Air Base; and (3) invite some (less than ten) former Japanese army and navy officers to movies at the base.

A pilot subsequently flew unofficially to Iwo Jima and brought back a big rock, which was cut by Major Ritchie into several pieces with a saw. Brigadier General Hudnell invited the wives of the late Lieutenant General Kuribayashi, Colonel Takaishi, Lieutenant Colonel Nakane, Lieutenant Colonel Nishi, and Major Yamanouchi, as well as my wife, to the base for the ceremony. Nakajima Shunji, mayor of Tachikawa City, was also invited. Pieces of the rock were presented to the widows by Mr. Nakajima, and the remaining part was given to my wife for the other bereaved families. They were distributed to the bereaved families at the Iwo Jima Memorial ceremony held at the Yasukuni Shrine in 1964.

Kuribayashi Taro, the son of Lieutenant General Kuribayashi, has been working at Tachikawa Air Base as an architect, occupying an important position.[2] For the movie showings, Lieutenant Generals Iimura Jo, Shibayama Kaneshiro, Nakamura Akihito, and Teshima Fusataro attended from the former Imperial Japanese Army, and Rear Admiral Horie and Captain Oi represented the Imperial Japanese Navy. Admiral Oikawa was also invited but at the last minute could not attend. General Imamura declined, saying that he would not be able to attend for the time being, as he was serving as an advisor to the Self-Defense Forces, the postwar military of Japan.

I believe the above events were good for the friendship between both countries. U.S. personnel pay attention to and respect the souls of both Americans and Japanese who were killed on Iwo Jima. My heart is filled with deep emotion as I look back on the past twenty years.

afterword

Several years ago, a Mrs. Takeoka Yuki wrote me a letter asking if I knew her son, Kanichi, who had been twenty-three years old in 1944 and who had belonged to the Special Secret Service Unit (Tokumu Kikan) on Iwo Jima. On March 17, 1963, when a memorial ceremony for the perished personnel of Iwo Jima was held at the Yasukuni Shrine in Tokyo, I was asked the following questions after my small speech.[1]

A young lady said to me, "My father was a first lieutenant. He loved me very much. He went to Iwo Jima when I was eight years old. What did my father look like when he was serving on Iwo Jima?"

A middle-aged lady asked me, "My older brother was a sergeant named Matsuno. He was from Saitama Prefecture. He went to Chichi Jima. Then, he wrote home that he was leaving there for Iwo Jima. Did you meet my brother?"

A girl of about twenty years old mentioned: "As I was a baby, I only saw pictures of my father, and I don't remember his face. Did he have a moustache on Chichi Jima and Iwo Jima?"

When I heard these questions, I could not stop weeping. The bereaved families were very anxious to know any and all things about their fathers and brothers. It was very hard for me to say, "I don't know." I felt like I was committing a crime by not giving them something more to hold on to, but I could not make up a story and tell a lie.

When I tried to crack some rocks from Iwo Jima with a hammer to distribute to the bereaved families, hundreds of people ran up to me to get a piece. Some of them wept, grasping for some fragments of the stone. Others just looked at the stone. Some pieces were wrapped in a cloth, and a lady put some dust from the stone on her cheek. There were tears, tears, and more tears. It is natural that everyone wants to know about the last moments of his or her child, husband, father, brother, or nephew. Today, years after the war, it is particularly sad that they do not know much about their losses. This is true of the American side as well, which emerged victorious. A writer (and later editor) with the *Saturday Evening Post* named Clay Blair Jr. interviewed Baron Nishi's widow during the recent Olympics in Tokyo (October 1964) and told her of a friend who had three sons who died in the war, one of whom died on Iwo.[2] Every country's sadness is similar to others.

Finally, I have two things I would like to ask the public. My first question is, "Is it all right for us to leave the bereaved people as they are?" My second question is, "How can we use the tragedy of Iwo Jima to prevent war in the future?"

In connection with the first question, has Japan sufficiently paid attention to those that perished? There are unknown soldiers' tombs in the United States, West Germany, the Soviet Union, etc. Each tomb is visited not only by the people of that country, but also by foreign dignitaries as well. What is the Japanese tomb? The Yasukuni Shrine?

In foreign countries, the bereaved families are well taken care of. In Japan, why are they given such meager pensions and poor treatment?

In connection with the latter question, why they are given such meager pensions and poor treatment, we must analyze Japanese tradition and improve on it. We must think about the problems emerging from the history of feudalism. While European countries expanded their territories abroad and established faits accomplis, Japan in those days, under the Tokugawa Shogunate, adopted a self-imposed seclusion policy. Historians say that the seclusion policy was adopted simply to protect the interests of the Tokugawa family exclusively and not for the nation as a whole. This policy ended up limiting the growth of Japan, and my generation ended up fighting to seek its expansion in the twentieth century.

Second is the tragedy that derived from the independence of the supreme command over the military. Modern countries place the military under political control when conducting war. In Japan, the prerogative of supreme command was independent of political control. The war had to be a national effort, fought at great distances. The decision to start the war, war advocacy, even the nonmilitary aspects of society were handled by the military. While the military is partly to blame, the system itself was most at fault.

Third is the tragedy originating from the education system. There was a trend to underestimate the capabilities and national wills of foreign countries and to overestimate those of Japan. This failure to understand other countries and cultures directly contradicted the principle of Sun Tzu, the great Chinese strategist, who said, "A general who knows both of the enemy and himself will always win the war." Japan did not know itself or others; it did not teach its people the truth about the populations, terrains, resources, industries, cultures, etc., of the other major countries or the actual position of Japan in relation to them.

We cannot really blame the so-called war advocates, in that case, as they received the same type of education. There were many phrases bantered around at the time such as, "The corners of the world under one roof, under the power of the Japanese emperor" and "One thousand bamboo spears would be enough to defeat the enemy." With the outbreak of war, the government prohibited the study of foreign languages. During the war, the Japanese mistreated prisoners of war. All of these problems originated from the wrong type of education, almost like the extremes of today, when young people either worship foreigners or despise them. While overestimating the spiritual factor, the Japanese also underestimated the material factor. Thinking too much of military matters, they forgot the importance of science.

The fourth point concerns problems in our national character. Those who said they were ready to die at any moment for the country were portrayed as brave men and patriots, but if someone pointed out the inability of Japan to win, he was, no matter how objectively he spoke, labeled a coward. We tended to judge people all too suddenly and irrationally. We thought it was better to be on the offensive than on the defensive. We were too ready to believe the army, navy, and big industry, who spoke arrogantly (and incorrectly, in retrospect) of their capabilities.

Fifth is a question of humanity. Japanese tended to place too little value on human life.

What should be done? What can we do to improve our ways as a country? I believe the realization of democracy in Japan is the best route to take. If we see democracy only as a condition of surrendering to the victors or as something that was forced on us because we lost the war, then we will likely see "another Iwo Jima" or "another Hiroshima" one day.

I know it will be difficult for us to change our ways, but it will be necessary to do so in order to avoid "another Iwo Jima." It is hard for us to break with traditions, no matter how bad they may be. We must continue to deepen and expand democracy and ensure the participation of everyone in governing the country, establishing new and better traditions. By doing so, we will let those who perished as victims of the old tradition sleep in peace.

I am very much concerned with the present state of Japan, because it has come to resemble that of Germany after World War I. In those days, the people in Germany shouted, "We were politically defeated but not overcome militarily!" and they dreamed of the revival of their former proud Germany. The German people, faced with massive economic inflation and social decay, looked for a hero. They welcomed Adolf Hitler with blind enthusiasm.

It is unnecessary to describe what happened afterward to Germany led by its "hero" Hitler. Japan does not need its own "hero." Japan should not seek a dictatorship. When our children or grandchildren can truly realize democracy, Japan will have a brighter future.

appendix I
explanation of japanese defense plan of chichi jima, december 23, 1945

By Major Y. Horie

[Editors' note: In order to show Horie's efforts at learning English and to leave it in his original voice, this text has been only slightly corrected.]

CONTENTS

1. Preface

It is indeed a great honor for me to have this golden opportunity of expressing my humble opinion regarding defense plan of Chichi Jima in the presence of many American Officers. My English is very poor and I am sure you will find many difficulties in my talk. But as I should like to express what I have in my mind thoroughly I venture to make my speech in English. I should like to have your permission for my discourtesy.

2. General Situation

a. History of Bonin Islands

About seventy years ago Bonin Islands became the territory of Japan. In connection with this history, Colonel Rixey knows better than I do, so I will not touch it. At 1914, just when the World War No. 1 [*sic*] occurred General of the Army Y. Uehara, Chief of the General Staff, insisted on the importance of fortifying Chichi Jima and Amami Oshima for national defense, and began to make fortress at Chichi Jima and after several years he placed one part of the heavy artillery.

i. But as a result of the Washington Conference we were obliged to stop the reinforcement of this fortress and at the beginning of the World War No. II we had only Fortress headquarters, 24cm howitzer 4, 15cm cannon 2 and 12cm howitzer 2 in Army.

ii. On the other hand, in Navy, we constructed the radio station at 1937, and made the Air Force at 1942, and at 1943 Naval Base Headquarters.

b. Situation of Spring, 1944.

"Truk" was raided by American task force at February and Palau at March 1944. On that time our strength of Sea and Air forces became about half of that of America. Therefore Japanese Imperial Headquarters made the Central Pacific Fleet Headquarters and the Central Pacific Fleet Headquarters (Commander in Chief was Vice Admiral T. Nagumo) and the 31st Army Headquarters (Commander was Lieutenant General E. Obata) at Saipan and endeavored to reinforce the Army and Navy of the Middle Pacific area thoroughly.

Our strength of Bonin Islands at March was as follows:

	IWO	CHICHI	MUKO	HAHA
Army	3,000	3,000	500	1,000
Navy	2,000	2,000	20	500

The Commander of the 31st Army instructed the Commander of the Chichi Jima fortress to bring Army and Navy of Bonin Islands under single control.

c. Situation of Summer, 1944.

From March to June Japanese Imperial Headquarters have sent about ten divisions to Middle Pacific area and specially did their very best to strengthen Saipan, Guam and Palau, and on the other hand endeavored to reestablish our Great Fleet.

In those days, at Tokyo, we were discussing many times regarding the value of Iwo Jima. At that time I was at Tokyo being appointed as a staff officer of the 31st Army and went on board with the first group of these repossessing forces under the command of the 5th Fleet. But on 19th of June our Great Fleet was completely defeated by your 5th Fleet at 270 miles north of Yap Island and lost nearly all of the carrier planes. Then Japanese Imperial Headquarters gave up their plan of repossessing Saipan, stopped the dispatch of the 5th Fleet and determined to reinforce the Bonin Islands with this first group and some other units.

On 30th of June the 109th Divisional Headquarters was at Iwo appointing Lieutenant General Kuribayashi as the Divisional Commander and I became a staff officer of this Division. Situation of Bonin Islands at 30th of June was as follows:

Army: Army was direct under Japanese Imperial Headquarters. Lieutenant General Kuribayashi placed his forces as follows:

At Iwo—Main power of Divisional headquarters 2nd mixed brigade and other troops.

At Chichi—1st mixed brigade and other troops under the (Ani, Muko) command of Colonel MASAKI.

At Chichi Jima was the only central base of supply and communication between Japan and Bonin Islands. Lieutenant General Kuribayashi placed here the dispatched headquarters as Major Horie the head of it.

I was ordered to supply materials to each island, communicate with Tokyo and each island.

Navy: At Iwo we had the 27th Air Force under the command of the 3rd Air Fleet [at the] newly constructed Kisarazu. The Commander of Chichi Jima Naval Base place[d the] Navy of Chichi

and Haha under his single control, and he was under the command of Yokosuka Admiralty Port.
  d. Situation of January, 1945.
      Strength of Bonin Islands was as follows:

	IWO	CHICHI	ANI	MUKO	HAHA
Army	17,500	8,000	350	600	3,500
Navy	5,500	6,000			3,000

3. Defense of Chichi Jima.

  a. My judgment regarding anti enemy's plan.
      Until American forces landed on Iwo I thought American forces
      will assault Iwo and Chichi or Haha at the same time.
        When American forces occupied Iwo and went to Okinawa I
      felt that Chichi may be by-passed.
        But in order to provide against your sudden attack and for
      my honor I did my best to make this fortress much stronger.
  b. My judgment in connection with American strength and land-
      ing direction, when American forces will assault Chichi Jima.

      (Comparison with the Japanese Division)

Land forces	Army or Marine Division		3	(3)
Sea forces	Battle Ship		6	(30)
	Cruiser		15	(15)
	Destroyer		40	(8)
Air Forces	Airplanes		3,000	(43)
	Total		(about 100)	

      In connection with the landing direction, I will explain on the
      sand model.
  c. My premise regarding Defense Plan of Chichi Jima we did have
      any fleet, air force, supply and reinforcement.
  d. Approximate number of our strength, arms and ammunitions
      (Army and Navy).

Officers and men			15,000
Arms (and ammunitions)	Big guns	100	50,000
	Small guns	15,000	9,000,000
Torpedo and Suicide boats.			150

  e. Special character of my Defense Plan.

(a) Complete fortification (after three years we were able to connect each position with gallery).

(b) Make depth position from beach to the top of the mountains.

(c) No offensive operation at the seaside.

(d) No reserves.

(e) Attach importance on sniping.

(f) Use anti-aircraft gun as artillery.

f. My Estimate of Enemy's loss and our fighting term.

(a) Estimate of Enemy's loss:

(The dead)

By big guns	50,000 (one man-one round)
By small guns	90,000 (one man-100 rounds)
By suicide boats and other	10,000 (" ")
Total	150,000

(b) Fighting term.
About three months.

g. Details of defense.
Refer to my booklet.

4. Conclusion

What gave decisive block to Japan in the World War No. II were American submarines and Air Forces. Japan lost most of her Navy and transport by the American submarines and Air forces.

I pay my respects to your greatness of mass-production, superior technique, skillful movement and especially pre-eminence of joint operation. I experienced bitterly how difficult it was to defend the island when there are no fleet, no air forces and no supply coming. Even though our death and fall of this island was evident we were to continue our fighting to the last and give tremendous damage to the enemy. For this purpose we need persevering spirit. I did my best to fight for the honor, reminding Lt. Gen. Anatoly Stoessel of Russia who was in charge of the defenses of Port Arthur 45 years ago. Best of all I thank you very much for your kind attention to my humble speech.

appendix II
explanation of japanese defense plan and the battle of iwo jima, chichi jima, january 25, 1946

By Major Y. Horie
(Ex-Staff Officer of General Kuribayashi)

[Editors' note: In order to show Horie's efforts at learning English and to leave it in his original voice, this text has been only slightly corrected. For reasons uncertain, in paragraph 8, "Battle," Horie's paper reverses the order of g and h. "h. Desperate fight of Army and Navy" precedes "g. Supply from Japan by aircraft."]

CONTENTS

4. Strength, Arms and Ammunitions (Army and Navy) at the 1st of February
5. Situation of Supply
   a. System of supply
   b. Damages of ships
   c. Working of unloading and loading at Chichi Jima as supply center and unloading work at Iwo Jima
   d. Supply crisis of November 1944
   e. Provisions at February 1, 1945 (army and navy)
6. Convoy Strategy to Cover the Supply Transportation
7. Everyday Life and Sanitary Situation of Officers and Men
8. Battle
   a. Landing operation of American forces on the First Airfield and our battle
   b. Fall of Mount Suribachi
   c. Appearance of American M4 tank
   d. Value of bombardment of American air forces and vessels
   e. Battle command of Lieutenant General Kuribayashi
   f. Value of cutting-in infiltration attacks
   g. Supply from Japan by aircraft
   h. Desperate fight of army and navy
   i. The last moments of Lieutenant General Kuribayashi
9. Why Japanese Soldier Does Not Surrender
10. Conclusion

INSTRUCTIONS OF WAR TELEGRAPHED FROM LIEUTENANT GENERAL KURIBAYASHI TO THE CHIEF OF THE GENERAL STAFF
1. Preface

I will state the outline of Japanese defense plan and battle of Iwo Jima by the kind advice of an American officer.

To tell the truth, I have a very deep impression in regard to this problem, because I was concerned in defense plan of Iwo Jima and especially devoted my body and soul to its supply under my respectful Lieutenant General Kuribayashi.

And every day since American forces landed on Iwo Jima on the 19th of February, 1945, I wrote on my map of all battle reports communicated from Iwo Jima and studied tactics noting my opinions on it, but I am very sorry to say, I had burned all of them when Iwo fell and I have to pick it out from my poor memory.

I am unable to state my opinion without rending my heart to many officers and men of Japan and America who sacrificed their respectful lives.

I express my grateful thanks to Colonel Rixey (Island Commander of American Occupation Forces, Chichi Jima) and Captain Kusiak (his staff officer) for their helpful criticisms to my humble booklet.

2. General Situation
   a. History of Iwo Jima

About seventy years ago Iwo Jima became the territory of Japan with Chichi Jima and Haha Jima. But we had no special product on this island and it had been written on the geographical book as only an island of sulphur spring, no water, no sparrow, and no swallow. And it was indeed after Truk was raided by American task force at February, 1944 and our great fleet retired from there, when we (except several officers) began to think much of this island in connection with our strategy.

   b. Situation in spring 1944

In 1943 our navy constructed the First Airfield (near Mount Suribachi) on Iwo Jima and made it an intermediate aircraft base from Japan to Marianas, and used it also as an aircraft base for our convoy strategy.

In February, 1944 we had only the following strength on Iwo Jima:

Naval Air Force	1,500 men
Aircraft	20

From February to March, Japanese Imperial Headquarters increased the strength of Iwo Jima and at the end of March our army and navy were as follows:

Army	3,000
Navy	2,000

In those days army was under the command of Chichi Jima fortress and navy was under the command of Yokosuka air force.

   c. Situation in summer and autumn 1944

From March to June Japanese Imperial Headquarters has sent about ten divisions to middle Pacific area and especially did their very best to strengthen Saipan, Guam, and Palau and endeavored to reestablish our great fleet.

On the other hand Japanese Imperial Headquarters came to recognize the value of Iwo Jima and began to study what exis-

tence influence of this isolated island does to the main land of
Japan when Marianas fell to the enemy's hand.

From March to June the Chichi Jima fortress commander was
under the command of the 31st Army of Saipan, and army and
navy of Bonin Islands was under the single control of Chichi
Jima fortress commander.

June 15, American forces landed on Saipan and on 19th our
great fleet was defeated by American 5th Fleet at 270 sea miles
north of Yap Island. And Japanese Imperial Headquarters gave
up their plan of repossessing Saipan and determined to reinforce Iwo Jima with a part of this repossessing strength.

On 15th of June about one hundred of our naval aircraft were
defeated by the first American air raids.

In those days we did not have any strong defense fortifications this island and it was as hazardous as a pile of eggs. At
that time if American forces had assaulted Iwo Jima, it would be
completely occupied in two or three days.

On 30th of June Japanese Imperial Headquarters made the
109th Division appointing Lieutenant General Kuribayashi on
the same day.

On the other hand, at the end of June, navy made the 3rd
Aircraft Fleet at Kisarazu and brought the air force of Iwo Jim
under the command of this fleet as the 27th Air Force.

We had the following army strength to be sent to Iwo Jima
from Chichi Jima after July:

145TH INFANTRY REGIMENT

3RD BATTALION OF THE 17TH MIXED REGIMENT

26TH TANK REGIMENT

Antitank-Gun Independent Battalion	5
Machine-Gun Independent Battalion	2
Mortar Company	1
Rocket-Gun Company	1
Assault Company	1
25-mm Machine-Gun Company	2
Other units	
Total	about 14,000 men

But enemy's disturbances by air forces and submarines were severe and we had bad weather many times, so the transportation
of this strength by sea delayed and continued to the very time
American forces landed on Iwo Jima.

Lieutenant General Kuribayashi placed the detached headquarters at Chichi Jima as Major Horie the head of it, and made
him in charge of transportation, supply and communication.

The navy also increased its strength on Iwo Jima by crushing
many difficulties.

d. Chief persons
(a) Lieutenant General Kuribayashi
(Commander, 109th Division)
Graduated Military Academy and Military College, cavalry
officer. Stayed in Canada for two years. Had a long service
in the War Office and mostly appointed as staff officer.

He was a poet, and wrote "Aiba Koshin Kyoku" (a song
of loving horses) and "Aikoku Koshin Kyoku" (a song of
loving his nation).

At Iwo Jima, one night, I talked with him thoroughly,
and he told me as follows: "When I was in Canada I went to
the United States and saw many factories. I pay my respects
to the greatness of American mass-production. I think that
'Victory or Defeat' of this War will be decided by the production power. Don't you think so?"

(b) Major General Osuga
(Ex-Commander of 2nd Mixed Brigade)
Graduated Military Academy and Military College, artillery
officer. Appointed as the Chichi Jima fortress commander in
March, 1944, from Kyurun fortress commander.

Appointed as the commander of 2nd Mixed Brigade on
30th of June when the 109th Division was made. In December, entered in field hospital of Iwo Jima, suffering from
paratyphus.

Had gentle and quiet personality.

(c) Major General Senda
(Commander of 2nd Mixed Brigade)
Appointed as the commander of 2nd Mixed Brigade in
December, 1944 as successor of Major General Osuga from
commander of Sendai Reserve Military Academy.

Graduated Military Academy. Served in Infantry School,
School for Noncommissioned Officers, etc. Had experience
of infantry regimental commander. Well acquainted with infantry battle.

(d) Colonel Hori (ex–Chief of Staff)
Graduated Military Academy and special course of Military

College. Had experience of teacher of Military Academy, infantry regimental commander and chief of staff of Homeland Division.

Appointed as the chief of staff of the 109th Division on 30th June. Was discharged from this position and was attached to the 2nd Mixed Brigade headquarters in December, 1944.

Had gentle and quiet personality.

(e) Col. Takahashi (Chief of Staff)

Graduated Military Academy and Special Course of Military College, Infantry Officer.

Appointed as the successor of Colonel Hori in December.

Well acquainted with infantry battle, very energetic and was a poet.

(f) Staff Officers (from old to young by age).

Lieutenant Colonel Nakane—Operation Staff.

Lieutenant Colonel Nishikawa—Supply Staff.

Major Yoshida—Fortification Staff.

Major Yamanouchi—Intelligence Staff.

Major Horie—head of Chichi Jima Detached Headquarters.

(g) Lieutenant Colonel Nishi.

(Commander of the 26th Tank Regiment)

Baron, cavalry officer, a champion of Olympic Horse Games.

(h) Rear Admiral Ichimaru

Graduated Naval Academy. Famous pilot of Naval Air Force.

(i) Naval Staff Officers.

Commander Mase—Senior and Operation Staff.

Lieutenant Commander Okazaki—Supply Staff.

Lieutenant Commander Akada—Defense Staff.

3. Defense Plan of Iwo Jima

a. Many discussions regarding the defense plan of Iwo Jima

Iwo Jima was very near to the main land of Japan and was able to place many aircraft. Then we thought much of this island and discussed the value of it many times at Tokyo and Iwo Jima.

First, at Iwo Jima, some officers said as follows: "We will not be left as an isolated force, we can keep on fighting by expecting the assistance of air forces and fleets from the main land of Japan, so the plan should be an offensive defense."

At Tokyo, some officers said as follows: "We must make a plan how to use this Iwo Jima and need not be anxious about the fall of Iwo Jima."

At that time, I, Major Horie, was one of the officers who observed the situation of this War most pessimistically and insisted on my opinion as follows: "Now we have no fleet and no air forces. If American forces will assault this island it will fall into their hands in one month.

"Therefore it is absolutely necessary not to let the enemy use this island. The best plan is to sink this island in the sea or cut the island in half. At least we must endeavor to sink the First Airfield.

"In the future, if by any chance we have an opportunity to take an offensive step again in the Pacific area, we will not use Iwo Jima."

At the General Staff Office and the Naval Staff Office, there were some officers who had the same ideas. Especially one staff officer asked me to calculate the necessary explosive quantity to sink Iwo Jima.

Lieutenant General Kuribayashi also concurred with me. But in September, 1944 he inspected the whole island of Iwo Jima with me and investigated how to dispose of this island, and in conclusion we found out that the disposition of this island was quite impossible and we should make this island much stronger by fortification.

However, we had the same idea that even if we placed any strength on the First Airfield it will be immediately defeated by the enemy under his severe bombardments of air forces and vessels, and it is better for us not to place any strength on this airfield.

Later, one staff officer on the 3rd Aircraft Fleet came to Iwo Jima and insisted on saying he should like to give many 25-mm machine guns and materials from the navy and make many pillboxes around the First Airfield.

And in October, he began to make pillboxes, using several battalions every day, and after three months he made 135. When American forces landed on Iwo Jima he could scarcely complete all of them.

In fact, this airfield was trodden by American forces in only two days. If we had infused this great strength, many materials and three months of labor which were used on the airfield, into the defense of Motoyama district and Mount Suribachi, we would have been able to make these areas much stronger.

b. Our judgment regarding enemy's plan

We got various information that many American vessels were gathering at Ulithi, Guam, and Saipan from the end of January, 1945 and we thought at Tokyo and Iwo Jima that American forces would land on Iwo Jima or Okinawa.

In my opinion the possibility of landing of American forces at Iwo Jima was 40 percent and that of Okinawa, 60 percent.

We thought that if American forces land on Iwo Jima, she will occupy the First Airfield and make an offensive base there and use many tanks. Therefore we endeavored especially to strengthen the defense of Mount Suribachi and the front of Minamiburaku, Tankuiwa, and Osakayama, and the training of antitank battle.

c. Many discussions regarding the location of the 109th Divisional headquarters

Many officers insisted on that since Iwo Jima is the first front line it is better to let the 2nd Brigade commander be island commander, and divisional commander should stay at Chichi Jima where it is convenient to control the supply and communications of all over the Bonin Islands. But the Vice Chief of the General Staff, General Ushiroku, and Lieutenant General Kuribayashi said as follows: "Iwo Jima is the most important island and the enemy will surely come to get it. So we should place the divisional headquarters at Iwo Jima."

And Lieutenant General Kuribayashi determined to place the detached headquarters at Chichi Jima in order to supply and communicate with each island.

d. Changes of the plan and execution of the defense dispositions

Until October, 1944, we had a plan not to place any strength on the First Airfield, but because of the above mentioned reason, we changed our plan and placed there two battalions.

e. A problem how army and navy should be disposed

Army had an opinion that they should be disposed for the defense of all over the island and naval troops should be disposed under the command of each district army commander.

But navy was very anxious to defense one district by himself and insisted on that it is better to make plans for mutual understanding, by strengthening the union and display the fighting power.

Then in conclusion, the main power of navy was put in charge of the defense of Minamiburaku district and army was in charge of the defense of all the rest of the island.

f. The defense plan of Lieutenant General Kuribayashi

In June 1944, the plan was to strengthen the Motoyama and Mount Suribachi districts and especially to hold a big reserve (including the 26th Tank Regiment), and if the enemy landed on the First Airfield to make offensive operations toward seaside and annihilate the enemy. In January 1945, the plan was changed to having each man think of his defense position as his graveyard, to fight until the last, and to give many damages to the enemy.

g. Discussions regarding the value of antiaircraft gun

I insisted on this problem as follows: "We should change our plan to use most of the antiaircraft guns as artillery and remain very small part of them as antiaircraft guns. Antiaircraft guns are good to protect the disclosed targets, especially ships, but are invaluable for the covering of the land defense."

But the opinion of the staff officers of Iwo Jima have inclined as follows: "At Iwo Jima, it is good to use antiaircraft guns both as antiaircraft guns and as artillery. And as the natural features of Iwo Jima are weaker than that of Chichi Jima, if we have no antiaircraft guns, our defensive positions will be completely destroyed by the enemy's air raids."

And so most of the three hundred antiaircraft guns were used in both sense as above mentioned.

But later, when American forces landed on Iwo Jima, those antiaircraft guns were put to silenced in one or two days. And we had the evidence that antiaircraft guns were not valuable. But 7.5-cm antiaircraft guns, prepared as antitank guns, were very valuable.

h. Fortification of an underground tunnel

In order to connect with each defense position of Motoyama district, we planned to make 28,000 meters underground tunnel, and began this work in December 1944. But by the time American forces landed on Iwo Jima we only made five thousand meters.

i. Training for battle

Lieutenant General Kuribayashi insisted on the following train-
ings:

(a) Bodily attacks against enemy tanks.

(b) Cutting-in attacks.

(c) Sniping.

Especially he made special badges for the men who were in
charge of bodily attacks against enemy tanks and men in charge
of cutting-in attacks.

4. Strength, Arms and Ammunitions (Army and Navy) at the 1st of February

Strength 23,000 (Army 17,500; Navy 5,500)

ARMS	NUMBER OF		AMMUNITION (ROUNDS)
Big guns (more than 7.5-cm)	120	Total	100,000
Antiaircraft gun (more than 25-mm MG)	300	Each gun	500
Small gun (including heavy and light Machine guns)	20,000	Total	22,000,000
Howitzer (8-cm, 12-cm)	130	Each	90
Mortar (20-cm)	20	Each	40
Rocket gun (20-cm)	70	Each	50
Antitank gun (47-mm)	40	Each	600
Antitank gun (37-mm)	20	Each	500
Tanks	27		

5. Situation of Supply

a. System of supply

Army and navy both had two systems as follows:

i. Tokyo–Iwo Jima (by destroyer, high speed transport and SB—something like the American LST but smaller in size)

ii. Tokyo–Chichi Jima (by ship and/or high speed transport) Chichi Jima–Iwo Jima (by sailing boats, fishing boats and SB) Most transportation belonged to the later system.

b. Damages of ships

Especially after August, 1944, the power of American air forces and submarines was very severe and from Tokyo to Chichi Jima, in Futami Ko and especially from Chichi Jima to Iwo Jima, we had many damages and on the sea we lost more than 1,500 men and 50,000 tonnages of materials.

c. Working of unloading and loading at Chichi Jima as supply center and unloading work at Iwo Jima

When materials were sent to Chichi Jima from the main land of Japan, we unloaded them on Omura during darkness and intermissions between the enemy's air raids, we dispersed them to the interior of this island.

To Iwo Jima we sent them by sailing boats and fishing boats. This was very hard work and many times we used two thousand men and fifty trucks a whole day without sleeping and resting. No harbor, rough waves, and severe air raids gave the greatest hindrance to the unloading work at Iwo Jima. At Iwo Jima we could not place *daihatsus* [landing craft] on the sea, and when we finished unloading, we had to pull them up on the land.

d. Supply crisis of November 1944

In November, 1944 we had only about thirty days of grain and fifteen days of supplementary food, and we came to a very dangerous situation. But afterward, we were able to increase the food a little by brave and self-sacrificing transportation.

e. Provisions at February 1, 1945 (army and navy)

Grain	about 70 days
Supplementary food	about 60 days

6. Convoy Strategy to Cover the Supply Transportation

Until June of 1944, American aircraft did not come to Chichi Jima areas, so we only thought of antisubmarine convoy. Namely our transports were protected primarily by our destroyers or coast defense ships and few assistance of aircraft from Tateyama, Hachijo Jima, Chichi Jima, and Iwo Jima.

After June American aircraft and submarines started attacking our transports in this area and we were obliged to think of night transportation and night work, and so as to protect our ships we have sent one army aircraft squadron to Iwo Jima.

I experienced bitterly how miserable our transportation by sea was when the air and sea were in the hands of enemy's control.

7. Everyday Life and Sanitary Situation of Officers and Men

Officers and men of Iwo Jima were suffering from lack of water; they gathered rain water in empty barrels and bottles and used it.

As they were unable to take both because of the water shortage, they were obliged to go to Kitakaigan to take hot sulphur springs. I also went to that hot spring once.

There were no fresh vegetables, and especially had many malnutrition and paratyphus patients. And in these days, I think 20 percent of all troops were patients.

8. Battle

a. Landing operation of American forces on the First Airfield and our battle

On the 19th of February, American forces landed on the First Airfield under cover of their keen bombardments of aircraft and warships. Although their landing direction, strength and fighting methods were same as our judgment, we could not take any countermeasures toward them, and 135 pillboxes we had at the First Airfield were trodden down and was occupied in only two days after their landing. We shot them bitterly with the artillery we had at Motoyama and Mount Suribachi, but they were immediately destroyed by the enemy's counterfiring.

At that time we had opportunities to make offensive attack against the enemy, but we knew well that if we do so we will suffer many damages from American bombardments of aircraft and vessels, therefore our officers and men waited the enemy of coming closer to their own position.

b. Fall of Mount Suribachi

We were very discouraged when we heard of the fall of Mount Suribachi after only three days of fighting. When I received the message at Chichi Jima from Iwo Jima that district commander of Mount Suribachi informed to Lieutenant General Kuribayashi by wire saying "Enemy's bombardment from air and sea and their assaults with explosions are very fierce and if we ever try to stay and defend our present positions it will lead us to self-destruction. We should rather like to go out of our position and choose death by 'banzai' charges." I burst with emotion.

I knew the fall of the First Airfield, but I never thought of losing Mount Suribachi in only three days.

c. Appearance of American M4 tank

When American M4 tank appeared in front of Osakayama, Lieutenant General Kuribayashi was very anxious to know how to dispose of this tank. Even our 47-mm antitank gun could not destroy it, and at last came to the conclusion that bodily attack with explosives was the only way to destroy it.

d. Value of bombardment of American air forces and vessels

  Lieutenant General Kuribayashi informed to Tokyo by wire as follows: "I am not afraid of the fighting power of only three American marine divisions if there are no bombardment from aircraft and warships. This is the only reason why we have to see such miserable situations."

e. Battle command of Lieutenant General Kuribayashi

  Lieutenant General Kuribayashi was usually at his commanding place in the cave. As soon as his staff officers made messages with the information which came into their hands from time to time from each troops, he inspected, revised, and ordered to dispatch them. As he was very skilful in making compositions, so his messages let all Japanese weep in those days.

f. Value of cutting-in infiltration attacks

  At first we received information that the value of our cutting-in (infiltration) attacks were giving great damages to the enemy. But at the beginning of March the information to Tokyo by wire was as follows: "The look-out American forces became very strict and it is difficult to pass through their guarded line. Don't overestimate the value of cutting-in attacks."

h. Desperate fight of army and navy

  According to the telegraphic reports of Lieutenant General Kuribayashi, we can find the following desperate fights:

  (a) 7th March—

  All troops of "Tamanayama" district are fighting desperately by facing the enemy with only eighty meter distance. Seven small units sent for infiltration attack from "Tamanayama" on the sixth night are not back yet and their results are unknown.

  (b) 8th, 1000—

  i.   Today, from 0630, the enemy is attacking northern district. His bombardments from mortars and warships are very severe.

  ii. Several troops of the enemy are advancing toward naval headquarters hill (near "Kitaburaku") and "Hyoriuboku."

  iii. All surviving fighting bases have sustained heavy losses, but their fighting spirits are running high and they are giving great damages to the enemy.

  (c) 8th, 1800—

  Troops at "Tamanayama" and northern districts are still

holding their position thoroughly and continued giving damages to the enemy. Their fighting situation believing their country's victory looks godlike.

(d) 8th, 2000—

I am very sorry that I have let the enemy occupy one part of the Japanese territory, but I am taking comfort in giving heavy damages to the enemy.

(e) 10th, 1930—

    i.   Although the attacks of the enemy against our northern districts are continuing day and night, our troops are still fighting bravely and holding their positions thoroughly.

   ii.   Divisional radio station was fighting under the siege of many enemy's troops from the 8th, but finally today at 1130 destroyed the radio telegraph.

  iii.   Two or three hundred American infantrymen with several tanks attacked "Tenzan" all day. The enemy's bombardments from one battleship (or cruiser), eleven destroyers and aircraft are very severe, especially the bombing and machine gun firing against divisional headquarters from thirty fighters and bombers are so fierce that I cannot express nor write here.

Before American forces landed on Iwo Jima, there were many trees around my Headquarters, but now there are not even a grasp of grass remaining. The surface of the earth has changed completely and we can see numerous holes of bombardments.

(f) 10th, 2000—

At "Tamanayama," the 2nd Mixed Brigade Headquarters became dangerous, and they might go out for "banzai" charge on the midnight of 8th, because we cannot contact with them after that.

(g) 11th, 1050—

    i.   Surviving strength of northern districts (army and navy) are now 1,500.

   ii.   On the 9th, we gave 798 men and one tank losses to the enemy.

(h) 11th, 1400—

    i.   On the 8th, one M4 tank stopped on the rugged ground of the northern district and one man was trying to go out from the canopy, just at that time, Superior Private Gondo sniped him, threw a hand grenade into the tank and burned it.

   ii.   We cannot contact with the commander of the "Tamanayama" district from yesterday.

   iii.   From this morning the enemy began to concentrate their shooting of warships, firing of mortars, heavy artillery and bombing of aircraft to northern districts.

(i) 13th, 0800—

By the captured documents, we found out that the enemy is the 3rd, 4th and 5th Marine Divisions, and the 5th Division is now in the "Tenzan" area.

On the 12th we gave the following damages to the enemy only in northern districts: Shot down one aircraft and killed about two hundred men.

(j) 14th, 1500—

The attack to the northern district from this morning became much severe than before, and at about noon, one part of the enemy with ten tanks broke through our left front line and approached to two hundred meters east of the divisional headquarters.

(k) 15th, 0800—

   i.   To: Chichi Jima Signal Corps Commander.
     From: Iwo Jima Signal Corps Commander.
     "Situation is very dangerous. Do your best to contact with us."

   ii.   Present strength of the northern districts are about 900.

(l) 15th, 0930—

Since the 10th main power of the 26th Tank Regiment and one part of the navy (about three hundred men together) near "Manburaku" repulsed the enemy several times.

(m) 16th, 0800—

Our surviving strength are now as follows:

Northern districts   500
Eastern districts   300

(n) 17th, 0200—

From: Lieutenant General Kuribayashi
To: All surviving officers and men

   i.   The battle situation came to the last moment.

   ii.   I want my surviving officers and men to go out and attack the enemy tonight.

iii. Each troop! Go out simultaneously at midnight and attack the enemy until the last. You all have devoted yourself to His Majesty, the emperor. Don't think of yourself.

iv. I am always at the head of you all.

(o) 17th, 0500.

The 145th Infantry Regiment fought bravely near "Hyori-uboku," holding their regimental flag in the center.

The last message sent to me on 15th was as follows: "Here we burned our brilliant regimental flag completely. Good-bye."

(p) 21st, 1200—

i. At midnight of 17th I went out from my cave and gathered all survivors of the 145th Infantry Regiment, "Tamanayama," Northern, Eastern and Western districts, westward of "Kitaburaku" and we are continuing our fighting.

I have four hundred men under my control.

ii. The enemy besieged us and at 18th and 19th approached us by firing and flame of their tanks.

Especially they are trying to approach to the entrance of our cave with explosives.

(q) 21st, 1300—

i. 20th and 21st, my officers and men are still fighting.

ii. The enemy's front line is two or three hundred meters from us, and they are attacking by tank firing.

iii. They advised us to surrender by a loudspeaker, but we only laughed at this childish trick and did not set ourselves against them.

(r) 22nd, 0910—

Naval headquarters came to our cave on 16th and are fighting together.

(s) 22nd, 1000—

Divisional commander, officers and men are continuing fighting.

g. Supply from Japan by aircraft

I pay many respects to two brave aviators who supplied weapons to Iwo Jima by aircraft. They made arrangements with Iwo Jima commander, and started Isamamatsu (Japan) airfield and supplied hand grenades and flame projectors.

It is indeed difficult to express how the hearts of the fighting youth of Iwo Jima who stood before their death were when they saw these brave flyers.

i. The last moments of Lieutenant General Kuribayashi
Lieutenant General Kuribayashi commanded his battle under the candle lights without having a single rest or sleep day after day. Radio broadcasts, newspapers and magazines of Japan encouraged him thoroughly. Especially, old and young men, boys and girls of his native place prayed God for his victory.

On 14th of March "Song of Iwo Jima," composed by the fighting men of Iwo Jima, before the American forces landed, was broadcast to Lieutenant General Kuribayashi, officers and men from Tokyo, and he sent his thankful message to all Japanese.

On the 15th of March, he informed Tokyo by wire as follows: "I am determined to go out and make 'banzai' charges against the enemy at midnight of the 17th. Now I say good-bye to all senior and friend officers everlastingly."

And he added three farewell songs in this message. From the morning of the 17th we were unable to communicate with him, and we thought that the 17th of March was his death day.

He was promoted to general on the 17th. But we were greatly surprised when we received his message suddenly on 21st morning. We knew from this message that he and his men (army and navy all together four hundred men) went out on the midnight of the 17th and shut themselves in the cave 150 meters northwest from his old cave.

He sent the last following message to us: "We have not eaten nor drank for five days. But our fighting spirit is still running high. We are going to fight bravely till the last."

I did my very best at Chichi Jima to send him the message of his promotion to general on the 17th of March. On the evening of the 23rd one radio operator informed me by wire "All officers and men of Chichi Jima, good-bye" from Iwo. I tried to communicate with them for three days after that, but finally I did not get their answer.

9. Why Japanese Soldier Does Not Surrender
In Japanese opinion, if the Japanese soldiers stand on a battlefield they ought to devote their body and soul, namely, the only way is to select victory or death for the honor.

From ancient time, this has been the Japanese soldiers' custom, tradition, or common sense, and if by any chance the prisoners of war return to their homeland after the war ceases they will be treated as a coward by all Japanese.

Therefore at Iwo Jima, on 23rd of March, even though there were about three hundred Japanese supervisors, most of them did not surrender to the enemy and fought till the very end of their lives.

10. Conclusion

When I look back the Japanese defense plan and battle of Iwo Jima, I must pay many respects to overwhelming material quantity and skillful operations of American forces.

On the other hand, I am bursting with emotion, seeing the sacred spirit of General Kuribayashi and his officers and men who fought bravely for their honor.

Ah! Many Japanese and American brave men died for their country on Iwo Jima and I cannot calculate how many families and relatives there are.

Now bloody war came to an end and feeling peace is here. There is no hatred and anger between Americans and Japanese.

I am very honored if my humble booklet will give mere suggestion to American officers and men now in Iwo Jima and all Japanese and American surviving families to remind the situation of those days.

INSTRUCTIONS OF WAR TELEGRAPHED FROM LIEUTENANT GENERAL KURIBAYASHI TO THE CHIEF OF THE GENERAL STAFF

I will write down the American tactics, effect of our arms, etc. following my memory.

1. From the landing of the enemy on Iwo Jima to February 20th, Second Lieutenant Nakamura attached to the 8th Independent Anti-tank-Gun Unit, destroyed one score of the amphibious tanks by handling himself the 47-mm antitank gun and died a heroic death.
2. However firm and stout pillboxes you may build easily at the beach they will be destroyed by bombardment of main armament of the battleships. It is better to build dummy pillboxes at the beach and concentrate the enemy's shooting to this point.
3. As the enemy is using plain language for reporting information, it is wise to listen to them and understand their plan and movement.

4. The violence of the enemy's bombardments is far beyond description. Especially a small isolated island like Iwo Jima when bombarded severely by hundreds of various warships day and night with forty and fifty aircraft always in the air ready to fire against every target they are able to find, not even one man can scarcely move a step during daytime. Even at night, it takes about more than ten hours for young officer to walk about one kilometer for communication. Telephone lines are completely cut off.

5. All positions, especially southern districts are almost completely destroyed by the severe bombardment from ships and had great damages on camouflaged installations and men. The bombardment from ships were not less than thirty thousand rounds per day.

6. We need to reconsider the power of bombardment from ships. The beach positions we made on this island by using many materials, days and great efforts, were destroyed within three days so that they were nearly unable to be used again. Every main position was also destroyed by day and night bombardment from ships and the lay of the land has changed completely. Beach-position firing was done from battleships and other warships anchored at the distance of one to two thousand meters.

   Firing against main positions is done by seaplane scouting and observing unsparing time and ammunition.

   Power of the American warships and aircraft makes every landing operation possible to whatever beachhead they like, and preventing them from landing means nothing but great damages, therefore for landing operations we must cut the number of coast guns and installations to the smallest and crush the ships. Defense of isolated island which lacks this condition could never exist.

7. If you want to use telephone, you must bury the line or at least equip gutter for them.

8. The enemy finds the radio station by using direction detector and concentrates their firing to them, therefore commanding post must be pretty far from the radio station, but at the time it is necessary to take measures so as to obtain communication.

9. Adjacent to the commanding post of the enemy is generally clamor, and there are some using lights.

10. Long period of time and enormous number of men used for the extension work of the first and "Motoyama" airfield have impeded the defense, fortification and drill greatly.

    We must avoid constructing hopeless airfields.

11. Position must be selected where it is out of the ships' range without being restrained from the direct covering of airfield. Especially we must attach great importance to the antitank defense.

    Antitank obstacles must be equipped in and front of the position.

12. It is no exaggeration to say that victory or defeat of fighting on land is decided by aircraft and tanks.

    In the future we must endeavor our best to construct this two arms.

13. For artillery middle-size mortar (20-cm) and rockets (20-cm). For antitank gun, Type-90 field guns are most effective (7.5-cm).

14. Nearly all army and naval guns placed near the beach for firing on landing craft and troops were destroyed before the enemy landed.

15. For defending an isolated island, it is absolutely necessary to accumulate large quantities of ammunition for guns, mortars, and hand grenades.

    On this island most guns except the one at the seaside existed pretty long, but the ammunition ran short in only a week.

16. The enemy's air control is very strong. One hundred or at least thirty aircraft are flying ceaselessly from early morning to night above this small island, and if they discover any symptom they began to attack it with obstinate bombardments from warships led by observation planes are quick and exact and give unimaginable damages to defense positions, and if our antiaircraft guns start firing the enemy's aircraft usually destroy our guns at once.

17. The enemy's tanks have strong destructive power, slow but steady advance, make full usage of material power and are extremely hard to destroy. If our antitank gun appears they retire quickly, let the naval guns led by observation planes, destroy them, and then advance.

18. The enemy has two or three handlers of flame projectors among fifty or sixty men, so it is necessary to snipe these handlers immediately.

19. The enemy's penetrating attack through our front line is done with tanks under cover of violent machine-gun artillery and mortar firing, then we have no means to counter them.

Notes

Unless identified as those of the author, the endnotes are supplied by the editors.

Editors' Preface

1. The editors use the more common name of the island, Iwo Jima, rather than the actual name, Iwo To, as most English-language readers are more familiar with the former. Horie used both in his writings and speeches, depending on the audience.

2. This information comes in part from the appendix titled "Japanese Command at Iwo" in Richard F. Newcomb, *Iwo Jima* (New York: Henry Holt, 1965). With the exception of the name of the author in the book's subtitle, Japanese names appear according to Japanese cultural tradition—that is, family name first.

3. For more on Komoto, see Kumiko Kakehashi, *So Sad to Fall in Battle: An Account of War* (New York: Ballantine Books, 2007), 162–63.

4. Chichi Jima is the largest island in the Ogasawara Islands group and, being north of Iwo Jima, served as an important transshipment point between Tokyo, Iwo Jima, and the islands in the Central Pacific.

5. Some authors have mistakenly written that Horie was sent to Chichi Jima by Kuribayashi due to a disagreement over a never-materialized plan to implode Iwo Jima and sink it into the sea. This misunderstanding appears in, for example, Robert Leckie, *Strong Men Armed: The United States Marines vs. Japan* (New York: Da Capo, 1997, first published in 1962), 427. Readers who saw Clint Eastwood's film adaptation, *Letters from Iwo Jima,* may remember the scene in which Lieutenant Colonel (and Baron) Nishi Takeichi (played by Ihara Tsuyoshi) speaks with Lieutenant General Kuribayashi (played by Watanabe Ken) in the latter's tent. In the movie, it is Nishi who proposes sinking the island. In fact, it was Horie who did so, but probably due to considerations of simplifying the movie's story and characters, in the movie Nishi's character makes the suggestion. Similarly, as is made clear in chapter

7 of this book, it is Horie who is asked by Kuribayashi to play the role of the enemy landing on the beach, not his aide, Lieutenant Fujita Masayoshi (played by Watanabe Hiroshi in the film). Horie's character does not, unfortunately, appear in the movie, despite his service in the preparations for the battle and his work in the postwar period explaining in English and in Japanese what took place.

6. See, for example, in chronological order: Tada Minoru, *Nanimo Kataranakatta Seishun* [The Youth I Could Not Speak About] (Tokyo: Mikasa Shobo, 1993); Akikusa Tsuruji, *17 Sai no Iwo Jima* [17 Years Old and on Iwo Jima] (Bunshun Shinsho, 2006); Kawashima Shoichi, *Iwo Jima Senki: Gyokusai no Shima Kara Seikan Shita Ichiheishi no Kaiso* [Diary of the Battle of Iwo Jima Diary: Recollections of One Soldier Who Returned Alive from the Island Where Almost Everyone Died] (Tokyo: Kojinsha, January 2007); and Hisayama Shinobu, *Eiyu Naki Shima: Iwo Jima Sen Ikinokori Motokaigun Chusa no Shogen* [The Island with No Heroes: An Imperial Japanese Navy Lieutenant's Testimony of Surviving the Battle of Iwo Jima] (Tokyo: Sankei Shimbun Shuppan, August 2008).

7. Ando Tomichi, *Aa Iwo Jima Kiroku ni Yoru Iwo Jima Senshi* [Oh, Iwo Jima: A Battle History of Iwo Jima based on Documents] (Kawade Shobo Shinsha, 2007), for example.

8. K. Mike Masuyama, *Iwoto: Nihonjin Horyo no Mita Amerika* [Iwo Jima: America as Seen by a Japanese Prisoner of War] (Tokyo: Haato Shuppan, June 2008).

9. The original book was titled *Tokon: Iwo Jima,* [Fighting Spirit: Iwo Jima]. It was published by Kobunsha Publishing, in Tokyo's Kanda District of Chiyoda Ward. A second edition was entitled *Iwo Jima: Gekito no Kiroku* [Iwo Jima: A Record of Heavy Fighting] (Tokyo: Kobunsha, 1973). The third edition, which was also titled *Tokon* and included the subtitle *Ogasawara Heidan Sanbo no Kaiso* [The Memoirs of a Staff Officer, Ogasawara Forces] was published by Kojinsha Publishers, in the Kyudan District of the same ward. For reasons unclear, the third edition eliminated chapter 18 ("Island of Tragedy, Iwo Jima"). As explained above, the editors have decided to retain it in this English edition. We have, however, chosen to eliminate the original chapter 13, "The Largest Operation in Marine Corps History," which provides an overview of the American chain of command and personalities involved in the battle of Iwo Jima, and chapter 16, "The Stars and Stripes Go Up on March 14," as it was written using American accounts of the battle, including long quotes from Lieutenant General Holland M. Smith's *Coral and Brass: "Howlin' Mad" Smith's Own Story of the Marines in the Pacific* (New York: Scribner's, 1949) and Leckie's *Strong Men Armed*. Furthermore, because of the length of the original chapter 15, we decided to break it up into smaller chapters, renumbering and retitling them. In addition to English-language articles and the articles and books discussed in the foreword and in the editors' preface, Horie also wrote a chapter about the battle titled "Dai 109 Shidan Sanbo no Kaiso" ["The Recollections of a Staff Member of the 109th Division"], in Hashimoto Eiya, ed., *Iwoto*

Kessen [The Decisive Battle for Iwo Jima] (Tokyo: Kojinsha, 2001), 87–117. This chapter was originally published as an article ("Iwoto Kessen Kaiko" [Recollections of the Decisive Battle of Iwo Jima]) in a special edition of the military affairs magazine *Maru,* no. 13, July 1989.

10. In an article for the Tachikawa Base newspaper, at which he would later work, Horie mentioned the English version of the manuscript as well and the hope that it was going to be published in the United States. See "Beisakka no Shuzai ni Kyoryoku: 'Tokon Iwojima' no Horie Shi" [Mr. Horie, Author of "Fighting Spirit: Iwo Jima," Interviewed by American Writer], *Kanto Kugun Shimbun* [Kanto Air Force Newspaper], September 15, 1966, copy courtesy of Horie Yoshibumi. The American author who came to interview Horie, and is shown in the photo in the story, was John Toland.

11. Consultations with the family of Major Horie led to the decision to publish the work through the prestigious U.S. Naval Institute Press, in light of its long history, strong collection of Iwo Jima–related works, and the fact that Major Horie had published his article on convoy escorts in the U.S. Naval Institute *Proceedings* in 1956 (see the discussion later in this editors' preface and in chapter 2).

12. Horie, "Iwoto Kessen Kaiko," 108.

13. Ibid., 107.

14. For more see Robert D. Eldridge, *Iwo Jima to Ogasawara o Meguru Nichibei Kankei* [Iwo Jima and the Bonin Islands in U.S.-Japan Relations] (Kagoshima: Nanpo Shinsha, 2008), chap. 3; James Bradley, *Flyboys: A True Story of Courage* (New York: Back Bay Books, 2003); and Chester Hearn, *Sorties into Hell: The Hidden War on Chichijima* (Guilford, Conn.: Lyons, 2003).

15. See Eldridge, *Iwo Jima to Ogasawara,* 142.

16. For one of the best detailed accounts of the investigation, see Hearn, *Sorties into Hell.* Also see Eldridge, *Iwo Jima to Ogasawara,* and Bradley, *Flyboys.*

17. Bradley, *Flyboys,* 318. It should be pointed out that although Horie writes about the prisoners in this book, he does not really address their fate here and seems to have publicly kept silent until his essay in 1984 shed light on that dark period and the details of their savage treatment. Horie Yoshitaka, "Chichi Jima Jinniku Jiken: Shidancho mo Kutta" [The Chichi Jima Cannibalism Incident: The Commanding General Also Ate (the Flyers)], *Rekishi to Jinbutsu* 14, no. 14 (1984): 120–35.

18. Colonel James H. Tinsley (USMC, Ret.) to Robert J. Snyder, Chichi Jima, Bonin Islands Marines Association, undated, courtesy of the son of Colonel Tinsley, USMC (Ret.) [hereafter Colonel Tinsley Jr.].

19. Major Yoshitaka Horie to Lieutenant Colonel James H. Tinsley Jr., February 1, 1946, courtesy Colonel Tinsley Jr.

20. Horie, "Chichi Jima Jinniku Jiken."

21. The editors have been unable to identify the full name of Davis. The son of Colonel Tinsley suggests that it might instead have been Brigadier General William E. Riley, assistant division commander, 3rd Marine Division, who assumed command of the division from Major General

Graves Erskine upon the end of hostilities and Erskine's departure in October 1945. Riley, according to Tinsley, "oversaw the period of disbandment, closing the books on the Third Division on December 28, 1945." Colonel Tinsley Jr., e-mail to Robert D. Eldridge, June 18, 2009.

22. Major Yoshitaka Horie to Lieutenant Colonel James H. Tinsley, February 1, 1946.

23. The 1973 edition used a slightly different title. It was published as *Iwo Jima: Gekito no Kiroku* [Iwo Jima: A Record of Heavy Fighting] (Tokyo: Kobunsha, 1973). See footnote 44 (this section) for more about this book.

24. See "Japanese Defense of Iwo Jima," *Marine Corps Gazette* 36, no. 2 (February 1952): 18–27, and "Defense Plan for Chichi Jima," *Marine Corps Gazette* 37, no. 7 (July 1953), 26–40. The editors would like to thank Robert Aquilina of the Reference Branch, Marine Corps History Division, for his outstanding assistance in providing copies of these articles.

25. See "This Month and Next," *Marine Corps Gazette* (February 1952).

26. Yoshitaka Horie to Colonel Tinsley, December 1953, courtesy Colonel Tinsley Jr.

27. The exchange rate at this time (until 1971) was 360 yen to the dollar.

28. Yoshitaka Horie, "The Last Days of General Kuribayashi," *Marine Corps Gazette* 39, no. 2 (February 1955): 38–43.

29. Yoshitaka Horie, "The Failure of the Japanese Convoy Escort," U.S. Naval Institute *Proceedings* 82, no. 10 (October 1956), 1073–81.

30. Walter B. McKenzie, chief, Editorial and Graphics Division, Office of the Chief of Military History, Department of the Army, to Yoshitaka Horie, January 8, 1964, courtesy of Horie Yoshibumi.

31. See Charles W. Tatum, *Iwo Jima: Red Blood, Black Sand—Pacific Apocalypse* (Stockton, Calif.: Chuck Tatum Productions, 2002). Tatum's book was referenced heavily when producing the HBO miniseries *The Pacific*, which aired in early 2010.

32. See footnote 14 for details.

33. Richard Wheeler, *Iwo* (Annapolis: Naval Institute Press, 1980), viii.

34. Wheeler, sadly, passed away half a year later, in the fall of 2008.

35. Kakehashi, *So Sad to Fall*.

36. For more on the coup, see Meirion and Susie Harries, *Soldiers of the Sun: The Rise and Fall of the Imperial Japanese Army* (New York: Random House, 1991), particularly 167–200.

37. "Brief Biographical Sketch of Author, June 19, 1951," courtesy of Colonel Tinsley. Eldridge subsequently met and interviewed retired Lieutenant Colonel Shaffer at his home in Salt Lake City, Utah, on August 17–18, 2009.

38. "TAB Japanese Employee Recalls Planning Historic Island Defense," *Kanto Plainsman* (Iwo Jima Supplement) 8, no. 25, June 21, 1968.

39. Horie Yoshibumi, e-mail on father's work to Robert D. Eldridge, May 25, 2009.

40. This document was shared with the author, courtesy of Horie Yoshibumi.

41. For more on Nakasone's time as president of Takushoku, see Yasuhiro

Nakasone, trans. and annotated by Lesley Connors, *The Making of the New Japan: Reclaiming the Political Mainstream* (Surrey: Curzon, 1999), 182–84.

42. The book was edited by the Ogasawara Senyukai (Association of War Veterans of Ogasawara) but was written in large part by Horie. It was published in order to commemorate the June 27, 1969, dedication of the Japanese memorial constructed on top of Mount Suribachi immediately next to the better-known memorial of the 5th Marine Division (which had been constructed by the navy's 31st Naval Construction Battalion [Seabees], which had participated in the battle of Iwo Jima and was attached to the 5th Marine Division in 1947) and had undergone some redesign in 1968 immediately prior to the reversion of the islands. For more, see Eldridge, *Iwo Jima to Ogasawara*, 437–39.

43. Traditionally, Japanese publishers provide not only the year but the month and day on which a book is published. Unfortunately, no month was given for the publication of this 1972 book.

44. This 1973 book, *Iwoto: Gekito no Kiroku*, was actually *Fighting Spirit*, revised and reissued under a different title. This practice is fairly common among Japanese publishers, especially regarding well known or popular books. Indeed, even the publisher became confused—the title and the title on the inside back cover differed, the latter reading "Iwoto: Tokon no Kiroku" [Iwo Jima: Record of Fighting Spirit]. For this book, Horie added sixteen pages' worth of photos and biographical information (pages 270–85) on some of the Japanese soldiers and sailors who died on Iwo, at the request of Kobunsha's president, Ikeda. He also added a new, but shorter, preface.

45. Bob Phelps, "Iwo Jima 20 Years after the Battle: Former Enemies Recall Opposing Sides of Invasion," *Kanto Plainsman*, February 19, 1965, 1–4.

46. Yoshitaka Horie, interviewed by Dr. Alvin D. Coox, "Japan's Self-Defense Force Today," *Marine Corps Gazette* 49, no. 2 (February 1965): 50–53.

47. There is no date on the essay, provided to Eldridge by the son of Major Horie, but its context suggests it was written in 1983.

48. John Toland, *The Rising Sun: The Decline and Fall of the Japanese Empire* (New York: Random House, 1970), chap. 26.

49. Horie, *Iwoto: Gekito no Kiroku*, 1.

50. Ibid.

51. The Fuji School is about a hundred kilometers west of Tokyo.

52. Sugita Ichita, the first director of the school, who had been a member of the Army Section of the Imperial General Headquarters (Nihon Daihonei Rikugunbu Sanbo) and worked on planning for the battle of Iwo Jima and later served as a chief of staff of the self-defense force (March 1960–March 1962), became aware of the talk and asked Horie to provide further documentation. Sugita also asked retired lieutenant general Shirai Akio, a military historian, to research this as well, and the latter corresponded with Horie. Eventually, Shirai was able to introduce his results in a 121-page study published in eighteen installments

in the Fuji Gakko's journal, *Fuji*. See Shirai, "Kuribayashi Shogun no Saigo ni Tsuite no Ichikosatsu: Horie Motoshidan Sanbo Kaiso no Kensho" [A Look into the Final Days of General Kuribayashi: Examining the Memoirs of Staff Officer Horie], *Fuji*, nos. 311–28, November 2005–April 2007). Also, citing Shirai's writings, one of Kuribayashi's biographers takes up this issue in a well-researched 2007 article. See Kakehashi Kumiko, "Kuribayashi Chujo Shogeki no Saigo: Noirooze, Buka ni Yoru Shinsatsusetsu no Shinso" [The Shocking Last Moments of Lieutenant General Kuribayashi: The Truth about (His) Neurosis and the Theory of His Killing by Subordinates], *Bungei Shunju* 85, no. 3 (February 2007): 114–29.

53. Horie, "The Last Days of General Kuribayashi."
54. Horie Yoshitaka, "Iwojimasen Kaiko" [Recollections of the Battle of Iwo Jima], *Maru*, November 1989.
55. Boeicho Kenkyusho Senshibu, ed., *Iwo Jima Sakusen ni Tsuite* [About the Iwo Jima Operation] (Tokyo: Senshishitsu, Boei Kenkyusho [National Institute for Defense Studies], March 1962), cited in Kakehashi, "Kuribayashi Chujo Shogeki no Saigo," 117.
56. The description of the relationships described in this paragraph draws from Horie's unpublished essay mentioned above, "Onshu o Koete" [Beyond Love and Hate].
57. Horie, "Onshu o Koete."
58. Wheeler, *Iwo*.
59. Richard Wheeler, trans. Horie Yoshitaka, *Chigoku no Senjo: Iwojima-Suribachiyama no Kessen* [Hell's Battle: The Fight for Iwo Jima and Suribachiyama] (Tokyo: Kobunsha, 1981).
60. John Keith Wells, *Give Me Fifty Marines Not Afraid to Die: Iwo Jima* (Abilene, Tex.: Ka-Well Enterprises, 1995), 303–4.

Foreword
1. Where the editors found obvious mistakes, we have tried to make appropriate corrections to the text in the form of annotations, footnotes, or parentheses.
2. For whatever reason, Horie does not seem to have completed or published the Japanese translation of the book. A list of his writings appears in the editors' preface.
3. In a letter to Horie shared with the editors by Horie's son (who maintains some of his father's papers), Colonel McKenzie added a personal, handwritten note to Horie saying that he had just completed a three-year tour at Camp Zama, the headquarters of U.S. Army, Japan, in June the year before (1963), and had "many wonderful friends in Japan." Colonel Walter B. McKenzie to Yoshitaka Horie, March 10, 1964.
4. There were several lines in the original edition in Japanese about Colonel Tinsley's career that were factually incorrect and that the editors decided to correct here. The text thus reflects Colonel Tinsley's actual career. The editors are grateful to Colonel James H. Tinsley Jr., USMC (Ret.), for help in clarifying the senior Colonel Tinsley's career. James H. Tinsley Jr. to Robert D. Eldridge, October 28, 2008, and James H.

Tinsley Jr., e-mail to Robert D. Eldridge, June 5, 2009. Tinsley was a student at the Amphibious Warfare School (AWS), Senior Course, at Marine Corps Schools, Quantico, Virginia, and then stayed on as an instructor at the AWS Senior Course until June 1951, when he was sent to Korea as part of the 1st Marine Division. It seems that during his time at Quantico he approached the editorial staff of the *Marine Corps Gazette*, which comprised active-duty personnel until the early 1970s, about Horie's materials. Colonel John A. Keenan, USMC (Ret.), e-mail to Robert D. Eldridge, June 5, 2009.

5. The three articles relating to the battle are discussed in the editors' preface.

6. The editors have chosen to use photos of Horie rather than those of the battle itself in this book, as most of the photos Horie used came from USMC sources.

Chapter 1. The Toughest Battle in World History

1. Figures for deaths and casualties vary, but those usually cited are: 21,570 killed on the Japanese side and 6,821 killed on the American side, with 26,038 Americans missing or wounded.

2. Rear Admiral Ichimaru was promoted posthumously to vice admiral in March 1945.

3. Their story has been brought to life in several books, documentaries, and movies, as well as in the Himeyuri Peace Museum (Himeyuri Heiwa Kinen Shiryokan) in Itoman, Okinawa.

4. The Iwo Jima Song went as follows: "Where dark tides billow in the ocean / a wink-shaped isle of mighty fame / guards the gateway to our Empire / Iwo Jima is its name. We brave men who have been chosen / to defend this island strand / filled with faith in certain triumph / yearn to strike for Fatherland. Thoughts of duty ever with us / from dawn to dusk we train with zeal / bound by Emperor's commanding to bring the enemy to heel. Oh, for Emperor and homeland / there's no burden we won't bear / sickness, hardship, filthy water / these are less to us than air. Officers and men together / work and struggle, strive and trust / till the hated Anglo-Saxons / lie before us in the dust." This English version of the lyrics for this song is taken from Leckie, *Strong Men Armed*, 423–33.

Chapter 2. Isolated Island: Where No Planes or Vessels Could Go

1. According to a recent book about the battle of Midway, aircrew losses were 110, and aircraft losses amounted to 246. See Jonathan Parshall and Anthony Tully, *Shattered Sword: The Untold Story of the Battle of Midway* (Dulles, Va.: Potomac Books, 2005), 450–51, 476.

2. The full quote comes from a secret meeting between Yamamoto and Prime Minister Prince Konoe Fumimaro on September 12, 1941: "If you insist on my going ahead I can promise to give them hell for a year or a year and a half, but can guarantee nothing as to what will happen after that." See Agawa Hiroyuki, *The Reluctant Admiral: Yamamoto and the Imperial Navy* (Tokyo: Kodansha International, 1979), 232.

3. See Louis Morton, *The War in the Pacific: Strategy and Command, the First Two Years* (Washington, D.C.: Office of the Chief of Military History, 1962), 285.

4. Ibid., 369.

5. Ibid., 119–20.

6. Horie noted here: "Regarding the surprise attack on Pearl Harbor, one U.S. official history states the following: 'The Japanese surprise attack against Pearl Harbor apparently succeeded and inflicted heavy loses to the U.S. vessels. But, it had the following three weak points: first, the U.S. aircraft carriers were out at the time, so the U.S. Navy could organize task forces immediately after to proceed with operations. Second, the U.S. supply tank facilities received no damage, so the U.S. Navy had no trouble in fuel supply. Third, no damage was made to the ship maintenance facilities, so the U.S. Navy could repair damaged vessels easily. Furthermore, the Americans became united after this saying, "Remember Pearl Harbor," while the Japanese, elated with the apparent success of the strike, were unaware of what was to come.'" It is unclear what work Horie was citing from, and thus the above text, retranslated into English from the Japanese, does not represent the original wording.

7. Horie, the author, was not related to Rear Admiral Horie, despite the same spelling of their family name.

8. *Kuretake* was not a class of ship per se but the name of an actual Imperial Japanese Navy destroyer, the second in the second class of destroyers known as the *Wakatake* class. It was launched in 1922 with the name No. 4 Destroyer, or DD4 (*Dai Yon Kuchikukan*), but was renamed in 1928. It had a displacement of 820 tons and a top speed of 31.5 knots. It carried a complement of 110, and was armed with three 4.7-inch guns; two antiaircraft machine guns and four 21-inch torpedo tubes arranged in two pairs.

9. The chapter Horie is likely referring to is chapter 18 ("The Grand Fleet and the Submarine Alarm: October and November, 1914") in Winston Churchill, *The World Crisis, 1911–1914* (London: Thornton Butterworth, 1923). The book was translated into Japanese as *Sekai Taisen,* vol. 2, in 1937 and published by Hibonkyaku.

10. Akiyama had served as the Japanese naval attaché in Washington, D.C., from 1897 to 1899, a period of tension in the U.S.-Japanese relationship due to the overthrow of Queen Liliuokalani of the Kingdom of Hawaii and other matters.

11. *Kaiyo* was the later name of a high-speed passenger ship launched in 1938 as *Argentina Maru*. In 1942, the Imperial Japanese Navy, desperate for aircraft carriers, converted it into an escort carrier.

12. For more on this, see Horie, "The Failure of the Japanese Convoy Escort."

13. Shikoku is one of the four main islands of the mainland of Japan, and thus the comment by the person Horie cites probably is meant to suggest a very desperate situation.

14. Maurice Matloff, *Strategic Planning for Coalition Warfare, 1943–1944* (Washington, D.C.: Center of Military History, U.S. Army, 1959), 330–31.

15. Horie begins a long description of this controversy as a footnote at the end of the paragraph: "The phrase 'the Army started the war,' was often heard. In connection with this story, many issues are intertwined, including, for instance, the 2.26 Incident (1936), the overthrow of Adm. Yonai Mitsumasa's Cabinet (in 1940), and the Japan-Germany-Italy Tripartite Pact (1940), etc. Apart from these problems, Lt. Gen. Suzuki, whom I respected most and who was killed in action at Leyte as the commanding general of the 35th Army (Daisanjugo Gun), used to tell me the following: that in the Navy they would say the Army started the war. In the Army they said that Adm. Nagano, Chief of the Naval Staff, stated in front of the Emperor on September 8, 1941, that we now have the chance to win the war, but in the future those prospects would gradually become worse. So we should start the war now. And thus the Army decided it should start the war. As the situation worsened, both the Navy and the Army criticized the other and tried to make themselves look better. Both seem to have a good reason. But, I believe the legal responsibility of the outbreak of the war must rest upon the two service chiefs and all ministers, and upon the public from the moral point of view. Because our activities must be based upon the Imperial Prescript, and the Meiji Constitution describes that the Emperor has no responsibility and every responsibility comes upon his advisors, the two service chiefs and all ministers who served as advisors to the Emperor should take responsibility regardless whether or not they were war advocates. Moreover, all the people must take moral responsibility because since the Sino-Japanese War and Russo-Japanese War, they have been happy to see the prosperity of Japan and they have made an atmosphere under which they have been apt to say, 'Defeat the foreigners.' They must take responsibility regardless whether or not they knew the real situation. Of course, few people have any malicious intent, and everyone likes peace and would prefer victory rather than defeat. As a result, no one takes responsibility even though the people are all responsible for having gone along with the Imperial Rescript. On this point, Adm. Oikawa used to say: 'All over the country, ninety-nine percent of the people have neither principle nor constancy. What course shall we take? We must just follow the course decided by the Emperor. That is to say, we should obey the Imperial Rescript.' But, there is one episode about Adm. Oikawa. After the war, with the death of Lt. Gen. Suzuki in Leyte, I had come to respect Adm. Oikawa the most. One of my friends in my office asked if he could see one of the important leaders of the war period. I wrote Adm. Oikawa, asking him if I could visit him with this friend at his convenience. He wrote me back immediately agreeing to meet and the friend and I visited him one Sunday afternoon. To my surprise, he did not say anything about the Imperial Rescript or principles and moral responsibility, but he criticized the Army at length, speaking ill of it for two hours without any stop. To begin with, he said, 'There were no politicians in the Army, although there were some politicians in the Navy. It led our country to

the Japan-Germany-Italy Tripartite Pact and the outbreak of WWII.' The friend of mine said, 'I had been looking for the opportunity to hear that kind of story. During the war we were unaware of what had happened.'"

Chapter 3. Saipan Was Said to Be Impregnable

1. The Imperial Japanese Army had established its Shipping Headquarters in Ujina in 1902, making the area an important logistical center. Prior to that, the headquarters had been in Tokyo.
2. Horie's cousin's husband had been working with Nanyo Kohatsu, KK (Kabushiki Kaisha). When Saipan was invaded he was drafted by the army and was killed in action at the beginning of July 1944. At the end of December 1943, Horie had stayed with him in Java when Horie was returning to Tokyo.
3. For more on Ugaki, see Ugaki Matome, *Fading Victory: The Diary of Admiral Matome Ugaki* (Pittsburgh: Pittsburgh University Press, 1991).
4. The admiral here is Toyoda.
5. Philip A. Crowl, *The War in the Pacific: Campaign in the Marianas* (Washington, D.C.: Office of the Chief of Military History, Department of the Army, 1960), 121–23.

Chapter 4. Iwo Jima Is Next!

1. Horie notes that Ando, as the commander of the Southern China Expeditionary Army (Nanshi Hakengun), had once been fired, along with the chief of staff, Prince Kanin no Miya, due to the invasion of French Indochina, and committed suicide after World War II.
2. Oi survived the war and wrote *Kaijo Goeisen: Taiheiyo Senso no Senryakuteki Bunseki* [The Convoy Escort War: A Strategic Analysis of the Pacific War] (Tokyo: Nihon Shuppan Kyodo, 1953). It has since been republished many times and is still available in paperback. No English-language version exists of which the editors are aware.

Chapter 5. Iwo Jima: An Island of Pineapples and Jungle

1. The name Iwo Jima changed to Iwo To in 2007, with Kita Iwo Jima becoming Kita Iwo (Io) To and Minami Iwo Jima becoming Minami Iwo (Io) To.

Chapter 7. Let's Sink Iwo Jima into the Ocean

1. Between May and September 1939, a desperate battle was fought between the Japanese army and the Soviet army at Nomonhan, Outer Mongolia.
2. Chikatabi are thick, socklike items of footwear with soles.
3. Edo is the old name for Tokyo.
4. Nagata was murdered by a fellow IJA officer (Lieutenant Colonel Aizawa Saburo) over doctrinal disputes.
5. Suzuki, shortly after this, went to serve as the commanding general of the 35th Army in the Philippines, where he died in April 1945. He

had previously served as the director of the Transportation Headquarters (Unyu Honbu) and simultaneously at the Shipping Division of the General Staff.

6. Ugaki was the brother of Vice Admiral Ugaki Matome and served as a major in the Russo-Japanese War. Between 1924–25 and 1930–31 he served as war minister four times and was looked at as the premier designate in January 1937. However, the army opposed him and refused to nominate a minister of war, thus preventing him from forming a cabinet at that time.

7. This is a reference to a fire that broke out at the Imperial Guard, otherwise known as the Konoe Division, which is an organization dedicated to protection of the emperor of Japan and his family, palaces, and other imperial properties.

8. The Japanese legation in Canada opened in 1929, and Tokugawa served there from 1929 to 1934.

9. This is presumably what Horie told Kuribayashi, but he was incorrect. *Kaga* and *Soryu* were fatally damaged by carrier planes and sank on June 4. *Akagi* was fatally damaged in the same attacks and sank the next day (June 5). *Hiryu* was also fatally damaged late on June 4 and sank the next day. This was not the entire 1st Air Fleet, as Horie writes, but only four of the six carriers that had raided Pearl Harbor. The other two carriers, *Shokaku* and *Zuikaku*, were not sunk until June and October 1944, respectively.

Chapter 8. Night Supply Operations via Chichi Jima

1. Although the names of the prisoners taken and those with whom Horie interacted are known, he does not provide the names here of prisoners 2 and 3.

2. Both men were from Hawaii.

3. Horie had befriended Nishi's widow after the war and was provided access to the letters from her husband.

4. The Tokyo School of Foreign Languages is now the Tokyo University of Foreign Studies (Tokyo Gaikokugo Daigaku).

5. Tachibana was executed along with four others, including Matoba, following trials in Guam, in which they were found guilty of murder and the prevention of honorable burials, with cannibalism as an aggravating factor.

6. Yonai served as navy minister and also as prime minister.

7. Nishikawa actually said, "You two *Tenposen* folks have a good time." Horie explains that the graduates of the Army War College would wear a pin that looked like a type of coin used during the Tenpo Era (1830–44), and thus the graduates would be referred to as "Tenposen" (Tenpo coins).

8. The seventeenth and eighteenth classes corresponded to the years 1903 and 1906; there was a gap due to the Russo-Japanese War of 1904–1905.

Chapter 9. Defensive Operations from the Caves

1. Smith, *Coral and Brass*, 200.

Chapter 10. Send More Weapons and Ammunition!
1. See, for example, Leckie, *Strong Men Armed*, 427.

Chapter 11. Defending Iwo Jima to the Death
1. Horie had become friendly with Kuribayashi's family after the war, and the latter's widow (Kuribayashi Yoshii) shared the general's letters to the family with Horie. He first published them in English in his article "The Last Days of General Kuribayashi," discussed in the editors' preface. The article was published in the February 1955 edition of the *Marine Corps Gazette*. The article includes a full translation of this August 2, 1944, letter and of several more.
2. Takako was Kuribayashi's third child, the second daughter of the family. She was eight years old at the time.
3. Teraki, who participated in the dissection of the American POWs after they were executed, wrote his memoirs some thirty years after the war. See Teraki Tadashi, *Kokuhaku no Ishibumi* [A Confession] (Tokyo: Ningen to Rekishisha, 1979). There is no English version of that book.

Chapter 12. Two Months before the Storm
1. See note 4, chapter 1, for the wording of the poem.
2. As was mentioned earlier, Horie had befriended Nishi's family after the war. Nishi's widow shared with Horie her husband's letters from Iwo.
3. This letter was published in full in Horie, "The Last Days of General Kuribayashi," 43.

Chapter 13. Farewell, Everyone, on Chichi Jima
1. Positions were arranged in two ways. The first one was a combat position, used when the enemy was expected to land. The other was when the enemy only used air raids or fired from the sea.
2. On the islands of Saipan, Tinian, and Guam, the Japanese defenders attacked at night against the invading forces. Even under the cover of darkness, the attackers lost about 50 percent of their troops within two or three hours. Later on Okinawa, the 32nd Army lessened its effectiveness by making counterattacks, ordered by higher authority. In the defense of Iwo Jima, the Imperial Japanese Headquarters never intervened. By around noon on the 19th, the U.S. landing forces already had about ten thousand marines and two hundred armored vehicles, including tanks and LVTAs (landing vehicles, tracked, armored—better known as Amtracs), ashore.
3. Kuribayashi's telegram was incorrect—there were no battleships sunk, and the number of tanks knocked out or destroyed was, while serious, less than a third of the reported number.
4. According to Horie, Tan, also pronounced "kimo," was the code name given to the Ogasawara Garrison.
5. At this time, Horie writes, the United States had committed the 3rd Marine Division to the frontline fighting.
6. NHK, or the Japan Broadcast Corporation, still exists today.

Chapter 14. Our Cave Became a Sea of Fire:
First Lieutenant Musashino Kikuzo's Story

1. According to Horie, Musashino was a member of the engineer company of the 2nd Mixed Brigade, but in fact he was in the engineer company directly under the command of the 109th Division.
2. It is unclear if it was Horie or Musashino who wrote it, but a note was added stating that Japanese forces were envious that U.S. forces had the capability of bringing water with them in large containers and thus were self-sufficient.
3. Nogi Maresuke was a famous general and Togo Heihachiro a famous admiral, both in the Russo-Japanese War.
4. Horie repeats this account, but as a "rumor," in chapter 17.
5. Horie added the following commentary here: "I heard from a lady who was evacuated from Saipan when she [was] 12 years old that in Saipan the Japanese officers and civilian leadership were always saying that Japan was a divine country, that reinforcements would come without fail the next day, and that the Combined Fleet would come to rescue them."
6. According to Newcomb, Maeda was the commander of the 2nd Mixed Brigade of the Brigade Artillery Group. See Newcomb, *Iwo Jima*, app., "Japanese Command at Iwo Jima," 308.
7. Horie offers figures for the number of dead and prisoners of war, based on U.S. data: Japanese deaths, slightly less than 19,000; American deaths, 5,521; and Japanese POWs, 1,125.

Chapter 16. Come Out! Seaman First Class Koizumi
Tadayoshi's Story

1. Horie notes that Koizumi's father used to be his senior in the 2nd Infantry Regiment. He was killed in action in northern China in 1937.
2. This is likely a reference to the underwater demolition teams (UDTs) that approached Iwo Jima's shores prior to the actual invasion on February 19. For more on their role, see Wyatt Blassingame, *The Frogmen of World War II* (New York: Random House, 1964), and James Douglas O'Dell, *The Water Is Never Cold: The Origins of the U.S. Navy's Combat Demolition Units, UDTs, and Seals* (Washington, D.C.: Brassey's, 2000).
3. Here Koizumi is referring to the crews of the midget submarines (five subs at two men each). One crewman was captured and was neither mentioned in propaganda accounts nor shown in the famous photograph of the attack with the faces of the nine men who perished arranged around the picture.
4. This is a reference to the "fire balloon" or "balloon bomb," an experimental bomb known as the *fusen bakudan*, or Fu-Go. Approximately nine thousand were launched between November 1944 and April 1945, and about three hundred were observed in North America. For more, see John McPhee, "Balloons of War," *New Yorker*, January 29, 1996, 60.
5. The editors were unable to determine Chapel's full name.
6. The editors were unable to determine Buckstar's full name.

7. Koizumi writes that the ship's name was the *General Weble,* but it in fact was *General William Weigel.*

Chapter 17. Warriors Remembered

1. Horie seems to have gotten the names of battalion commanders confused here. There were two battalion commanders in the 145th Regiment with names written similarly, but neither being "Ando." The commander of the 2nd Battalion was Yasutake Sueki; the commander of the 3rd Battalion was Anso (or Ansho) Kenro. The beginnings of both names are written with the same Chinese character, and Horie could have misread the name at the time or misremembered it over the years. He was probably referring to Anso (or Ansho), but the editors have decided to keep "Ando," as he had originally written it in the Japanese version of the book.
2. The statement that every Japanese warship had radar installed is clearly in error.
3. A letter Ichimaru had penned to President Franklin D. Roosevelt was found among the admiral's belongings after the war. It has been translated by Warrant Officer Mikami Hirofumi, and it reads:

> Rear Adm. R. Ichimaru of the Japanese Navy sends this note to Roosevelt. I have one word to give you upon the termination of this battle. Approximately a century has elapsed since Nippon, after Commodore [Matthew C.] Perry's entry to Shimoda, became widely affiliated with the countries of the world. During this period of intercourse Nippon has met with many national crises as well as the undesired Sino-Japanese War, Russo-Japanese War, the World War, the Manchurian Incident, and the China Incident. Nippon is now, unfortunately, in a state of open conflict with your country. Judging Nippon from just this side of the screen you may slander our nation as a yellow peril, or a blood thirsty nation or maybe a protoplasm of military clique. Though you may use the surprise attack on Pearl Harbor as your primary material for propaganda, I believe you, of all persons, know best that you left Nippon no other method in order to save herself from self-destruction. His Imperial Highness, as clearly shown in the "Rescript of the Founder of the Empire," "Yosei (Justice)," "Choki (Sagacity)," and "Sekkei (Benevolence)," contained in the above threefold doctrine, rules in the realization of "Hakko-ichiu (the universe under His Sacred Rule)" in His Gracious mind. The realization of which means the habitation of their respective fatherlands under their own customs and traditions, thus ensuring the everlasting peace of the world. Emperor Meiji's "The four seas of the world that are united in brotherhood will know no high waves nor wind" (composed during the Russo-Japanese War) won the appraisal of your uncle, Theodore Roosevelt, as you yourself

know. We, the Nippon-jin, though may follow all lines of trade, it is through our each walk of life that we support the Imperial doctrine. We, the soldiers of the Imperial Fighting Force take up arms to further the above stated "doctrine." Though we, at the time, are externally taken by your air raids and shelling backed by your material superiority, spiritually we are burning with delight and enjoying the peace of mind. This peacefulness of mind, the common universal stigma of the Nippon-jin, burning with fervour in the upholding of the Imperial Doctrine may be impossible for you and Churchill to understand. I hereupon pitying your spiritual feebleness pen a word or two. Judging from your actions, white races, especially you Anglo-Saxons at the sacrifice of the coloured races, are monopolizing the fruits of the world. In order to attain this end, countless machinations were used to cajole the yellow races, and to finally deprive them of any strength. Nippon in retaliation to your imperialism tried to free the oriental nations from your punitive bonds, only to be faced by your dogged opposition. You now consider your once friendly Nippon a harmful existence to your luscious plan, a bunch of barbarians that must be exterminated. The completion of this Greater East Asia War will bring about the birth of the East Asia Co-Prosperity Area, this in turn will in the near future result in the everlasting peace of the world, if, of course, it is not hampered upon by your unending imperialism. Why is it that you, an already flourishing nation, nip in bud the movement for the freedom of the suppressed nations of the East. It is no other than to return to the East that which belongs to the East. It is beyond our contemplation when we try to understand your stinted narrowness. The existence of the East Asia Co-Prosperity sphere does not in any way encroach upon your safety as a nation, on the contrary, will sit as a pillar of world peace ensuring the happiness of the world. His Imperial Majesty's true aim is no other than the attainment of this everlasting peace. Studying the condition of the never ending racial struggle resulting from mutual misunderstanding of the European countries, it is not difficult to feel the need of the everlasting universal peace. Present Hitler's crusade of "His Fatherland" is brought about by no other than the stupidity of holding only Germany, the loser of the World War, solely responsible for the 1914–1918 calamity and the deprivation of Germany's reestablishment. It is beyond my imagination of how you can slander Hitler's program and at the same time cooperate with Stalin's "Soviet Russia" which has as its principle aim the "socialization" of the World at large. If only the brute force decides the ruler of the world, fighting will everlastingly be repeated, and never will the world know peace nor happiness. Upon the attainment of your barbaric world monopoly never forget to retain in your mind the failure of your predecessor President Wilson at his heights.

Chapter 18. Tragic Island, Iwo Jima

1. This "fear" may have been a reference to the suicide on May 7, 1951, of an Imperial Japanese Navy veteran of Iwo Jima, Yamakage Kofuku, who had been able to return to Iwo Jima purportedly to retrieve his diary and personal effects, only to jump off of Mount Suribachi as he and his escorts were about to return to Tokyo. This incident is discussed in more detail in Robert D. Eldridge, *Iwo Jima and the Bonin Islands in U.S.-Japan Relations: American Strategy, Japanese Territory, and the Islanders In-Between,* forthcoming, chapter 7.
2. Taro passed away in 2006.

Afterword

1. It would be another decade, in the mid-1970s, before the Yasukuni Shrine would become as controversial as it is today.
2. The editors inquired of the *Saturday Evening Post* if Blair ever produced a story using Mrs. Nishi's interview, but the archivist there was unable to locate one. Blair left his position as editor of the *Post* shortly afterward, on November 14, 1964. Diana Denny, archivist, *Saturday Evening Post,* e-mail to Robert D. Eldridge, April 5, 2010.

index

Army Mixed Brigade, 2nd (Konsei Daini Ryodan): Artillery battery, 88; Artillery Regiment, 86; banzai charges of, 111, 112; Engineer Company, 40, 86, 88; field hospital (Konsei Daini Ryodan Yasen Byoin), ix, 31, 86; Iwo Jima, orders to, 42; Iwo Jima battle, 85, 102, 188; officers in, 43; organization of, 42; Pioneer Company, 87; visit to, 74

Army Provisional Field Ordnance Unit (Japanese), 87

Army Provisional Field Supply Unit (Japanese), 87

Army Shipping Headquarters (Senpaku Shireibu), xx, 9, 18, 29, 204n1 (chap. 3)

Army Special Secret Service Unit (Japanese), 87

Army Tank Regiment, 26th (Sensha Dainijuroku Rentai), 31, 43, 56–57, 68–69, 86, 183, 189

Army War College (Rikugun Daigaku), x, xx, 9, 47, 62, 72, 80, 205n7 (chap. 8)

Arnold, Henry H., 43, 45

Asada Shinji, 116–17

Atsuchi Kanehiko, 39, 46, 47, 73, 88, 101, 110, 158

Awatsu Hokatsu, 85

Awatsu Katsutaro, 110

B-24 bombers, 66, 93, 126, 140, 143
B-29 bombers, 45, 125, 126, 140, 143
balloon bombs, 141, 207n4 (chap. 16)
banzai charges: on Iwo Jima, 102, 109–11, 112, 114, 115–17, 119, 153, 154, 155, 156, 158; on Saipan, 22–23; U.S. control of Iwo Jima and, 1

beach line, defense of, 46–47, 70

Benitani Seizo, 113, 115, 116, 149

Biak Island, 4, 21, 27, 28

Blair, Clay, Jr., 166, 210n2 (afterword)

Buchstar, First Lieutenant, 143, 207n6 (chap. 16)

Bushido, 121

cannibalism, xi, xxiii, 205n5

casualties and losses during battle, 2, 101, 102, 104, 109, 110, 112, 113, 114,

120, 121, 141, 201n1 (chap. 1), 206n3 (chap. 13), 207n7

caves: antiaircraft guns in, 70; arms and ammunitions for use from, 3; attack by U.S., 110; attack on by U.S., 101, 107, 110, 115, 122, 137–39; banzai charges from, 115–17, 119; on Chichi Jima, 82; conditions in, 94, 132, 134, 136; dead bodies in, 119; digging of, 90–91, 96–97; effectiveness of fighting from, 75–76, 78; encouragement to leave, 137–38; entrance to, location of, 133; explosion of entrances to, 1, 107, 117, 118, 122, 134; hiding in, 136–37; of Kuribayashi, 154, 155; radio communications from, 1; size of, 129; suffocation gas in, 138; tanks use from, 63; as tombs, 90–91, 101–2

Central Pacific Fleet (Chubu Taiheiyo Homen Kantai), 15

Chapel, Captain, 143, 207n5 (chap. 16)

Chichi Jima: air raids on, 61, 62, 63, 66, 69, 94, 148; air transport to, 56–57, 58; assignment to, ix, xx–xxvii, 33, 83, 195–96n5; attack by U.S., 93–94, 99; caves on, 82; conscience, Chichi Jima's, x; convoy escorts for troops and shipments to, 34; defense of, 69–70, 71; defense strategy for, xi–xii, 169–73; English-language studies on, x; evacuation of islanders, 60, 62, 89; farming and fishing practices, 70–71, 94; food and water supply on, 94; Futami Harbor, 33, 42, 58, 66–67, 93; hospital on, 69; invasion of, 160; location of, ix, 195n4; military installations on, 42; prisoners on, treatment of, x–xi, 197n17; shipping through, ix, 33, 42, 49, 65, 66–69, 93, 195n4; Tiger of Chichi, x; troops ordered to, 34

Chichi Jima Fortress (Chichi Jima Yosai Shireibu), 42, 43, 65

Chichi Jima Military Police (Japanese), 87

China, xviii, 89, 203–4n15

Cho Isamu, 22, 23, 24–25, 30, 33

Christmas celebration, 143

about the author
and editors

Horie Yoshitaka was born on August 15, 1915, in Sashima County, Ibaraki Prefecture, in the northeastern part of Japan. He was a graduate of the Sakai Kenritsu Chugakko (Sakai Prefectural Middle School) and of the Imperial Japanese Army Academy, the latter in 1936. He was commissioned October 1, 1936, and attached to the 7th Company, 2nd Infantry Regiment. In 1937 he became the regimental flag bearer as well as an instructor of the Army Officer Candidate School. He was sent to China in 1938 as a communications officer about a year after the outbreak of fighting there and was seriously wounded in the city of Kaifeng in December 1939. He graduated from the Army War College in 1942. He served on the staff of the Army Shipping Headquarters as a liaison officer to the Navy, in the 31st Army (although aerial attacks on Saipan prevented his going there), and at Iwo Jima. As a major he helped Lieutenant General Kuribayashi Tadamichi plan the defense of Iwo Jima. After the war he worked for the U.S. Air Force in Japan at Tachikawa Air Base and served as a lecturer at the University of Maryland's Asia Division and at Takushoku University. He was an honorary lifetime member of the U.S. Marine Corps 5th Division Association. He died in August 2003.

Robert D. Eldridge, PhD, is currently the deputy assistant chief of staff, G-5, Marine Corps Bases Japan, and was a tenured associate professor of U.S.-Japanese relations at the School of International Public Policy, Osaka University, Japan, from 2001 to 2009. He earned his PhD in Japanese political and diplomatic history at Kobe University's Graduate

School of Law and is an award-winning author of numerous works on the bilateral relationship, including *The Origins of the Bilateral Okinawa Problem* (Garland, 2001), *The Return of the Amami Islands* (Lexington, 2004), *Secret Talks between Tokyo and Washington: The Memoirs of Miyazawa Kiichi, 1949–1954* (Lexington, 2007), *Japanese Public Opinion and the War on Terrorism* (Palgrave, 2008, coedited with Paul Midford), and a book in Japanese titled *Iwo Jima and the Bonin Islands in U.S.-Japan Relations* (Nanpo Shinsha, 2008), forthcoming in English from Marine Corps University Press. He was a Scholar-in-Residence at Marine Corps Forces Pacific at Camp Smith, Hawaii, between August 2004 and August 2005, and he serves on the Board of Directors of the Pacific War Memorial Association in Honolulu.

Charles W. Tatum was in the 1st Battalion, 27th Marines, 5th Marine Division, U.S. Marine Corps, and, as an eighteen-year-old machine gunner, was in the first assault wave in the battle of Iwo Jima. Wounded there, he was awarded the Bronze Star. He is the author of numerous works, including *Iwo Jima: Red Blood, Black Sand — Pacific Apocalypse* (Chuck Tatum Productions, 2002); the critically acclaimed documentary of the same title; and another about the life of Medal of Honor and Navy Cross winner Gunnery Sergeant John Basilone, *The Saga of Manila John, February 23, 1945*. He lives in Stockton, California, and is active in Marine Corps affairs, having served twice as president of the Stockton Marine Corps Club. He maintains a Web site dedicated to Iwo Jima–related affairs at www.marineswwii.com/.